Cinema at the Margins

New Perspectives on World Cinema

The *New Perspectives on World Cinema* series publishes engagingly written, highly accessible, and extremely useful books for the educated reader and the student as well as the scholar. Volumes in this series will fall under one of the following categories: monographs on neglected films and filmmakers; classic as well as contemporary film scripts; collections of the best previously published criticism (including substantial reviews and interviews) on single films or filmmakers; translations into English of the best classic and contemporary film theory; reference works on relatively neglected areas in film studies, such as production design (including sets, costumes, and make-up), music, editing and cinematography; and reference works on the relationship between film and the other performing arts (including theatre, dance, opera, etc.). Many of our titles will be suitable for use as primary or supplementary course texts at undergraduate and graduate levels. The goal of the series is thus not only to address subject areas in which adequate classroom texts are lacking, but also to open up additional avenues for film research, theoretical speculation and practical criticism.

Series Editors

Wheeler Winston Dixon – University of Nebraska, Lincoln, USA
Gwendolyn Audrey Foster – University of Nebraska, Lincoln, USA

Editorial Board

Thomas Cripps – Morgan State University, USA
Catherine Fowler – University of Otago, New Zealand
Andrew Horton – University of Oklahoma, USA
Valérie K. Orlando – University of Maryland, USA
Robert Shail – University of Wales Lampeter, UK
David Sterritt – Columbia University, USA
Frank P. Tomasulo – City College of New York, USA

Cinema at the Margins

WHEELER WINSTON DIXON

ANTHEM PRESS
LONDON · NEW YORK · DELHI

Anthem Press
An imprint of Wimbledon Publishing Company
www.anthempress.com

This edition first published in UK and USA 2013
by ANTHEM PRESS
75–76 Blackfriars Road, London SE1 8HA, UK
or PO Box 9779, London SW19 7ZG, UK
and
244 Madison Ave #116, New York, NY 10016, USA

Copyright © Wheeler Winston Dixon 2013

The author asserts the moral right to be identified as the author of this work.

All rights reserved. Without limiting the rights under copyright reserved above,
no part of this publication may be reproduced, stored or introduced into
a retrieval system, or transmitted, in any form or by any means
(electronic, mechanical, photocopying, recording or otherwise),
without the prior written permission of both the copyright
owner and the above publisher of this book.

British Library Cataloguing-in-Publication Data
A catalogue record for this book is available from the British Library.

Library of Congress Cataloging-in-Publication Data
Dixon, Wheeler W., 1950–
Cinema at the margins / Wheeler Winston Dixon.
  pages cm. – (New perspectives on world cinema)
Includes bibliographical references and index.
ISBN 978-0-85728-186-9 (hardcover : alk. paper) – ISBN 978-1-78308-016-8 (pbk. : alk. paper)
 1. Motion pictures–History. I. Title.
PN1993.5.A1D53 2013
791.43'7–dc23
               2013041436

ISBN-13: 978 0 85728 186 9 (Hbk)
ISBN-10: 0 85728 186 0 (Hbk)

ISBN-13: 978 1 78308 016 8 (Pbk)
ISBN-10: 1 78308 016 7 (Pbk)

Cover photo © Kristen Glaze 2013

This title is also available as an ebook.

For Gwendolyn Audrey Foster

It's the movies that have really been running things in America ever since they were invented. They show you what to do, how to do it, when to do it, how to feel about it, and how to look how you feel about it.

—Andy Warhol

CONTENTS

Acknowledgments   ix

Introduction   xi

PART I. GENRE

1. The Future Catches Up with the Past: Peter Bogdanovich's *Targets*   3
2. Surrealism and Sudden Death in the Films of Lucio Fulci   11
3. *Flash Gordon* and the 1930s and '40s Science Fiction Serial   19
4. Just the Facts, Man: The Complicated Genesis of Television's *Dragnet*   31
5. The Disquieting Aura of Fabián Bielinsky   43

PART II. HISTORY

6. Fast Worker: The Films of Sam Newfield   61
7. The Power of Resistance: *Les Dames du Bois de Boulogne*   77
8. Beyond Characterization: Performance in 1960s Experimental Cinema   91
9. Vanishing Point: The Last Days of Film   105

PART III. INTERVIEWS

10. "Let the Sleepers Sleep and the Haters Hate": An Interview with Dale "Rage" Resteghini   119
11. *Margin Call*: An Interview with J. C. Chandor   135
12. "All My Films Are Personal": An Interview with Pat Jackson   147
13. Working Within the System: An Interview with Gerry O'Hara   157

14. Andrew V. McLaglen: Last of the Hollywood Professionals   179

15. Pop Star, Director, Actor: An Interview with Michael Sarne   195

Works Cited and Consulted   205

About the Author   213

Index   215

ACKNOWLEDGMENTS

This collection of essays has never been published before in book form; in addition, when they have appeared in smaller journals or on the web, they were cut for reasons of space which, in many cases, severely diluted the impact of the pieces and made their arguments incomplete. Thus, I'm very pleased to have the opportunity to bring these essays together in one volume, available for easy reference, so that these texts – like many of the films they examine – do not become phantoms themselves.

Versions of Chapters 1, 2, 4, 5, 11 and 15 all first appeared in the journal *Film International*; my thanks to Daniel Lindvall, editor, for permission to reprint these essays in this volume.

Chapter 10, originally from the *Quarterly Review of Film and Video*, and Chapter 12, first published in the *Journal of Popular Film and Television*, appear through the kindness of Taylor and Francis Publishers; my sincere thanks to them. Versions of Chapters 3, 8 and 13 all first appeared in *Screening the Past*; my thanks to Anna Dzenis, editor, for permission to reprint these essays.

Versions of Chapters 6, 7, 9 and 14 first appeared in *Senses of Cinema*; my thanks to Rolando Caputo for his permission to reprint these pieces in this volume. My other thanks must go to Dana Miller, whose superb typing of all my manuscripts makes my continued work possible, and Jennifer Holan for her typically comprehensive index. In addition, I want to thank Tej Sood of Anthem Press for commissioning this volume and my wife, Gwendolyn Audrey Foster, who remains my most perceptive critic and advisor.

INTRODUCTION

There can be no doubt that we are in an age in which the cinema as we know it has been transformed. The era of film is ending and the era of digital cinema is already hard upon us. While some movies are still shot on actual film, the vast majority of "movies" are created with digital cameras and hard drives, so much so that one of the industry's largest equipment suppliers, Birns and Sawyer, recently sold off their entire collection of cameras simply because no one was renting them. There are a few holdouts in the area of actual film production: Steven Spielberg remains a traditionalist, in more ways than one, and no less a figure than Christopher Nolan, who also embraces film over digital media and whose reboot of the *Batman* series proved incredibly influential. As Nolan noted in a recent interview with Jeffrey Ressner in the *DGA Quarterly*,

> For the last 10 years, I've felt increasing pressure to stop shooting film and start shooting video, but I've never understood why. It's cheaper to work on film, it's far better looking, it's the technology that's been known and understood for a hundred years, and it's extremely reliable. I think, truthfully, it boils down to the economic interest of manufacturers and [a production] industry that makes more money through change rather than through maintaining the status quo. We save a lot of money shooting on film and projecting film and not doing digital intermediates. In fact, I've never done a digital intermediate. Photochemically, you can time film with a good timer in three or four passes, which takes about 12 to 14 hours as opposed to seven or eight weeks in a DI suite. That's the way everyone was doing it 10 years ago, and I've just carried on making films in the way that works best and waiting until there's a good reason to change. But I haven't seen that reason yet. (Ressner 2012)

And yet, as Nolan himself acknowledges, he's playing a losing game. Digital is taking over; it's cheaper to shoot, can be viewed instantly, edited with the touch of a button and cuts cost on every level – from production to final delivery – to the bone. It's a shift that's been one hundred years in the making, even since film evolved from paper roll film to cellulose nitrate film and then safety film. Digital is simply the next platform. But make no mistake: 35mm is gone. I predicted this in a lecture at the University of Stockholm, Sweden on 3 December 2000, after the first movie theater in New York had just made the shift to digital and Hollywood studio executives attending the inaugural screening were ceremonially photographed gleefully throwing 35mm film canisters into a large trash barrel. Digital had arrived and there was no looking back.

The members of the Stockholm audience – distinguished academics from around the world – were aghast at this and couldn't accept the fact that 35mm was heading for its final spin. But, as I pointed out, Alan Crosland's *The Jazz Singer* opened in Manhattan in precisely one theater in 1927 and revolutionized the industry with the advent of "talkies"; this was just the same sort of platform shift playing out yet again. The industry is constantly changing and adapting, relentlessly driven by the bottom line, at once an industry and an art form, but one which, in recent years, seems eager to forget its past and exist exclusively in the present – except, of course, for those few cinephiles who still order DVDs of their favorite titles.

As for the 35mm prints of existing films, they're being aggressively junked by the studios in favor of DCPs (Digital Cinema Packages) that are unlocked by computer codes called KDMs (Key Delivery Messages) for each individual screening, giving studios an unprecedented control over their product and taking a great deal of discretional leeway out of the hands of theater owners. Want to run an extra midnight screening? You'll have to clear it first. Want to screen a film for a local critic? Again, you'll have to log in to the studio's website, get a clearance, pay a fee and then screen it. With 35mm prints, you could just thread them up and go. Now, that freedom is gone – and, along with it, the ability to shift a film from one screen to another within a multiplex for maximum profitability. The studios are firmly in charge. If you want to screen a classic film – say Blake Edwards' *Breakfast at Tiffany's* (1961) – you can no longer get a 35mm print; it's either a DVD, a DCP or nothing at all. Then, too, as the prints become scarcer, so also do replacement parts for conventional 35mm projectors; in an all-digital world, the filmic image has been relegated to museums and archives.

This is the last wave of film, the last chance to capture images with dyes and plastics, the last chance to embrace grain and other filmic characteristics, before the brave new world of digital, perfect cinema takes over. There are all sorts of issues involved here; in particular, archiving digital cinema – a task that this volume will discuss in the essay "Vanishing Point" – since the new image capture systems reduce everything to pixels, ones and zeros, and have to be

INTRODUCTION   xiii

constantly upgraded to new platforms to make sure that they continue to exist in an uncorrupted form. It should come as no surprise that the major studios are still creating 35mm fine grain negatives of all their films as a backup in case something happens to the digital masters and often use them when digital files become corrupt. This in itself says something about the ephemerality of the digital image. If everything is converted to digital in the future, what happens to the past of cinema? What happens to the more than one hundred years of cinema that lies in the studio vaults, most of which isn't inherently "commercial" and so will never see the light of day?

For example, one studio in particular – Republic Pictures, which operated from the mid-1930s until the late 1950s and produced literally hundreds of films – has all of its films stored in long-term cold vaults, but almost none of them are available in screening copies for the contemporary viewer. When VHS was first introduced, Republic put out much of its back catalogue on tape, but modern audiences weren't interested in the vast majority of their films, simply because they weren't aware of either the studio or the films' existence. William Witney – one of Republic's most prolific directors and one of Quentin Tarantino's acknowledged influences – created a vast amount of material for Republic, but when the jump to DVD came, almost none of Republic's films were introduced in the new format. Thus, much of Witney's work became invisible; it wasn't profitable enough to warrant a DVD release and so it was consigned to oblivion. Some titles, including many by Republic – and rather eccentric choices at that – have been picked up by Olive Films, a small DVD distribution outlet, but who knows how long that will last? For most films, if they don't make money, the studio will put them in a vault and forget about them. Everything must go. As critic Dave Kehr noted,

> It's bad enough, to cite a common estimate, *that 90 percent of all American silent films and 50 percent of American sound films made before 1950 appear to have vanished forever.* But even the films we have often live on in diminished states. An astonishing number of famous titles – like [Ernest B. Schoedsack and Merian C. Cooper's 1933 film] *King Kong* and [Howard Hawks' 1940 film] *His Girl Friday* – no longer exist as original camera negatives, but survive only as degraded duplicates and damaged release prints. A great deal of important material – not just features but shorts, newsreels, experimental work, industrial films, home movies and so on – remains on unstable nitrate stock, and must be transferred to a more permanent base before the films turn to goo. And once the endangered material has been stabilized (the preservation step), it often must undergo an even more expensive process of restoration to recover its original luster: the removal

of dirt and scratches, the replacement of lost footage or missing intertitles, the cleaning up of degraded soundtracks. (Kehr 2010, emphasis added)

The other thing that's surprising is that all of this happened in plain sight, so to speak, through neglect and or willful destruction of films that were no longer deemed commercially viable. Also, that the complete digitization of the industry came as such as surprise to everyone – even professionals within the field. As Jan-Christopher Horak, director of the UCLA Archives, noted in an essay in 2012, discussing the 1993 United States Congressional Hearings on Film Preservation, "A Study of the Current State of American Film Preservation,"

> having been a witness myself at those hearings […] I'm struck today by how *clueless* literally all the participants of those hearings were about the digital tidal wave that would wash over the field in only a few short years. Not one person predicted the end of analog cinema, certainly not within a little more than a decade. (Horak 2012)

And yet that time is now here and there's no going back. The ruthlessness with which studios are embracing the new digital world should come as no surprise given the enormous cost savings involved in every area – except, of course, in archiving the past. More and more, just a few canonical classics – like Michael Curtiz's *Casablanca* (1942) or Victor Fleming's *Gone with the Wind* (1939), to name just two very obvious examples – are "standing in" for the entire output of an era for a new generation that knows nothing of the past and is encouraged by popular media to live only in the eternal present. What will happen to the rest of the films that enchanted, informed and transported audiences of the 1930s, 1940s and even the more recent 1960s?

For the most part, they will be forgotten and their makers forgotten with them. As someone who teaches a film history class on a regular basis, I can confirm that even such an obvious historical marker as Alfred Hitchcock's *Psycho* (1960) is unknown territory for a vast majority of my students. And yet – and here is the nub of my argument with this book, which is an act of historical recovery – once they are exposed to these films that they would never seek out otherwise, they are enthralled by them and wonder *why* they've never heard of them before. Even with films that are readily available as either digital downloads or on DVDs, you have to know that they exist in order to seek them out. In the 1980s and 1990s, at least, the more adventurous video stores served as a useful tool for browsing through the annals of classic cinema, encouraging patrons to sample films they would never have heard of otherwise. Now those stores are gone, along with bookstores and record stores as well, and the days of browsing are over. Much is available, but you have to know it's there; if you don't, then how on earth would you even know that it existed? But, as my students' continued interest demonstrates, it's still worthwhile to examine these non-mainstream films and filmmakers. They, as much as any of the more popular titles, have something to offer us, and their claim on our memory is more persistent precisely because they have often been neglected in conventional cinema histories.

In the first section of this volume, "Genre," I discuss Peter Bogdanovich's *Targets*, a prescient film that chronicles the shooting spree of a young Vietnam veteran and is based on real life events from the 1960s – which, in light of recent events in Newtown, Connecticut and elsewhere, seems more relevant than ever before. I also examine the violent and surreal horror films of the late Italian director Lucio Fulci – reviled during their initial appearance, but now acclaimed as classic example of Gothicism – as well as the world of constant peril inhabited by the protagonists of motion picture serials in the 1930s and '40s, such as *Flash Gordon* and other films that inspired many of the comic book blockbusters that fill today's cinemas – George Lucas's *Star Wars* (1977) and its many sequels, for example, as well as the continuing series of entries in the Marvel superhero canon. I take a look at the genesis of the television series *Dragnet*, which is usually credited solely to Jack Webb, but which, as the reader will see, had many hands involved in its creation – not the least of which was Anthony Mann and Alfred Werker's *He Walked by Night* (1948), in which Webb appeared as a police forensics expert, and then appropriated the entire structure of the film to create his long running series. And, finally, I cover the more recent, more sophisticated caper and crime thrillers of the late Argentinean director Fabián Bielinsky, who was most famous for his 1998 art house hit *Nine Queens*, but who found greater depth and resonance in what would sadly be his last film, *The Aura* (2005).

The second section, "History," begins with the works of director Sam Newfield, the most prolific director of the American sound cinema. Newfield labored for the bottom-rung Hollywood studio Producers Releasing Corporation, making sharp and efficient films in every conceivable genre throughout the 1940s – sometimes, as many as fifteen per year under his own name and two pseudonyms. "The Power of Resistance: *Les Dames du Bois de Boulogne*," meanwhile, recounts the production and reception of a key work of French Resistance cinema. Created under the Nazi-directed Vichy government in WWII-era France by director Robert Bresson and scenarist Jean Cocteau, *Les Dames* marks the pair's only collaboration on a film. "Beyond Characterization: Performance in 1960s Experimental Cinema" examines the fringe world of 1960s experimental filmmaking in New York and the ways in which these filmmakers and performers used their own lives as material for the films they created. Finally, "Vanishing Point: The Last Days of Film" considers the end of actual film production and distribution and the rise of digital cinema, a momentous shift that is taking place even as I write these words and which raises numerous archival, distribution and exhibition questions – all of which are still quite unresolved.

The final section, "Interviews," features discussions with the prolific music video director Dale "Rage" Resteghini – who is now moving into feature films – and examines how changing distribution patterns are changing the face of cinema; J. C. Chandor, the director of the excellent 2011 film *Margin Call*, which considers the 2008 financial meltdown on Wall Street from the vantage point of one hectic night at a brokerage concern; the final interview given by pioneering British filmmaker Pat Jackson, whose credits range from one of the first Technicolor documentaries to the cult television series *The Prisoner*, starring Patrick McGoohan; director Gerry O'Hara, who talks about his long career in cinema working with such luminaries as Laurence Olivier, Ronald Neame, Michael Powell, Carol Reed and Otto Preminger; Andrew V. McLaglen, perhaps the foremost exponent of the commercial Western in the last half of the twentieth century; and, finally, director and pop star Michael Sarne, whose notorious film *Myra Breckinridge* is just the most visible work of a long and varied career.

All of these essays and interviews explore the careers and works of filmmakers who operated in an inherently commercial medium to create films of lasting worth and value – filmmakers who bridged the artificial gap between "high" and "low" art to reach audiences through genre films, commercial television or underground films in the 1960s and really get their vision out before the public. Sometimes their works were coded as mainstream entertainment and sometimes they were presented as unvarnished bulletins from the front; but, in all cases, these are films and filmmakers who are vanishing from the cinematic record, unjustly and through no fault of their own.

The marginalization of these artists – and all of them, no matter how commercial they might have been, merit that distinction – is convenient for mainstream historians, but distorts our picture of both the past and present of cinema. As Geoffrey O'Brien, one of the most instructive of all film critics and theorists and something of an enigmatic figure in academia, noted:

> [The] decades slid by so quickly in the dark. What year was it, anyway, in which of the worlds you'd lived in simultaneously? A life spent watching movies could best be described by certain movie titles: *A Double Life, I Died a Thousand Times, I've Lived Before*. Caught up in the shifting celluloid waters, living in reverse and playback, you ended up craving an anchor, something that had definitely happened at a definite time, a Great

Real Thing providing ballast for the phantoms. Could anything real be inscribed on those liquid surfaces, anything harsh and durable? If you could find your way back to it you could trace another route, a road on which the world could be seen truly as it was. (O'Brien 1995, 78–9)

Val Lewton, producer of some of the most evocative commercial films ever made – a series of dark and deeply personal Gothic films made on shoestring budgets and breakneck schedules at RKO Radio Pictures during the 1940s, such as Jacques Tourneur's *I Walked with a Zombie* (1943) – once remarked to an associate in an echo of Keats' famous self-composed epitaph, "here lies one whose name was writ in water," that "making films is like writing on water" (Dixon and Foster 2011, 20). In other words, nothing is permanent. Everything is fixed only for the moment and only comes to life for that brief fraction of a second when the cinematic image is projected on the screen. If a film isn't available, it can't really be said to exist.

Unlocking these phantom visions, then, and seeking the work that comes from the margins is the task that I have set for myself with these essays and interviews. My goal is to document the films that have moved me deeply and yet have been omitted from the dominant canon of film history. Film history is dynamic, not static, but values that we have inscribed in our hearts and minds – values that often have been passed on to us and which we have accepted without fully understanding – keep us from a deeper understanding of our cinematic heritage. No, everything must *not* go. Instead, as film archivists around the world are fond of saying, everything must be saved. Not all films will be, certainly, and many of the films described in this volume are phantoms already, but brought to light, these oft-obscured titles can teach us much about life as it really was during certain eras – life not as the dominant cinema wishes us to remember it, but rather, as it actually was.

Even as I write these words, the present is inexorably receding into the past. Film, by its very nature, is the sarcophagus of the eternal return of the past, resurrected with each new screening again and again on demand, but only if that demand exists. This is the realm of the cinema, which captures life or, in the words of Jean Cocteau, "photographs death at work" – a machinery of phantoms, dreams and desires in which constructed realities compete with each other for our collective attention. The world presented here is at once remote and omnipresent, tactile and elusive, present and inextricably linked to the past. And, yet, by the very act of discussing these films and their makers, we can bring them back to a sort of life and celebrate both their existence and their collective hold on our imaginations. The cinema is endless, boundless, too rich to be encompassed by any one history, or even any one set of histories. But, with this book, there is the hope that at least a part of that history is brought to light.

Part I
GENRE

Chapter 1

THE FUTURE CATCHES UP WITH THE PAST: PETER BOGDANOVICH'S *TARGETS**

Targets *are people ... and you could be one of them!*
(Tagline for *Targets*)

Peter Bogdanovich got his start as a critic and historian, conducting interviews with some of cinema's most illustrious directors in their twilight years and publishing them first in a variety of books and magazines, then as a collection in his 1998 volume *Who the Devil Made It: Conversations with Legendary Film Directors*. Bogdanovich realized early on, however, that these interviews were not enough; he wanted to do more. So he moved to Los Angeles, fell in with the Roger Corman circle at the height of its creative brilliance and soon found himself working on such landmark exploitation vehicles as *The Wild Angels* (1966), doing double duty as an assistant director and an extra.

After this, the next logical step was directing a movie himself and Corman – then able to green light films with modest budgets that would actually wind up in a theater as opposed to going straight to tape, VHS, DVD, Blu-Ray or VOD – famously offered Bogdanovich a deal. The actor Boris Karloff, famous for his roles in the *Frankenstein* films, owed Corman two days of work on a multipicture deal and Corman offered the fledgling director these two days with Karloff, twenty minutes of footage from the recently completed film *The Terror* (1963, ostensibly a Corman film, but one which nearly everyone in Corman's circle – including Francis Ford Coppola, Monte Hellman, Jack Hill and Jack Nicholson – had a hand in directing), a minimal budget and a shooting schedule. Corman told Bogdanovich that if the finished film was any good he'd distribute it through Paramount; if not, he'd dump it in drive-ins through American International Pictures.

---

* A version of this chapter was first published in 2013 by *Film International* (online) as "The Future Catches Up With The Past: Peter Bogdanovich's Targets" (17 January): http://filmint.nu/?p=6778.

Figure 1. *Targets.*
Source: Author's collection.

Absorbing this, Bogdanovich went home and, working with his then-wife, Polly Platt, and an uncredited Samuel Fuller, who contributed considerably to the final script, drafted a screenplay about the last days of an aging horror star, Byron Orlok (Boris Karloff) who wants to quit the business because he's sick of starring in one rotten horror film after another. Orlok feels that his brand of Gothicism has become outdated and that he should exit gracefully while he's still in demand. At the same time, in a parallel story, young all-American Vietnam veteran Bobby Thompson (Tim O'Kelly, in a terrifyingly realistic performance) is having trouble readjusting to society after his hitch in the service; he goes on a murderous rampage as a sniper, picking off unsuspecting people from the top of a huge oil refinery tank and, later, from behind the screen of a drive-in theater. Thompson does all of this quite casually, as if the entire rampage was simply a sporting event – which, of course, it is for him. He is incapable of empathizing with his victims – he has no feeling for anyone. All of his victims are simply targets, as the title states with succinct finality.

It is at this point that the two stories converge: Orlok is persuaded to make one final public appearance at the drive-in to plug his final film and, during the screening, Bobby starts killing attendees in their cars with a high-powered rifle. Taking command of the situation, Orlok summons all of his strength and confronts Bobby, knocking him down in front of the screen. He benefits from the fact that Bobby can't distinguish between on-screen Orlok, striding through the opening of *The Terror*, and Orlok in real life, walking towards him in a similar outfit (Samuel Fuller suggested this touch and it's a brilliant one). Once Bobby is subdued, Orlok looks down at the pathetic figure before him and murmurs, "Is this what I was afraid of?" And thus the film ends. When Corman saw the finished product, made for less than $100,000 and on which Karloff wound up working five days instead of two – the three extra days were a gift to Bogdanovich from Karloff, who correctly sensed that the project would be an important film – he immediately realized that he'd gotten a much better film than he'd originally bargained for. Corman sold it to Paramount, where it received a desultory release before vanishing into oblivion, resurfacing on DVD and VHS only years later.

But *Targets* (1968) was and remains a brilliant, stunningly prescient film and perhaps Bogdanovich's finest work, precisely because he had nothing to work with. When you have nothing, you have to give everything to a project to make it work – unless, of course, you don't care and Bogdanovich certainly cared. He even cast himself in the film as Sammy Michaels – the man who desperately wants Orlok to make another film and secure Sammy's big break as a director – simply because he had no money for anyone else. Despite the fact that the film got only a limited release, critics quickly recognized it for the masterpiece it was. Thus, the film ultimately fulfilled its primary function: getting Bogdanovich on the map as a director. Shortly after that, Bogdanovich directed *The Last Picture Show* (1971) and his career was assured.

The topicality of *Targets* was also a plus because, for the sniper section of this bifurcated film, Bogdanovich didn't have to go far to find a story line. The inspiration for *Targets* was utterly contemporary: the reign of terror inflicted on the citizens of Austin, Texas by Charles Whitman on 1 August 1966 when Whitman, armed to the teeth with an arsenal of legally acquired weapons, ascended to the top of the University of Texas Tower and began randomly shooting anyone who came into view. Before this attack, during which Whitman killed 14 people and wounded 32 others with deadly, methodical precision, Whitman killed both his wife and his mother, leaving behind a suicide note as more than ample evidence of his unbalanced mental state. The partially typewritten note, which was later recovered by police, is dated 31 July 1966 and begins with these chillingly prophetic words: "I do not quite understand what it is that compels me to type this letter. Perhaps it is to leave some vague reason for the actions I have recently performed. I do not really understand myself these days. I am supposed to be an average, reasonable and intelligent young man. However, lately (I cannot recall when it started) I have been a victim of many unusual and irrational thoughts" (Whitman 1966).

Then, after adding several additional sections of text to his note, some in ballpoint pen, Whitman went out to kill. In the end, the Austin police finally stormed the tower and shot Whitman dead. He was 25 years old. The weapons the police found at the shooting site included a machete, a Remington 700 ADL 6mm rifle, a Universal M1 carbine rifle, a 12 gauge semi-automatic shotgun, a Smith & Wesson M19 .357 Magnum revolver, a Luger PO8 9mm pistol and a Galesi-Brescia .25 ACP pistol.

At the time, the Whitman rampage was seen as an utterly aberrant act. If we look at the era more closely, however, we can see that, alongside the Peace movement and Flower Power era many remember with affection, dark events were occurring in American society with regularity, including the endless Vietnam War itself, the assassinations of John F. Kennedy, Martin Luther King, Jr., Robert Kennedy and Malcolm X, the Watts riots and numerous other societal disruptions – all of which, in their own way, pointed inexorably to an ever more ominous future. Violence became the cultural currency of the era and, even then, the nation was split between those who embraced guns and the culture they were a part of and those who sought to restrict guns to forestall a repeat of the Whitman incident. Now, in 2013, we confront in the United States a similar wave of terror brought on by gun violence – by a series of mass shootings too mind-numbing to recount and too terrifying to fully comprehend.

Bogdanovich himself has confessed his own bewilderment over the current state of affairs surrounding the gun culture in the United States and the protests that seem to grow ever more vocal every day, essentially deaf to the wishes of the majority of Americans for stricter gun control. As Bogdanovich wrote in an op-ed piece for the *Hollywood Reporter* shortly after the massacre in Colorado at a midnight screening of *The Dark Knight Rises* on 20 July 2012,

> We made *Targets* 44 years ago. It was based on something that happened in Texas, when that guy Charles Whitman shot a bunch of people after killing his mother and his wife. Paramount bought it, but then was terrified by it when Martin Luther King was killed and Bobby Kennedy was killed. The studio didn't want to release the film at all. So they released it with a pro-gun-control campaign, but that made the picture seem like a documentary to people, and it didn't do too well. It was meant to be a cautionary fable. It was a way of saying the Boris Karloff kind of violence, the Victorian violence of the past, wasn't as scary as the kind of random violence that we associate with a sniper – or what happened last weekend. That's modern horror.
>
> At first, some of the people [at *The Dark Knight Rises*] thought it was part of the movie. That's very telling. Violence on the screen has

increased tenfold. It's almost pornographic. In fact, it is pornographic. Video games are violent, too. It's all out of control [...] Back in the '70s, I asked Orson Welles what he thought was happening to pictures, and he said, "We're brutalizing the audience. We're going to end up like the Roman circus, live at the Coliseum." The respect for human life seems to be eroding [...] It's too easy to show murders in movies now. There are too many of them and it's too easy. There is a general lack of respect for life, because it's so easy to just kill people. Nothing's changed in 44 years [since *Targets*]. Things have gotten worse when it comes to the control of guns. This guy in Colorado legally had an arsenal. What's an AK attack rifle for? What is that for but to kill people? It's not for hunting. Why is it for sale? It boggles the mind. (Bogdanovich 2012)

And, of course, there's much more to it than that. The *Saw* films, the *Hostel* series and the *Texas Chainsaw* films all deal in the "cheapness" of human life and invite the audience to vicariously identify with the killer. These nihilistic slasher films degrade both the audience who watch them and the people who make them, but neither group will stop, especially in view of the genre's continued profitability. There is also the issue of the essential emptiness of American culture on a mass basis; we have become a landscape fueled by fear and a desire to consume, consume, consume, even as the "news," skewed either to the left or right, is so stage-managed and leveraged with "expert opinion" that the facts in any given situation are often impossible to discern.

What makes *Targets* an altogether different experience from the films mentioned above, however, is that it relentlessly and with scalpel-like precision examines the complete failure of American society to either address the social causes behind such rampages or provide audiences with print, television or cinematic material that has any real content – essentially, to stop functioning just like an endless diet of junk food. In *Targets*, Bobby's father, Robert Thompson, Sr. (an appropriately militaristic Tom Brown) knows only guns and mindless television as recreational activities; in a scene early on in the film, Thompson Sr. goes out on the practice field of a shooting range to pick up some targets during a session and Bobby levels the sight of his gun on his father, idly considering whether or not to kill him. Bobby's father catches him in the act and severely reprimands him. Bobby sheepishly apologizes for his "error" in judgment, but it's already been rendered clear what will happen as Bobby's mental state continues to spiral into free fall.

At night, in a superbly executed dolly sequence through a house utterly barren of any intellectual sustenance – no books in sight other than cookbooks and the Bible, mass produced paintings on the wall and conversations that never go beyond, "Hi, how are you?" and, "What's on TV tonight?" – Bobby and his family watch television. We never see what's on the TV, but it's obviously a late night talk show à la Johnny Carson. There is no real contact between any members of the family.

As the camera prowls the barren, air-conditioned nightmare that is their Southern California dream home, we hear them chuckle mindlessly at the antics on the screen, their faces illuminated only by the bluish glow of the television screen. At length, the family members peel themselves away from the electronic hearth to go to bed, but there's no real conversation, no communication, no sense that this family is a unit or that they even *know* each other. They're just four people in a room, thrown together by chance and circumstance: a son who's about to go off the deep end, a by-the-book father with no emotional or intellectual depth, an equally blank slate for a mother, Charlotte (Mary Jackson), and Bobby's similarly uncomprehending wife, Ilene (Tanya Morgan).

Shortly before going out to kill, Bobby makes one last desperate attempt to break through to his wife in a scene that is as economical as it is chilling. He tries to explain to her that something is wrong – he doesn't know what, but something is happening to him that he can't explain – and, though Ilene tries to listen, she simply doesn't have the depth to understand anything more than fashion magazines and Southern California pop culture. As the pair slouch against a wall in their bedroom, Bobby's face lit only by the glow at the end of his cigarette, it becomes clear to the viewer that nothing will stop Bobby now because the people around him lack the social reference points – indeed, any real *feeling* for anything other than the instant gratification that throwaway culture so relentlessly provides – to provide him with the understanding that he craves. Fittingly, Bogdanovich lights the scene so that Ilene gets some illumination, but Bobby is shrouded in darkness – the darkness that will soon consume both himself and those around him.

It's also interesting to note that there's no music in the film other than synthetic top 40 pop music – complete with a motor-mouthing disc jockey pouring forth endlessly from the radio in Bobby's car – and, if one wants to count it, Ronald Stein's original score for *The Terror*. Like Hitchcock's *The Birds* (1963), which used only "sound patterns" created by Bernard Herrmann, Remi Gassmann and Oskar Sala based on the sound of birds in flight calling to each other, *Targets* is set in a world that is all the more realistic because it eschews the extra-diegetic music that audiences have come to rely on for emotional response cues. Even the nature of the film itself mirrors Bobby Thompson – it's never apologize, never explain.

The other thing that's remarkable about Bobby, of course, is his complete *lack* of remarkability. Bobby Thompson seems like an utterly reliable, responsible, straight-ahead citizen who smoothly engages in idle chit chat with both his family members and those outside the home so casually and easily that his ferocious eruption is made all the more terrifying and all the more credible as a result. As he prepares for his shooting spree by buying even more guns and ammunition at a local gun shop, for example, Bobby seems to be an absolutely balanced individual – hiding in plain sight, a normal, easy going guy who has nevertheless completely lost touch with reality. And, indeed, there's nothing for him to hang on to. The society that has created Bobby Thompson is one in which there is nothing more to fill his mind with other than guns, violence and junk culture; significantly, he's a horror movie fan and early on in the film recognizes Byron Orlok outside a Los Angeles screening room (while purchasing still more weapons). It is this sighting that later influences his decision to pick the drive-in where Orlok will be appearing for his last murderous stint as a sniper.

Clearly, there is nothing here that's even remotely sensationalistic. *Targets* is a masterly depiction of the emptiness of conventional American life – sports, guns, video games, junk movies and junk television, plus junk novels – a life that offers nothing for something and that leaves the reader, listener or viewer both unsatisfied and undernourished, still empty after two-and-a-half hours of a mind-numbing spectacle at the multiplex, or knowing nothing new or useful after consuming yet another pop culture serial killer novel. It's all junk and there's nothing to be gleaned from it. Bogdanovich's film all too accurately depicts what the world was becoming in the late 1960s, even as many struggled against the idea of a culture ruled by mob consensus, fear and conspiracy theories, all of which people with nothing better to do were more than happy to propagate.

In the late '60s, we began the move toward where we are now in American society: total emptiness. There is nothing challenging, nothing sentient, nothing to believe in. One might try to dismiss Orson Welles's comment that "we're going to end up like the Roman circus, live at the Coliseum," but the fact is that we're already there. This is the terrifying prophecy of *Targets* – a vision that now has come to be true after decades of cultural neglect and the devaluation of both the humanities and humanity itself. Karloff's final courageous act in the film – confronting the sniper at the drive-in – is the act of one of the old guard; the rest of the patrons, however, run for their lives, heedless of offering any aid or assistance to others. In showing us the future of America – whether he knew he was doing so or not – Bogdanovich has given us a clear blueprint of what happens and what will continue to happen unless we take steps to rein in both the violence and the culture that embraces and glorifies it.

Chapter 2

SURREALISM AND SUDDEN DEATH IN THE FILMS OF LUCIO FULCI*

The films of Lucio Fulci, the Italian horror filmmaker, are usually lumped in with those of other "gore" specialists. It seems to me, however, that this gore is just one component of Fulci's work. Also running through all his films is a strangely dreamlike, hyper-violent abandonment of narrative which seeks to disrupt normative social preconceptions, perhaps as a result of Fulci's youthful excursions into Marxist political thought. In such films as *The House by the Cemetery* (1981), *The Beyond* (1981), *City of the Living Dead* (1980) and other works, Fulci continually operates against audience expectations in terms of both characterization and plot. In *The Beyond*, for example, a young blind woman's faithful guide dog turns on her without warning, tearing her throat out; in *City of the Living Dead*, a young couple is caught making out in the front seat of a car by the girl's father, who promptly drags the young man to a drill press and uses it to push a huge bolt through his skull.

Zombies roam hospitals, highways lead into the ocean with no end or beginning in sight, protagonists discover themselves trapped inside oil paintings and there's no logic to any of this. Fulci usually makes some desultory stab at a framing story, but once a central premise is set forth, the rest of the film is given over to unconnected and seemingly unmotivated sequences that follow with no discernible order or reason. I would argue that the chaotic non-narrative structure of Fulci's films is very much like the work of Luis Buñuel or Jean Cocteau; he creates a walking dream state from which the sleeper never awakes.

Born in Rome on 17 June 1927, Fulci studied medicine in college before becoming an art critic, then a screenwriter and then, oddly enough, breaking

---

* A version of this chapter was first published in 2012 by *Film International* (online) as "Surrealism and Sudden Death in the Films of Lucio Fulci" (24 December): http://filmint.nu/?p=6616.

Figure 2. Lucio Fulci.
Source: Author's collection.

in as a specialist in comedy – although, when one considers it, perhaps this isn't so odd after all. Fulci had studied at the famed Centro Sperimentale di Cinematografia (the Experimental Film Center, or Italian National Film School, founded by none other than Benito Mussolini in 1935) and, as he later told Robert Schlockoff:

> I studied at the Experimental Film Center in Rome, with teachers like Antonioni and Visconti. Incidentally, when I took the oral exam to be admitted to the Center, Visconti asked me what I thought of his film *Ossessione* [1943; actually an uncredited film version of James M. Cain's novel *The Postman Always Rings Twice*; MGM, who had purchased the rights to the book, was not amused, and a flurry of lawsuits ensued. *Ossessione* was soon withdrawn from circulation, finally resurfacing in the 1980s], which was then regarded as a masterpiece and, with the unconsciousness of my youth, I pointed out that he had "ripped off" quite a few pictures from Renoir's films! The rest of the jury looked at me as if I was a monster, but Visconti told me: "You are the first person to have told me the truth; you know films and you have a lot of courage – which is what a director needs to have!" And so they took me in! (Schlockoff 1982, 51)

After this auspicious beginning, Fulci provided the story for *A Day in Court* (1953) – I'll confine myself to the English titles for this chapter, in the interest of simplicity – then scripted an additional ten comedy/genre films up until 1958, when he finally got the chance to write and direct *The Thieves* (1958). The film created very little impact and was followed by his work as an associate producer on Mario Bonard and Sergio Leone's scrumptiously over-the-top 1959 version of *The Last Days of Pompeii* starring Steve Reeves and with Fernando Rey as Arbacès, the high priest and villain of the piece.

After this, more routine genre films followed in rapid succession, but Fulci was still, at this point in his career, just another journeyman filmmaker pounding out predictable, moneymaking entertainments. Among these were *Oh! Those Most Secret Agents* (1964) and *How We Robbed the Bank of Italy* (1966) – one of a series of broad comedies that also included *How We Got the Army in Trouble* (1965) and *How We Stole the Atomic Bomb* (1967). Fulci eventually found his true métier, however, with the surreal and deliriously violent *A Lizard in a Woman's Skin* (1971) and *Don't Torture a Duckling* (1972). He was traveling in a new direction, inspired by his contemporaries in the horror field; as he told Robert Schlockoff, "At that time, I would do comedies and rock 'n' roll films, [but] I was a great admirer of Tourneur and Corman – I love Corman's Poe series. After a while, I was fed up with comedies and would not do any more" (Schlockoff 1982, 51). As one of Fulci's most perceptive critics, Patricia MacCormack, notes,

> While Fulci contextualized the erotics of male homosociality through comedy and reaffirmation of machismo in the adventure films, he was simultaneously venturing into the horror territory with his *gialli*. These films adhere to the traditional *giallo* narrative structure while questioning and doubling standard cinematic concepts [...] even though, as in his previous films, Fulci's mind strained against the parameters of generic convention, through violence and dream sequences, special effects and a fascination with perversion (human rather than specifically sexual) he expressed a vision at once fascinatingly resonant with its horror genealogy and unique in its imaginative vision [...] the project of describing the best of Fulci's films, his gory horrors, is a paradoxical one. Being required to describe these films might expose them as poverty stricken within the constraints of signification of images, narrative and their capacity to be viewed as a readerly text.
>
> In order to evoke the powers of Fulci's best films, the reader must let go of: narrative as a temporalization of viewing pleasure which accumulates the past to contextualize the present and lay out an expected future; images as deferrals to meaning, signs to be read or interpreted; characters

as integral to plot, both in film in general and horror in particular as that which must be conceptually characterized in order to be meaningfully killed off or destroyed; narrative as intelligible contextualizer of action; exploitation as gratuitously existing for its own sake or to affirm and intensify traditional axes of oppression in society; gore as demeaning or a lesser focus in the impartation of visual expression; pleasure as pleasurable; repulsion as unpleasurable; violence as inherently aggressive; horror as dealing only with notions of returned repression, infantilism or catharsis. I ask the reader, in the tradition of Lyotard's economy of libidinal pleasure, to shift their address from *why* or *what* the images mean to *how* they affect [the viewer]. (MacCormack 2004)

Indeed, the bulk of Fulci's reputation as an authentic visionary of surrealist violence rests primarily on a mere handful of films: *City of the Living Dead* (1980), *The Black Cat* (1981), Fulci's uncontested masterpiece *The Beyond* (1981) and *The House by the Cemetery* (1982), perhaps the least interesting and most linear of these four projects. To this list must be added *Zombie* (1979), aka *Zombi 2* – although Fulci was really piggy-backing on George Romero's 1978 *Dawn of the Dead* with *Zombie*, extending Romero's images of the flesh-eating undead further into the realm of graphic specificity. Shortly after this, however, Fulci directed perhaps his most violent and repellent film, *The New York Ripper* (1982); too over-the-top even for his most hardcore fans, the film serves as a testament to the waning of Fulci's career. For, after the 1969 suicide of his wife, the death of his daughter Camilla in a car accident in the early 1970s and estrangement from his longtime scenarist, Dardano Sacchetti – the man responsible for the screenplays of Fulci's most famous films – over "credit" issues, the director's career went into steep decline.

At his peak, Fulci was compared to such horror experts as Dario Argento, Mario Bava and Jacques Tourneur and, though his current "fan" reputation rests almost entirely on his status as a purveyor of gore effects, Fulci himself viewed his films in a very different light. As he told Schlockoff in 1982:

> Horror is not a goal in itself to me. I am basically interested in the fantastic. As a matter of fact, there are few horror scenes in *City of the Living Dead*; *tension* is the important thing in this film. I have given up on horror for horror's sake; instead, I wanted to make a nightmare film where horror is ubiquitous, seen in apparently innocuous forms. Horror only appears in two scenes in a spectacular way, let alone the fact that the drill scene is a warning I wanted to give against a certain type of fascism, the girl's father killing the young guy in such an abject way just because the young guy is different, a frightened victim who, like the so-called witch in

Long Night of Exorcism, does not understand all this hostility towards him. I wanted to show this boy as a dropout whom girls protect because of his kindness, but unfortunately, I was not able to develop the conservatism of some Dunwich inhabitants. *City*, to me, is a visual rendering of the metaphysical side of bad dreams. [...]

I'd like to point out that the audience usually applauds once a horror scene is *over*, not while the horror is on the screen. People are wrong when they accuse my films of gratuitous horror; censorship is wrong about my films being an incentive to violence. Far from participating in this violence, the spectator, on the contrary, is rid of it, freed from horrors he holds within himself, the film being the catalyst for this liberation. [With *The Beyond*] my idea was to make an *absolute* film, with all the horrors of our world. It's a plotless film; a house, people, and dead men coming from *The Beyond*. There's no logic to it, just a succession of images. *The Sea of Darkness*, for instance, is an absolute world, an immobile world where every horizon is similar. I think each man chooses his own inner hell, corresponding to his hidden vices. So I am not afraid of Hell, since Hell is already in us. [...]

Curiously enough, I can't imagine that Paradise exists, though I am a Catholic – but perhaps God has left me? – yet I have often envisaged Hell, since we live in a society where only Hell can be perceived. Finally, I realize that Paradise is indescribable. Imagination is much stronger when it is pressed by the terrors of Hell [...] This may seem strange, but I am happier than somebody like Buñuel who says he is looking for God. I have found Him in the others' misery and my torment is greater than Buñuel's. For I have realized that God is a God of suffering. I envy atheists; they don't have all these difficulties. It is true that all my films are terribly pessimistic. The main characters in *The Beyond*, for instance, become blind, as their sight has no *raison d'être* anymore in this lifeless world. But humor and tragedy always join, anyway. If they emphasize the tragic side of things, it may have a comical effect. Everything considered, having directed so many comedies when I started my film career turns out to be very useful for my true cinema, the cinema of the fantastic. (Schlockoff 1982, 53–4)

The Beyond, of all of Fulci's films, remains the most resonantly mysterious and mesmerizing in its insistent avoidance of logic. It consists of a dreamlike series of set pieces revolving around a decaying New Orleans hotel, shot partially on location with interiors completed in Rome – a typical Fulci tactic, as his films were always made with the international market in mind rather than for native consumption in Italy where the market for horror films remained surprisingly limited. He also used American stars down on their luck in many of his films, such as Christopher George in *City of the Living Dead*, to increase the films' box-office appeal and worked in English and Italian interchangeably on the set. As Chas Balun recounts, in *The Beyond*:

> after a sepia-tinted prologue set in 1920s era Louisiana, a renegade [Warlock, who is also a painter] is chain-whipped, crucified with railroad spikes and drenched with acid [...] [The action then shifts] to the present day [and] the living dead are restless and ravenous [...] a curious plumber has one of his [eyes] savagely poked out – [a Fulci trademark] – only moments before an equally curious housemaid is trapped by a zombie and forced to forfeit one of her own eyeballs. It's no coincidence that Fulci's films are full of eyes, usually seen in extreme close-ups and often sightless and clouded, in addition to being on the receiving end of various sharp implements. [As] Fulci explains, "they are the first thing you have to destroy, because they have seen too many bad things" [...]
>
> [As *The Beyond* continues], lips, tongues and eyes are munched by marauding tarantulas, throats are ripped open by a guide dog gone to the Devil, partially dissected corpses run rampant and a little pigtailed girl has a hole blown clean through her cranium. All of this seems to support Fulci's thesis that 'life is often a really terrible nightmare, [and] our only refuge is to remain in this world, but outside time.' [*The Beyond*] ends enigmatically but triumphantly. The two surviving protagonists, [Fulci veterans] David Warbeck and Catriona MacColl, are chased into the basement of the hotel and are confronted with an eerie, surreal landscape littered with corpses. The climactic denouement [thus] brings the film full circle – the survivors, eyes now clouded and sightless, have entered the "Sea of Darkness" portrayed in the painting seen on the Warlock's easel during [the film's] prologue. (Balun 1996, 39–40)

Frozen in space and time, the camera pulls back to show the viewer that Warbeck and MacColl have become part of the painting, entombed forever in darkness, death and decay. Balun is correct in describing the conclusion of *The Beyond* as "triumphant," but it is the triumph of death, evil, violence and mortal immortality that the film ultimately embraces. All of this proceeds with a complete absence of logic or reason, as if no such concepts existed in Fulci's universe; things happen because they do and they obey no other order except for chance and circumstance. *The Beyond*'s framing story of the crucified Warlock is simply the jumping-off point for a series of grotesque and disturbing set pieces that have no reason for existence in the film other than the director's will to bring them to the screen. There's really no reason why any of what we see *should* happen; it's just the cruel illogic of an uncanny world in which human ambition, hope and striving are all but superfluous. The triumph of *The Beyond* is the erasure of causality and the subsequent rule of random events and circumstance that are completely beyond our control. As Fulci noted, "People who blame *The Beyond* for its lack of a story have not understood that it's a film of *images*, which must be received without any reflection." He complained that "any idiot" could understand a film with a plot, but that he was aiming for an "*absolute*" cinema that existed outside of narrative constraints (Schlockoff 1982, 54). Yet, after the completion of *The Beyond* – his finest film – Fulci's life was never really the same. Almost as soon as Fulci reached the summit of this achievement, his cinematic future ironically began falling away from him – just as it had for his doomed protagonists in *The Beyond*.

Faced with ever-shrinking budgets, trapped in a cycle of extreme violence as his sole stock in trade with producers and distributors alike and further incapacitated by poor health and depression, Fulci was reduced in his later years to lending his still-commercial name to a series of undistinguished horror films. These, he had little or nothing to do with other than appearing in a cameo role in some of them (a practice of long standing with Fulci that dated back to his earlier works – films he had actually directed), but allowed them to be released under the banner "Lucio Fulci Presents." These productions brought in a little much-needed cash, but further undermined Fulci's reputation as he was not allowed to publicly disassociate himself from them in return for payment for the use of his name. The final films that Fulci actually scripted and directed – *A Cat in the Brain* (1990), *Voices from Beyond* (1991) and *Door to Silence* (1991) – opened to scathing reviews and couldn't hope to match the power of his earlier works; sadly, they were of such poor quality that one has to agree with their contemporary reviews, which found the films to be almost amateurishly inept. Clearly, Fulci was going downhill; he had lost the energy and vision that had propelled him to genre stardom just a decade earlier.

Fulci's last major public appearance was as a guest of honor at the Fangoria Horror Convention in New York City in January 1996. On 13 March 1996, Fulci died in his modest apartment in Rome. Earlier, he had predicted that, after his passing, he and his films would swiftly be forgotten, but, if anything, Fulci's work is now more revered than ever. In fact, Fulci just missed the 1998 United States theatrical re-release of *The Beyond* in its original uncut version by Quentin Tarantino's Rolling Thunder Films. I was lucky enough to attend the midnight premiere at the Angelika Film Center in New York City and can attest that a discerning yet deeply enthusiastic crowd warmly received the film. In view of the fact that Fulci's films had routinely been recut, retitled, censored and shuffled off into VHS oblivion during his lifetime – indeed, even his *name* was omitted on some occasions, with directorial credit instead assigned to a variety of pseudonyms, such as "Louis Fuller," in an attempt to "Americanize" the films – it's a pleasure to note that a plethora of the director's films are now readily available on DVD and Blu-Ray in their original, unedited form and often with the original language (Italian) soundtracks as an option.

For someone who grew up admiring the works of Antonioni and Visconti and revering Renoir, Marcel L'Herbier and other renowned cineastes, yet spent most of his life laboring in the genre trenches, such posthumous acclaim will have to suffice. In the years since his passing, no one has come along with a similarly original vision of malevolent incoherence and cosmic indifference in the horror genre, and thus Fulci's achievements as a director and a genre game-changer have grown continuously more evident. A monster on the set, possessing a terrible temper with both actors and crew – "I do not like stars," he told Robert Schlockoff quite frankly – Fulci worked essentially for himself, an artist seeking to create his films for an audience of one. And, indeed, even at the end of his life, he never gave up the hope of making another film. As he told Schlockoff,

> René Clair, once asked what he intended to do after *Le Silence est d'or*, simply answered: "Another film." And for us, film directors, that is the question: to be or not to be able to shoot another film. I ruined my life for [the cinema]. I have no family, no wife, only daughters. All women left me because I never stop thinking of my job. My only two hobbies are my dogs and my sailing boat. Work is very important to me. John Ford once said, "I know that in bars they are saying bad things about me. But I am shooting films in the mountains with Indians while they are talking [...]" (Schlockoff 1982, 54)

Fulci labored on his own terms to create a forbidding world of unreal reality – a world that may be the truest "reality" of all. His is a legacy that any director would be proud of, no matter how much she or he had to sacrifice to create it; in the end, to quote Gustave Flaubert, another extravagant personality, if "the man is nothing, the work – all" ("*l'homme n'est rien, l'oeuvre – tout*") (Flaubert 1875). Through his work, Fulci brilliantly discharged his debt to the cinema and to the world of the Gothic.

Chapter 3

FLASH GORDON AND THE 1930s AND '40s SCIENCE FICTION SERIAL*

Motion picture serials, the forerunner of today's serialized television dramas, have been around since the earliest days of the narrative cinema. Exhibitors rapidly realized that, in order to assure continued audience attendance, open-ended "cliff hangers" were needed, as they keep viewers returning week after week to find out the latest plot twists, character developments and, of course, how the hero or heroine escaped from the previous week's peril. The first real serial – with multiple episodes and a running weekly continuity – was Charles Brabin's *What Happened to Mary?* (1912), starring Mary Fuller as an innocent young woman who inherits a fortune while the villain of the piece tries to separate her from her newfound wealth.

The sequel to the serial, *Who Will Mary Marry?* (1913), serves as proof of the new format's success. But the real breakthrough came in 1914 with Louis Gasnier's *The Perils of Pauline*, starring Pearl White. *Pauline* established the hectic, action-packed formula that would persist until the production of the very last serial – Spencer Gordon Bennet's *Blazing the Overland Trail* – in 1956. Fistfights, nonstop action, minimal character exposition and a sense of constant, frenetic danger permeated *The Perils of Pauline* and this recipe generated a host of imitators.

Soon the "damsel in distress" format used in *The Perils of Pauline* was being employed by a number of other serials, including Francis J. Grandon's *The Adventures of Kathlyn* (1913), starring an equally athletic Kathlyn Williams, and Louis Feuillade's epic mystery *Fantômas* (1913). Early serials were shown in weekly installments, a practice that continued throughout the lifetime of the genre, but early serial chapters could run as long as an hour – particularly

---

* A version of this chapter was first published in 2011 by *Screening the Past* (online) as "Flash Gordon and the 1930s and 40s Science Fiction Serial" (number 32): http://www.screeningthepast.com/2011/11/flash-gordon-and-the-1930s-and-40s-science-fiction-serial/.

Figure 3. *Flash Gordon.*
Source: Author's collection.

in the case of Feuillade's *Les Vampires* (1915), one of the most popular of the silent serials. These weekly screenings usually took place as a major part of the cinema program and early serials were aimed at both adults and children. Occasionally, an enterprising entrepreneur would run a serial chapter throughout the week to maximize attendance.

By the late teens and early '20s, a fairly rigid structure had been defined through trial and error. Serials ran 12 to 15 episodes, with the first episode usually running a half-hour to set up the situation and introduce the protagonists (and their adversaries) to viewers. Subsequent episodes clocked in at roughly 20 minutes. Each episode ended with what the industry termed a "take-out" – a scene of violent peril from which the hero or heroine could not possibly escape. The next chapter would pick up the action at the same point, but offer a "way out" for the lead character: a trap door offering a convenient escape, jumping from a moving car, or breaking free from some sort of fiendish device created by the serial's chief villain.

The central characters in serials were more often types, rather than fully fleshed-out characters. In the early silent days, women were the protagonists of many of the action serials, thrown into situations of continual danger until the final reel unspooled. With the advent of women's voting rights in 1920, the lead character became, more often than not, a heroic male – blindingly handsome and often endowed with above average mental acuity (as an investigator, adventurer or soldier of fortune). A female companion was then introduced to support the hero's efforts, with the possible addition of a young boy or girl "sidekick" to encourage adolescent identification with the serial's characters. The hero was aided by a number of associates who usually worked as a team to support the lead's efforts. Lastly and most importantly (for the leads in serials were usually rather bland), there was the chief villain, often masked, whose identity was not disclosed until the final moments of the last chapter. Known in the trade as "brains" heavy, the villain would, in turn, be aided by a variety of henchmen, or "action" heavies, who would unquestioningly carry out the orders of their leader in a campaign of mayhem and violence that kept the serial's narrative in constant motion. Indeed, though the serial format would serve as the template for weekly television series starting in the early 1950s, serials were far more violent than early television fare; they were noted for their extreme, nonstop action, their propulsive music scores and seemingly impossible stunt work. Unlike contemporary television series, which are open-ended and conclude only when audience interest has evaporated, serials were designed as a "closed set" – fifteen episodes and out, shot on breakneck schedules of 30 days or fewer for completed films that could run as long as four hours in their final, chapter-by-chapter format.

Serials embraced nearly every genre – jungle serials (*Jungle Menace* [1937], with Frank Buck); crime serials (Alan James' *Dick Tracy* [1937], with Ralph Byrd); the supernatural (Normal Deming and Sam Nelson's *Mandrake the Magician* [1939], with Warren Hull); Westerns (William Witney and John English's *The Lone Ranger Rides Again* [1939], with Robert Livingston); and, of course, science fiction. Some of the earliest serials made were sci-fi efforts, including Robert Broadwell and Robert F. Hill's *The Great Radium Mystery* (1919), Otto Rippert's *Homunculus* (1916) and Harry A. Pollard's *The Invisible Ray* (1920); all were successful with the public, who clamored for more.

Note that, in almost all of these cases, two directors were assigned to a serial. This was because of the sheer bulk of material involved. Sometimes, directors worked on alternate days to keep from becoming burnt out; in other instances, one director would handle all the action scenes while another would shoot all the narrative exposition sequences. Serial scripts were immense, often running to 400 pages or more (or four times the length of an average feature), yet shooting schedules and budgets were often minuscule and directors were expected to shoot as many as 70 "setups" (complete changes of camera angle and lighting) a day to stay on schedule. Nat Levine – head of Mascot Studios, prime purveyor of serial fare until his company merged with Republic Pictures and arguably the most accomplished of the sound era serial makers – used ruthless cost-cutting to bring in such films as *The Phantom Empire* (1935), a 12 chapter science fiction/Western hybrid serial directed by Otto Brower and B. Reeves "Breezy" Eason and starring a young Gene Autry.

Pushing his directors and crews to the limit, Levine also cut corners on actors' salaries and other production costs so that every dime he spent showed up on the screen. Actors, directors and stunt men were left to fend for themselves; all that Levine cared about was finishing on time and on schedule. Levine also had an improvised dormitory set up on the Mascot lot in some vacant studio space; there, exhausted stuntmen, actors and technicians could catch a few minutes of sleep in between setups, then grab a cup of coffee and some doughnuts to wake up before being dragged back to the set. This arrangement allowed Levine to keep an eye on his employees at all times – something like the production system used by the Shaw Brothers studios in Hong Kong in the 1970s. If you stayed on the lot all the time, Levine always knew where to find you.

As veteran serial director Harry Fraser recalled in his memoirs (Fraser would go on to co-script the first *Batman* serial in 1943, which was directed by Lambert Hillyer), Nat Levine was "the real Simon Legree without a whip" (Fraser 1990, 102). Wrote Fraser:

> I recall doing a Rin-Tin-Tin for him, released under the title *The Wolf Dog* (1933, co-directed with Colbert Clark), as I recall. I had an *eighty* scene schedule one day, with the dog as the star and involved in most of the scenes. In addition to [former D. W. Griffith stock company member] Henry B. Walthall playing the human lead, there was a long list of supporting actors and actresses. Well, I came out with seventy scenes at the end of the day, but pushing everyone to the limit. But when the Serial King heard I was behind schedule by ten scenes, he practically accused me of causing the company to go bankrupt. My Scottish ire aroused, I listened to Nat rave on, then finally threw the script on the table and walked out of his office. (Fraser 1990, 102)

Conditions at the other studios were little better. By now firmly consigned to the "kiddie trade" where before they had also attracted adult audiences, serials were seen as bottom-of-the-barrel product and the major studios that churned them out (Columbia, Republic and Universal) saw them as strictly bottom line propositions. However, in many cases, viewers went to the theater each week not to see the feature attraction, but rather the serial, which kept them coming back for the next thrilling installment. Always cost-conscious, serial makers would usually spend most of their production budget on the first three or four chapters to entice exhibitors to book the serial and capture audience attention; subsequent episodes were then ground out as cheaply as possible.

To top it off, the seventh or eighth chapter of many serials would be a "recap" chapter, in which expensive action sequences from earlier episodes were recycled for maximum cost benefit. Then, too, stock footage from earlier serials, as well as newsreel sequences, were often employed to keep costs down. Thus, most serials were compromised from the start. Occasionally, a serial hero would emerge who would rate slightly better treatment than usual – often a comic book hero transferred to the screen. *Dick Tracy* was one of the first of these; *Flash Gordon* was another, the star of three Universal serials produced between 1936 and 1940. *Flash Gordon* began its life as a comic strip with a lavish, full color Sunday episode on 7 January 1934, as created by Alex Raymond. The strip proved popular almost immediately and, in 1936, Universal decided to gamble a significant amount of time and money on bringing *Flash* to the screen.

While estimates range widely, the serial was roughly budgeted at $350,000 – far more than the average serial at the time, which was usually brought in for $100,000 or less. Despite the generous budget, *Flash Gordon* was an ambitious project, requiring spectacular sets (many of them borrowed from other Universal productions), a plethora of special effects and a fairly large cast of principal actors. Director Frederick Stephani – who also co-wrote the film's script – was given a six-week schedule, but the circumstances surrounding the production were by no means luxurious. Even with an uncredited assist from co-director Ray Taylor, Stephani faced a daunting challenge. As Buster Crabbe – the star of the serial and, for many, the archetypal, iconic Flash Gordon – remembered years later:

> [They] started shooting *Flash Gordon* in October of 1935, and to bring it in on the six-week schedule, we had to average 85 setups a day. That means moving and rearranging the heavy equipment we had, the arc lights and everything, 85 times a day. We had to be in makeup every morning at seven, and on the set at eight ready to go. They'd always knock off for lunch, and then we always worked after dinner. They'd give us a break of a half-hour or 45 minutes and then we'd go back on the set and work until ten-thirty every night. It wasn't fun, it was a lot of *work*! (Kinnard 1998, 39)

In addition to Crabbe in the leading role, Jean Rogers was cast as Dale Arden, Flash's nominal love interest. Charles Middleton, then in his sixties, made an indelible impression as Ming the Merciless – perhaps the most memorable of all serial villains for his pure cruelty and sadism. Frank Shannon portrayed Dr. Zarkov, Flash's scientific advisor and mentor, and Priscilla Lawson appeared as Princess Aura, Ming's daughter, who vacillates between loyalty to her father and a more than passing interest in Flash. Buster Crabbe – who, as Clarence Linden Crabbe, won a gold medal for swimming in the 1932 Olympics – was only 26 when he took on the role of Flash. While others – including future *Ramar of the Jungle* star Jon Hall – tried out for the part, Crabbe was seemingly destined for the role.

As he told Karl Whitezel in 2000, Crabbe went to the audition for the role purely as a lark, with no real interest in the part. As he was watching Hall and others try out for the role from the sidelines, however, Crabbe was noticed by the serial's producer, Henry MacRae. After a brief conversation and with no audition at all, MacRae surprised Crabbe by offering him the part. Under contract to Paramount at the time and not happy about it, Crabbe expressed polite disinterest: "I honestly thought *Flash Gordon* was too far-out, and that it would flop at the box office. God knows I'd been in enough turkeys during my four years as an actor; I didn't need another one." But MacRae persisted and, finally, Crabbe told him that it was up to Paramount: "if they say you can borrow me, then I'd be willing to play the part" (Whitezel 2000, 52).

The two men shook hands on it and, a month later, Crabbe found himself on a Universal sound stage, tackling the role that would become his lifetime calling card. His dark hair bleached blonde for the role, Crabbe dove into the hectic production schedule with a sense of cheerful fatalism; fate had given him the role, so he tried to make the best of it. As filming progressed, Crabbe grew more confident and the cast and crew realized that they were working on something that was – to say the least – a notch above the usual serial fare. When production wrapped a few days before Christmas 1936, there was no wrap party; that would have cost money. A few actors went across the street to a local bar for drinks, director Stephani patted Crabbe on the back, thanking him for a "nice job," and that was all.

At the time, *Flash Gordon* seemed like just another assignment for the young actor, who had made six other features in 1936 alone as part of his Paramount contract. But, to Crabbe's surprise, *Flash Gordon* made him a star overnight when it was released in March of that year. As the pseudonymous "Wear" in *Variety* enthused:

> Universal's serialization of the *Flash Gordon* cartoon character in screen form is an unusually ambitious effort. In some respects, it smacks of old

serial days when story and action, as well as authentic background, were depended upon to sustain their vigorous popularity. Here, instead, feature production standard has been maintained as to cast, direction, writing and background [...] Buster Crabbe is well fitted for the title role, a robust, heroic youth who dares almost any danger. Character calls for plenty of action, which places him in a favorable light. Charles Middleton, best known of late for his Western character portrayals, is a happy choice as the cruel Ming, [and] brings a wealth of histrionic ability to the part. Jean Rogers and Priscilla Lawson, besides being easy on the eyes, are entirely adequate, former as Dale Arden and Miss Lawson as Emperor Ming's daughter. Frank Shannon indicates promise from his portrayal of the wild-eyed inventive genius [...] *Flash Gordon* should be a top grosser in the serial field. (Willis 1985, 49)

Thus, as Flash, Crabbe achieved a certain sort of cinematic immortality – although, to the end of his days, he maintained a love/hate relationship with the role, convinced (perhaps correctly) that it had typecast him permanently as an action hero when he longed for more serious parts. When the original film proved a box-office bonanza, Crabbe was called back for two sequels, the first of which was Ford Beebe and Robert Hill's *Flash Gordon's Trip to Mars* (1938). For his second outing, however, the production was no longer a first-class affair. As Crabbe remembered:

We started the routine of long days and short nights again, to grind out what would become a lesser product than the first had been, quality-wise. The producer took short-cuts, such as reusing some of the rocket ship footage filmed earlier, and replaying some of the landscape shots, assuming that audiences wouldn't know the difference [...] I never attempted to learn how well it did for Universal. Judging from the fact that, two years later, I would be called back for a third *Flash Gordon* serial [Ford Beebe and Ray Taylor's *Flash Gordon Conquers the Universe*, 1940], I assume it was almost as successful as the first had been. (Whitezel 2000, 56)

In between these three iconic serials, in an attempt to break away from the Flash Gordon character, Crabbe also portrayed Buck Rogers in a 1939 Universal serial (*Buck Rogers*) that was cranked out quickly on a modest budget and directed by Ford Beebe and Saul A. Goodkind. All the while, Crabbe kept appearing in "B" feature fare at Paramount – much to his chagrin, as he kept hoping for more substantial roles. But Paramount apparently saw little potential in the actor and, to Crabbe's shock, dropped him as a contract player in late 1939 despite his success with *Flash Gordon*. Screen tests at other studios, including Twentieth Century Fox, yielded nothing. Twentieth Century Fox studio head Darryl F. Zanuck, after seeing Crabbe's test, dismissed him with the words, "he's a character actor. We can hire all of them we need" (Whitezel 2000, 57).

Crabbe's next film would seal his fate in Hollywood; he agreed to appear in a string of no-budget Westerns for PRC (Producers' Releasing Corporation, arguably the cheapest studio in Hollywood). As astonishing as it seems today, of all the studios, only PRC would agree to put Crabbe in a starring role. His salary was roughly $1,000 a week for each six-day picture with star billing, such as it was, thrown in as an added inducement. From there, it was all downhill. Crabbe had achieved lasting fame as Flash Gordon, but he would be forever identified with the role; now, the future seemed to promise only bottom-of-the-barrel action pictures.

The die had already been cast even with the cost-conscious production of *Flash Gordon Conquers the Universe* (1940). Most of the cast had been replaced by lesser-known actors for reasons of economy, with only Charles Middleton and Frank Shannon reprising their roles as Ming and Zarkov. As Crabbe remembered, with evident sadness:

> I didn't like the final *Flash Gordon* serial. We used a lot of scenes that we'd done before, the uniforms were the same, [and] the scenery was the same. Universal had a library full of old clips: Flash running from here to there, Ming going from one palace to another, exterior shots of flying rocket ships and milling crowds. It saved a lot of production time, but I thought it was a poor product that was nothing more than a doctored-up script from earlier days. (Whitezel 2000, 59)

Yet, for all the compromises and production shortcuts, the *Flash Gordon* trilogy stands as a major achievement in science fiction cinema history; indeed, the first *Flash Gordon* serial was selected in 1996 by the Library of Congress National Film Registry as being "culturally, historically, or aesthetically significant" (Wikipedia 2013). No matter that it used recycled sets and costumes, nor that its score comprised almost entirely of stock music from other Universal films – such as James Whale's *The Invisible Man* (1935), Whale's *Bride of Frankenstein* (1935), Lambert Hillyer's *Dracula's Daughter* (1936), Edgar G. Ulmer's *The Black Cat* (1934) or Rowland V. Lee's *Son of Frankenstein* (1939) – interspersed with snippets of new music by house composer Clifford Vaughan and "lifts" from Liszt, Brahms, Tchaikovsky and Wagner (this last music cue from *Parsifal* fitting in quite nicely). The trio of serials had made in indelible impact on popular culture.

The rocket ships were generally ineffective miniatures, the plots were predictably preposterous and the special effects were often primitive, but somehow, none of this mattered. For the first two serials, at least – as *Variety* noted in their review – the cast performed with a sense of conviction and cohesion that lifted the project out of the ordinary and into the realm of myth and wonder. There is a genuine chemistry between Crabbe and Jean Rogers and, although the first serial in particular is clearly geared towards a juvenile audience, it nevertheless has an adult feel to it – perhaps because all the principals took their roles seriously and didn't condescend to the audience.

Charles Middleton, for example, had been a song and dance man earlier in his career and had worked in films with everyone from Laurel and Hardy to director Cecil B. DeMille (in *The Sign of the Cross*, 1932). He also provided a memorable foil for the Marx Brothers in Leo McCarey's *Duck Soup* (1933) and appeared in a typically villainous role in John Ford's adaptation of John Steinbeck's *The Grapes of Wrath* (1940). In all, Middleton appeared in more than 190 films and worked in every imaginable role right up to his death in 1948. Like the other actors in the *Flash Gordon* films, Middleton played his role with conviction and sincerity and, as Ming, lent a certain gravitas to the entire enterprise. The world of *Flash Gordon* is at once fantastic and real; one feels for the characters, which are drawn with greater depth than traditional serial protagonists so that they seem to be actual personages in an actual world, albeit one far removed from our own.

In the wake of the *Flash Gordon* trilogy, other science fiction serials would follow – most from Republic Pictures. Many of the Republic efforts were quite effective, with high production values and superb special effects by Howard and Theodore Lydecker. These included Spencer Gordon Bennet and Fred C. Brannon's dystopic *The Purple Monster Strikes* (1945), which dealt with an alien invasion from Mars; William Witney and Brannon's memorably sinister *The Crimson Ghost*, in which the titular villain attempts to steal a counteratomic weapon known as a Cyclotrode in order to achieve the (somewhat predictable) aim of world domination; Spencer Gordon Bennet, Wallace A. Grissell and stuntman extraordinaire Yakima Canutt's *Manhunt of Mystery Island* (1945) with its plot device of a "transformation chair" to bring to life the serial's villain, one Captain Mephisto (Roy Barcroft, Republic's go-to heavy in residence), and a plot centering on the theft of a "radioatomic power transmitter"; and Harry Keller, Franklin Adreon and Fred C. Brannon's *Commando Cody: Sky Marshall of the Universe* (1953), the only serial directly designed as a syndicated television series, thus providing a link between the nonstop frenzy of the serial format and the more intimate domain of domestic TV fare.

Using recycled footage from Brannon's *King of the Rocket Men* (1949), *Radar Men From the Moon* (1952) and *Zombies of the Stratosphere* (1952), *Commando Cody*'s format was a definite departure from the usual serial template; each 30-minute episode was self-contained, yet the series maintained continuity so that each episode could be run as a "stand alone" or as part of a group. Released theatrically in 1953, the series of 12 episodes was picked up by NBC as a network series and ran from 16 July 1955 to 8 October 1955 (Hayes 2000, 124). However, despite this attempt to move into television, Republic's operation was winding down; the company's last serial was Franklin Adreon's nondescript *King of the Carnival* (1955). Republic officially closed its doors as a production entity on 31 July 1959, although it still exists today as a holding company and a distributor of past products (Flynn and McCarthy 1975b, 324).

Though the later Republic, Columbia and Universal sci-fi serials provided predictably pulse-pounding entertainment, there seemed at length to be a perfunctory air about many of the serials in the mid-to-late 1940s. They were predictable, their plots unfolded like clockwork, they did the job and got out. All nuances and much of the human element were gone. The serials had become a well-oiled machine, delivering predicable thrills on an assembly line basis with characters that lacked depth, personality or individuality. Serial leads were utterly replaceable, as were serial heroines – they did their job and went home – and dialogue was confined to exposition, with more and more repetition and recapitulation creeping in as the years passed by. The *Flash Gordon* serials created a world in which its characters lived and took on definite human shape; subsequent serials, no matter how well-crafted, lacked this three-dimensional quality.

Universal had been producing serials since 1914 and had 137 productions in all to their credit and more chapter plays than any other company when the ignominious end finally came with 1946's *Lost City of the Jungle* (directed by Ray Taylor and Lewis D. Collins and shot almost simultaneously with *The Mysterious Mr. M*, directed by Collins and Vernon Keays). *Lost City of the Jungle* has achieved a certain notoriety as famed character actor Lionel Atwill's last film; the actor was fighting what would ultimately prove to be fatal bronchial cancer and pneumonia and was forced to leave the film in the midst of production. Ironically, Atwill agreed to film his "death scene" for *Lost City of the Jungle* as his last work in front of the camera, leaving much of his role in the serial incomplete. Atwill then departed the Universal lot, never to return, and died on 22 April 1946. To finish *Lost City of the Jungle*, Universal used a double, created a new subplot to make Atwill's character an underling instead of the "brains" heavy and used outtakes for Atwill's reaction shots. It didn't work. *Lost City of the Jungle* was released on 23 April 1946 – the day after Atwill's death – to generally dismal results. When *The Mysterious Mr. M*, a nondescript science fiction serial, was released to a similarly lukewarm reception, Universal called it quits.

Columbia fared a little better. Lambert Hillyer's incredibly racist *Batman* (1943), for example – the first appearance of the caped crusader on the screen –

had a strong sci-fi element in the "mad lab" of Dr. Daka (J. Carrol Naish), a Japanese spy working to sabotage the Allied war effort. While it was a solid enough effort, it relied on characters that were sketched in broad, charcoal strokes with little shading or detail. The *Superman* serials from producer Sam Katzman's Columbia unit – 1948's *Superman*, directed by Spencer Gordon Bennet and Thomas Carr, and 1950's *Atom Man vs. Superman*, directed by Bennet alone – also have strong sci-fi elements, including disintegrator rays, teleportation machines and, of course, the person of Superman himself. Superman was played in both serials by Kirk Alyn and took the form of "a strange being from another planet who came to Earth with powers and abilities far beyond those of mortal men," as the narrative introduction for the subsequent *Superman* TV series – in which George Reeves took over the title role – would have it. But, in the two Columbia serials, whenever Superman was called upon to fly to the rescue, the legendarily cost-conscious Katzman would switch to two-dimensional animation rather than using the more expensive live action footage, seriously compromising the production as a whole. The television incarnation of *Superman* ultimately served the franchise much more effectively, with vastly improved live action special effects.

Thomas Carr, for example – whose career as an actor stretched back to the silent era and who actually played the role of Captain Rama of the Forest People in *Flash Gordon's Trip to Mars* – switched to directing program Westerns in the 1940s and would go on to direct a number of the early episodes of the *Superman* TV series, bringing much of the serial sensibility with him. But many viewers criticized the first season of the TV *Superman* series for its "excessive," serial-like violence; it took a regime change at the producer level to create a more "user-friendly" *Superman* for home consumption. What had worked in the theaters – usually out of the view of parents and guardians on a Saturday morning – raised eyebrows when Mom or Dad watched along with their children in the family den.

Thus, a "softer" *Commando Cody* and *Superman* paved the way for 1950s Saturday morning children's sci-fi, including a filmed West German, half-hour version of *Flash Gordon, Captain Video and His Video Rangers, Tom Corbett, Space Cadet, Captain Midnight* and *Rocky Jones, Space Ranger* – which had, arguably, the best production values of the lot (Dixon 2008). These Saturday morning teleseries would soon lead to more adult sci-fi, with *The Twilight Zone, The Outer Limits, Star Trek* and *Battlestar Galactica* all in prime time and the children's serial, as it had flourished in the past, fading into the mists of our collective memory.

Yet, of all these serials, it is the *Flash Gordon* trilogy that still commands our attention today. Its scrolling titles and futuristic gadgetry clearly inspired George Lucas's *Star Wars* series – particularly the initial episode, released in 1977. It has also inspired a host of remakes; after the 1954–55 West German series, there was an animated series entitled *The New Adventures of Flash Gordon* (1979–80), Mike Hodges' 1980 feature film featuring Max von Sydow as Ming the Merciless – which failed to live up to expectations – as well as Michael Benveniste and Howard Ziehm's X-rated parody *Flesh Gordon* (1974) and a sequel, Ziehm's *Flesh Gordon Meets the Cosmic Cheerleaders* (1989). As of this writing, director Breck Eisner has announced that plans are in the works for a new 3D version of *Flash Gordon*, which will bypass the 1980 film *and* the Universal serials and go straight back to Alex Raymond's comic strip for inspiration. So, it seems that Flash will always be with us and that the original serials – tacky and art deco in design though they may be – will remain talismans of our cinematic past.

As for the sci-fi serial format itself, the serial truly paved the way for the television series of the 1950s and beyond; it offered compact thrills and a continuing storyline within the confines of a twenty to thirty minute template and, just like contemporary television serials, kept audiences coming back for more week after week. Today's teleseries are considerably more sophisticated – both in their technology and in their narrative structure – and the characters that inhabit them are, for the most part, fully dimensional human beings and not cardboard archetypes. Yet, they owe a considerable debt to the serials, which inhabited a world of constant action, peril and imagination, but were ultimately too simplistic for contemporary audiences. The half-hour television series format simply erased the serial from public consciousness; the theatrical serial had become obsolete.

People didn't have to go out anymore to see the latest adventures of their favorite sci-fi heroes and heroines; they could watch them on TV. And so, just as *Flash Gordon* and its sci-fi serial brethren predicted much of our future technology (rockets, telescreens, the possibility of interplanetary travel), it also paved the way for the medium of television, with its chaptered format, rigorous schematic structure and cliffhanging plot lines. The future of sci-fi television, as well as theatrical series (the *Star Wars* and *Star Trek* feature films are two obvious examples), played out in the '60s, '70s and '80s and continues up to the present day; many of the plots are as fantastic as the early science fiction serials, even if the special effects have markedly improved. But the *Flash Gordon* serials played in important part in the creation of contemporary televisual formats – as well as in the serial-like sequel formats of many contemporary theatrical science fiction franchises – and offered to audiences a sense of wonder and amazement that still both resonates today and continues to gesture towards the future.

Chapter 4

JUST THE FACTS, MAN: THE COMPLICATED GENESIS OF TELEVISION'S *DRAGNET**

All I want to do is make a million dollars.
—Jack Webb, 1953 (Hayde 2001, 59)

Jack Webb had a lot of help when he created the hit series *Dragnet*. The series marked a significant departure from existing models of "crime and punishment" police and detective shows – which had, in the past, existed only in exaggerated versions. With *Dragnet*, the quotidian, everyday aspects of police work came to the fore, portrayed in minute detail. But the origins of *Dragnet* are shrouded in a good deal of contentious disputation and it's clear that series creator, Jack Webb, was not the only person involved in establishing the format for the show. Born in Santa Monica, CA, on 2 April 1920, Webb never knew his father, Samuel Webb, who deserted Jack's mother and filed for divorce shortly before Jack's birth (Hayde 2001, 9). Samuel Webb then vanished completely from Jack's life – swallowed up by the Depression – leaving Jack, his mother, Margaret, and her mother, Emma, to get by as best they could (Hayde 2001, 9–10).

As a child, Jack Webb was plagued by a variety of debilitating illnesses and thus forced to spend many hours in bed. There, he compensated for his incapacity by becoming an omnivorous reader of books borrowed from the public library or magazines scavenged from trash cans outside the family's cramped apartment (Hayde 2001, 10). Indeed, Webb was so ill during his childhood that he was unable to walk up a flight of stairs and had to be carried up by his mother; he didn't start attending school until he was nine years old, simply because his health was so precarious (Hayde 2001, 10). After graduating from Belmont High School – where he put on variety shows and

---

* A version of this chapter was first published in 2012 by *Film International* (online) as "Just the Facts, Man: The Complicated Genesis of Television's Dragnet" (25 November): http://filmint.nu/?p=6348.

Figure 4. Jack Webb and Ben Alexander in *Dragnet*.
Source: Author's collection.

got his first exposure to the technical aspects of radio production – Webb tried his hand at standup comedy, amazingly enough. Later, he worked as a disc jockey on *The Coffee Club*, assembling a voluminous record collection in the process, as well as creating and starring in a now-forgotten series entitled *One Out of Seven*, which was written by future *Dragnet* co-creator Jim Moser, whom Webb met while working as a staff announcer at radio station KGO, San Francisco (Hayde 2001, 11–12).

Indeed, in his early years, Webb's career focus seemed scattered, yet his drive and determination were never in doubt. Growing up during the Depression, like many others, Webb found escape at the movies; at one point, he became so enamored with Walt Disney's production of *Snow White and the Seven Dwarfs* (1937) that he parlayed his nascent skill as an amateur cartoonist into a scholarship at the Chouinard Art Institute in Los Angeles and even applied to the Disney Studios for work as an animator. Webb dropped off his portfolio at Disney's personally, convinced that his future lay in animation – yet, amazingly, forgot to include his return address. Predictably, Disney never got back to him (Hayde 2001, 11).

After that, Webb attended Los Angeles City College and created the radio series *A Half-Hour to Kill* – an early attempt at a murder mystery – for the college's radio station. He also began spending his nights at jazz joints – where he met his future wife, singer Julie London – then worked in a steel mill before impulsively joining the Army Air Force. There, he was assigned to a desk job as a clerk typist while directing USO variety shows on the side, eventually earning a dependency discharge in 1945 so he could work to support his ailing mother (Hayde 2001, 11). Desperate for cash, Webb worked as a bit actor in a variety of film roles in the late 1940s and early 1950s in addition to playing the wisecracking lead in *Pat Novak, for Hire*, a private eye radio series that ran for one season in 1946–47.

Most notably during this period, Webb appeared in the role of an assistant director in Billy Wilder's classic drama *Sunset Boulevard* (1950). When he got the chance to play a bit role as a forensic crime lab technician in Alfred L. Werker and Anthony Mann's noir classic *He Walked by Night* (1948), however, he saw that the gritty style the film embraced offered a new approach to the detective genre – a new angle that he had been looking for. Webb promptly appropriated the no-nonsense documentary style of *He Walked by Night* to create the hit radio series *Dragnet*, right down to the "this is the city, Los Angeles, California" opening narration; he also used the same deadpan, procedural approach for *Dragnet* that had worked so well in *He Walked by Night*. *Dragnet* was an immediate hit on radio, but Webb – who had been angling for a shot at the big time for decades – saw that radio was a dying medium.

With television rapidly draining away radio audiences, Webb saw that he had to make the jump to TV and, with the aid of director/editor Herbert L. Strock, Webb did just that. During his long career, Strock helmed the prescient science fiction feature *Gog* (1954), as well as numerous episodes of the early television series *Highway Patrol*, starring Academy Award winner Broderick Crawford. Strock was also a pioneer in the TV medium, directing the early teleseries *The Cases of Eddie Drake*, produced for CBS in 1949. Strock also directed episodes of *Bonanza, Maverick, Colt .45, 77 Sunset Strip, Cheyenne, The Alaskans, Sky King, Sea Hunt, The Veil, Science Fiction Theater, I Led Three Lives* and other series; another significant credit Strock notched up was as the editor of Herk Harvey's remarkable fantasy film *Carnival of Souls* in 1962, as well as Curt Siodmak's *The Magnetic Monster* (1953), Richard Carlson's *Riders to the Stars* (1954) and, as late as 1992, post-production supervisor on Wade Williams' remake of Edgar G. Ulmer's 1945 noir classic *Detour* (1992). So, Strock certainly knew his way around a sound stage. Yet, if Strock had one personal failing, it was his inability to stand up for himself in the face of opposition and so his credits as both director and editor fall into two distinct groups: projects on which he had a sympathetic and/or supportive producer, who left him alone to get the job done, and other projects, where he received little or no credit at all despite significant contributions because of his self-effacing nature.

Webb, on the other hand, had never directed film or television before; so, though he knew what he wanted, Webb needed Strock's technical expertise to help bring his vision to life and hired Strock to direct the pilot for the TV version of *Dragnet*. Shooting on sets that matched the interior of the Los Angeles Police Department down to the last detail, Webb and Strock's *Dragnet* had a distinctive visual look (tight close-ups on the faces of the actors as they delivered their lines; mechanical, repetitive editing which cut on each line, waiting for the response from the other actor; the use of drab locations and equally utilitarian sets; flat, harsh lighting to give the series a documentary feel) that set it apart from other television series of the era. Webb also insisted that all the actors in the series read their lines off teleprompters, thus eliminating rehearsals and forcing the actors to read their lines with the robotic air that Webb wanted. Yet, the collaboration between Strock and Webb was an uneasy one. When Webb felt confident enough to take over after watching Strock direct the pilot for the series – for which Strock received only an editorial credit – Webb summarily fired Strock in 1952 and began directing the series himself, although the visual and editorial style the two men had co-created remained intact.

While *Dragnet*'s social and cultural vision is largely attributable to Jack Webb, Strock's influence on the visual stylization of the series cannot be discounted. And, indeed, Strock was there at the very beginning of the series, working alongside the demanding and deeply insecure Webb, who saw *Dragnet* as his one "make it or break it" shot at the big time. As Strock recounted in his autobiography, *Picture Perfect*,

> I was introduced to Jack Webb and Homer Canfield, the *Dragnet* radio producer at NBC, and was eventually employed as director and editor on the pilot of the original *Dragnet* television series. Because I had plunged into television with a smattering of knowledge of TV production, actors' deals, photography, and techniques of the day, and because I had helped to form the Television Producers Association and aided in getting the Television Academy off to a start, I was hired by Jack Webb [...] I hired some of my crew from the *Eddie Drake* series and from feature productions, and we were off and running with *Dragnet*, which was a tremendous success. (Strock 2000, 16)

However, the two men soon clashed. Webb was, in Strock's view, "a lonely man, in constant search of someone to intimidate [...] he would call me at all hours of the night, and demand that I meet him at the studio to discuss a problem that often did not really exist" (Strock 2000, 18). Webb's shooting schedule was draconian; as Strock notes, "we were virtually shooting around the clock and over [...] holiday weekend[s]" (17). It was Strock who showed Webb how to give *Dragnet* the individual visual look that set it apart from other television series of the era. Surprisingly, despite the fact that the actors were simply reading their lines from teleprompters on the set during shooting rather than memorizing them – which should have saved time – the production pressure was relentless:

> For dramatic reasons, lines would sometimes be rewritten and have to be changed on all the various prompter sheets with large, permanent brush pens, which made reading more difficult. It was time consuming, but radio actors read lines, they don't learn them, and most of the cast, in the earlier shows, came from radio. The tension on these shows was unbearable, and not just because of tight schedules and prompters. Webb was tough on everyone. [...] I recognized his innate acting ability and quick mind. He was in his element when he was giving orders. In spite of his posturing, he was an extremely energetic and brilliant man and a fast learner. It didn't take him long to decide to be star, producer, *and* director of the show, and he did it very well. In fact, when I finally decided I'd reached the end of my rope with him, he told me I was a damn good teacher who taught him too fast how to direct, and he would now direct his own shows. (Strock 2000, 18)

The situation was ultimately untenable for Strock, who was essentially a gentle man and no match for Webb's authoritarian abrasiveness. But the *Dragnet* saga had an ironic coda for Strock. As he recalls, "years later, when we accidentally met on a plane, [Webb] surprised me by saying he owed his success to me – praise that came a little late!" (Strock 2000, 18). Bleak, unrelenting and highly stylized for all of its embrace of skid row realism, *Dragnet* mirrored the dark side of the Eisenhower era and became an iconic milestone in television history.

Before the series went off-the-air in its first incarnation (it would be revamped by Webb in a desperate attempt to salvage his flagging career in 1966 with a TV movie that spawned a short-lived, tone deaf revival of *Dragnet* from 1967 to 1970), the *original* television series of *Dragnet* racked up no fewer than 276 half-hour episodes, effectively spanning the entire decade of the 1950s from 16 December 1951 to 23 August 1959. At the same time, to wring every last possible dollar out of the franchise, *Dragnet* continued as a radio show from its original airdate of 3 June 1949 to 26 February 1957, even as the television series took firm hold of the nation's consciousness.

The 1950s version of *Dragnet* was, in many ways, an "outlier" in the contemporary televisual landscape; easily burlesqued and imitated, there was still nothing else like it in terms of hard-nosed stylization, grimly procedural story lines and, for the period, grimy authenticity. A look at some of the plot lines demonstrates just how out of sync *Dragnet* was in a world populated by the likes of *The Adventures of Ozzie and Harriet*, *The Donna Reed Show*, *Leave It to Beaver* and other enormously popular, family-oriented series of the era. *Dragnet*, by contrast, concentrated almost entirely on the downsides of 1950s American existence; misfits, psychos, drifters, con men and ne'er-do-wells collectively comprised the series' world. *Dragnet*'s world was the netherworld of American society and every episode made it clear that only the LAPD was holding back the tide of scum that threatened to engulf Los Angeles and, by extension, the entire nation.

In "The Big Death" (17 January 1952), an unsuspecting husband hires Joe Friday, LAPD detective and protagonist of the show, as a hit man to kill his wife; in "The Big Mother" (31 January 1952), a newborn infant is abducted from a hospital by an unstable young woman who is unable to have children herself; in "The Big Speech" (28 February 1952), Friday delivers a lecture warning on the evils of drug addiction at his former high school, even as he tracks down a teenage hoodlum who, in seeking his next fix, beats up and robs a friendly druggist; in "The Big Blast" (10 April 1952), which Webb both wrote and directed, a young mother is killed in her bed by a shotgun blast as her infant son slumbers next to her; in "The Big September Man" (8 May 1952), an unbalanced sociopath feels divinely inspired to kill "a sinner" and his former fiancée is his most recent victim; in the justly infamous ".22 Rifle for Christmas" (18 December 1952, *Dragnet*'s first "Christmas episode"), co-written by Moser and Webb, a young boy prematurely opens a Christmas gift – a .22 rifle – and accidentally kills one of his friends while playing with it, subsequently hiding the young victim's body in the brush on Christmas Eve.

In "The Big Lay Out" (16 April 1953), a high school honors student becomes strung out on heroin; in "The Big Hands" (21 May 1953), a young woman is found strangled to death in a cheap hotel room; in "The Big Nazi" (25 November 1958), Friday uncovers a high school neo-Nazi ring; and on and on it goes, a parade of beatings, stabbings, murders, rapes, robberies and wanton brutality that seems to have no end in sight, an unstoppable tidal wave of human greed, violence and corruption (Hayde 2001, 264–87). Compared to the 1960s version of the series, which kicked off with an unintentionally risible episode on the dangers of LSD – the "Blue Boy" episode, actually titled "The LSD Story," first broadcasted on 12 January 1967 – the 1950s version of *Dragnet* bristles with menace, energy and simmering social disruption; no one even thinks of "Mirandizing" suspects because, of course, no such law existed. Instead, Joe Friday and his partner, Frank Smith (Ben Alexander), sweat out an assortment of lowlifes, stoolies, drug addicts and convicted felons, quickly resorting to physical violence when even the slightest excuse to do so presents itself. Of course, in this, the original TV version of *Dragnet* effectively mirrors the racist, homophobic and right-wing Los Angeles Police Department of the period – then under the direction of Chief W. H. Parker, who was similarly adrift in the 1960s, oblivious to the demands and concerns of a new generation that was better educated, more independent, not afraid to challenge authority and, as the decade progressed, almost universally opposed to the war in Vietnam.

For all intents and purposes, however, Strock's work on the series seems to have been conscientiously erased in one manner or another. But an assiduous search of the archives at the Margaret Herrick Library of the Academy of Motion Picture Arts and Sciences reveals two tantalizing pieces of information. The *Daily Variety* for 7 January 1952 lists Strock as the film editor for the series – as he is credited in "The Human Bomb" pilot episode – yet, by 11 February 1952 (just one month later), *Daily Variety* records that Strock had been dropped from the series and replaced by Robert Leeds. In addition, in their review of "The Human Bomb" printed on 19 December 1951, *Weekly Variety* failed – in a departure from their usually scrupulously complete credits for all the films and television shots they covered – to assign any editorial credit *at all* to the series, while writer Jim Moser and Webb are both prominently credited ("Jose" 1951, 27).

What makes all of this even more suspect – at least in my eyes – is that only two days earlier in *Daily Variety* (17 December 1951), in another unsigned review, Strock is given credit as "Associate Producer" for the pilot, which is certainly a few notches up from merely being the editor. Thus, having spoken personally with Strock at great length in a detailed telephone interview before his death on 30 November 2005 and having also reviewed not only the materials in the Margaret Herrick Library, but also in the Jack Webb Papers at UCLA, and taking into account Strock's career path as a whole, I, for one, am inclined to believe his version of events. Strock was far from the only person whom Webb used and then summarily disposed of during his march to the top of the Nielsen ratings.

Webb's politics – though he always insisted that *Dragnet* was entertainment and not social engineering – leaned resolutely to the far right and impatience and intolerance with any differing points of view were shared equally by the actor in real life and the character he played. On the set, Webb was a classic bully, threatening actors and technicians and – once the yoke of Joe Friday had been indelibly placed upon him – increasingly consumed by a desire to get the day's shooting over as fast as possible; episodes of the second iteration of *Dragnet*, such as "The Big Prophet" (11 January 1968) – essentially, a half-hour tirade on the evils of drugs – were knocked off in less than *one day* of shooting as Friday and Joe Gannon, his new partner (Harry Morgan), interrogate a Timothy Leary-esque messiah figure who espouses the "mind-expanding" use of LSD.

Where the black-and-white *Dragnet* episodes of the 1950s would often take three to four days to film and involve numerous camera setups and carefully designed lighting, camera movement and narrative structures, "The Big Prophet" was in fact shot using only *five* camera setups for the entire half-hour; the camera gazes in somnolent stupefaction as Friday delivers yet another of his patented "Jesus Speeches," intended to set miscreants firmly on the path to law-abiding righteousness.

Sure enough, the 1967–70 incarnation of *Dragnet* lasted only 3 years and 98 episodes. Shot in garish, cheap color on garish, cheap sets with "hotspots" abounding on the walls and doors, the series lacks both care and conviction; any attempt at authenticity has vanished. In the 1960s *Dragnet*, we're left with a threadbare scold who doesn't understand what's going on in the world, doesn't want to know and, much like Mitt Romney, the failed Republican candidate in the 2012 presidential election, would love to return to the 1950s forever – to when gays were "sexual deviants" and women were fit only to be fashion accessories or baby machines. Perhaps this is why the 1960s shows – which only marginally scraped by in their original network turn – found their largest and most enthusiastic audience when they were run as camp artifacts in the late 1980s on *Nick at Nite*. While the 1960s version of *Dragnet* was the product of a tired, irascible, out-of-touch reactionary, the 1950s version brought home the reality of American life in the 1950s like no other show before or since.

But Webb's interaction with Herbert L. Strock in the early days of *Dragnet* is far from an isolated instance. Having come up the hard way and having appropriated so many ideas from others on his way to small screen stardom, Webb was well known to use people in the most brutal fashion as long as they could help him and then discard them without a backward glance. Not only was he tough on his crews and actors throughout *Dragnet*; he was equally rough on his business partners. From the start, Webb was ruthless in his desire to get whatever he wanted. To get *Dragnet* off the ground as a radio series, for instance, Webb required the assistance of agent Robert Rosenberg – who, in fact, owned the series outright, while Webb was merely a salaried employee. Needless to say, Webb wasn't happy about this and he refused to sign any contracts to bring *Dragnet* to television with NBC until he gained full ownership of the series. Rosenberg, erroneously reasoning that Webb needed *Dragnet* more than *Dragnet* needed Webb – in short, that Webb could be replaced with another actor/director – refused to sell out.

Thus began an intricate game of brinksmanship – the details of which are still somewhat obscure to this day – in which the series producer, Michael Meshekoff, somehow talked Rosenberg into signing over ownership to Webb. Webb then promptly fired Rosenberg, who immediately sued him for $300,000 in damages (Hayde 2001, 40–41).

With NBC and sponsor Liggett & Myers on his side, Webb now had the upper hand and Rosenberg settled out of court while Mike Meshekoff, who had worked for the agency headed by Rosenberg, resigned to become *Dragnet*'s new producer (Hayde 2001, 41). As payback for Meshekoff's help in pulling off this coup, Webb offered the erstwhile agent 25 percent of the show – which Meshekoff accepted – while Rosenberg was reduced to a mere $625 per week of the series' net profits; now *he*, not Webb, was the salaried employee (Hayde 2001, 41). But manifestations of Webb's inherent insecurity continued to pop up. When Webb was in the final negotiations with NBC for the *Dragnet* television pilot, he suddenly insisted that he was wrong for the leading role of Joe Friday and suggested that veteran actor Lloyd Nolan play the role. NBC wouldn't hear of it; Webb *was* Joe Friday whether he liked it or not and, if he wanted to direct the series, they'd give him a shot, but only if he also took on the leading role. Reluctantly, Webb, who was afraid he was spreading himself too thin, acquiesced to the network's demands (Hayde 2001, 41).

This was not the end of the off-screen turmoil. In 1954, as Lucanio and Coville, co-authors of "Behind Badge 714: The Story of Jack Webb and *Dragnet*," recount, Webb moved against Meshekoff, whom he now regarded as a "moneyman" and not a creative person, as Webb thought himself to be; he replaced him with Stanley Meyer, who immediately began negotiations for a big screen feature version of *Dragnet*, which came out in 1954 (Lucanio and Coville 1993b, 80). Nor was this the only legal or personal battle Webb faced in 1954; on 25 November, his divorce from Julie London became final, with Webb being required to pay alimony and child support for the couple's two daughters, as well as $500,000 in a property settlement. Significantly, not only did Webb not contest the ruling, but he wasn't even present in court as he was busy wrapping up shooting on the *Dragnet* episode "The Big Gangster" at the time – and, obviously, work came first (Hayde 2001, 75). During the same period, Webb gave an uncharacteristically unvarnished interview on the split with both Rosenberg and Meshekoff, in which he griped, "what the hell have [Rosenberg and Meshekoff] done since they left me? You just show me their track records […] some of these money men even tell me they create, too. They don't create as much as the worst bit actor in the show" (Lucanio and Coville 1993b, 80).

Shortly after this, Jim Moser – who had been the principal writer and, in many respects, not only the narrative, but also the ideological architect of the series' bleak worldview (only the police are competent; average citizens are either incompetent or obstructions to police work; criminals permeate every level of society and are at constant war with the common good – in short, rampant Cold War era paranoia) – got into a heated argument with Webb over Moser's freelancing work. In particular, they contended over Moser's scripts for the new hospital drama *Medic*, starring Richard Boone, which Webb viewed as direct competition to *Dragnet*; further, Webb accused Moser of appropriating *Dragnet*'s flat, matter-of-fact style in his scripts for *Medic* to bring a new degree of realism to the series, which was indeed a healthy departure from the *Dr. Kildare* vision of the medical profession (Lucanio and Coville 1993b, 80).

What made the situation more peculiar was that Moser had pitched *Medic* to Webb's Mark VII Productions as a possible series, but Webb, surprisingly, was convinced that a hospital drama would be too grim to attract a mass audience (Hayde 2001, 102). Webb was wrong; *Medic*, despite being slotted by NBC directly opposite *I Love Lucy*, lasted for two full seasons (1954–56) and was lauded by critics. When it eventually folded, however, Moser found himself drawn back into *Dragnet*'s monolithic production machine along with *Medic*'s producer, Frank La Tourette (Hayde 2001, 201).

Nevertheless, at the time, the feud between Webb and Moser was hot copy for the trade journals (Lucanio and Coville 1993b, 80) and relations between Webb and Moser were indeed strained – so much so that, on Friday, 18 December 1954, Moser filed suit against Mark VII Productions for back pay on no fewer than 47 radio scripts that Moser had written for the radio version of *Dragnet*, which then had been recycled for scripts for the TV series. Moser had only been paid for the use of 19 of the 47 screenplays and sued for $9,100. The matter was almost immediately settled out of court, but the acrimonious atmosphere between the two men persisted; Webb was simply driving Moser too hard and was jealous of any "outside" projects he might pursue (Hayde 2001, 78).

Privately, Webb hoped that he would be able to take a hiatus from *Dragnet* to launch a television series based on his 1951 radio series *Pete Kelly's Blues*, starring a trumpet player in 1920s Kansas City. In what little downtime he had available to him, Webb was an inveterate fan of New Orleans jazz – a holdover from his turbulent youth – and he saw this new show as a way to expand his horizons. There had been 13 radio episodes of *Pete Kelly* in 1951; now, Webb wanted to translate *Pete Kelly* to the small screen, but the unceasing demands of *Dragnet* proved overwhelming. Webb directed and starred in a 1955 feature film based on the old radio scripts – also entitled *Pete Kelly's Blues*, in which Lee Marvin's performance completely overshadowed Webb's work in the film – and, in 1959, finally brought *Pete Kelly* to television for a 13 episode run, starring William Reynolds in the lead role. Critical and audience response for the show, however, was tepid.

But with *Dragnet* firmly established, Webb was able to make his biggest deal yet: cashing in on *Dragnet*'s popularity to make a fortune overnight. As the 89th episode – "The Big Crime," about the abduction and sexual molestation of twin girls, age four, by an "alcoholic delivery man" who later admits he would have killed them both had not Friday and his partner apprehended him – wrapped production on 23 December 1954 and Webb, under doctor's orders, decamped to Hawaii for a month's vacation to recuperate from his round-the-clock work on the series, the actor/director was preparing for his biggest coup of all: selling out all rights to the television version of *Dragnet* to MCA (the Music Corporation of America) for a cool $5 million in cash (Hayde 2001, 78–9).

Dragnet was now *very* hot property indeed. The big screen movie version from Warner Bros. (in color) was in the offing and NBC further affirmed their faith in the continuing pull of the series on 28 December 1954 with an order for an unprecedented *95 additional episodes* (Hayde 2001, 79). Whether he liked it or not – and there is ample evidence that Webb was growing weary of the Joe Friday straitjacket – *Dragnet* had become an unstoppable, seemingly endless franchise. Whether he wanted to accept it or not, Jack Webb was hopelessly typecast; the public wanted him as Joe Friday or they didn't want him at all. Ever the realist, Webb decided to give the public what they wanted.

With Webb still in Hawaii, attorneys for Mark VII Productions and MCA in Los Angeles hammered out a final deal for the TV rights to *Dragnet* on the last day of the year, 31 December 1954. The MCA deal was both straightforward and complex. For $5 million, MCA got all rights to *Dragnet* as a television show – both all episodes so far produced, as well as all episodes to come – with Webb receiving an additional $100,000 a year in salary and royalties, as well as retaining complete creative control over the series through Mark VII Productions, extending into perpetuity (which is why when the series was relaunched in 1967, it remained firmly in the hands of MCA/Universal, as the company later became known) (Hayde 2001, 79). Additionally, MCA set up an entirely separate arm of their television production unit, Sherry TV, exclusively to manage both *Dragnet* and *Badge 714*, as the series was known in syndication; with more than enough episodes in the can, it was time to cash in on the nationwide "network" of independent television stations with reruns as *Badge 714* while the network version, *Dragnet*, continued on its course until 1959 (Hayde 2001, 79).

With the paperwork finalized, Meshekoff – long departed from the show, yet still the owner of 25 percent of Mark VII Productions – sold out to MCA, who immediately sold the 25 percent back to Webb as part of the overall deal. In the end, Meshekoff got roughly $2 million for his interest in Mark VII by holding out until the MCA deal was finalized; Stanley Meyer, who had set up a deal with Warner Bros. for the *Dragnet* feature, got out with $1.25 million;

Webb walked away with $2.5 million (Hayde 2001, 79). Webb no longer owned *Dragnet* outright, but he had fulfilled his initial ambition: he was now a millionaire – *more* than a millionaire. That was all he had ever wanted and now he had achieved his goal. The rest of his life would be a postscript.

Chapter 5

THE DISQUIETING AURA OF FABIÁN BIELINSKY*

I said no to Hollywood. There you have no freedom to create.
—Bielinsky to Federico Fahsbender (Fashbender 2005)

Film audiences won't find in [The Aura] an accessible or agreeable story. Also, the film doesn't show a bit of sympathy or good intentions for any of the characters. I'm talking not only about the near total lack of humor, but also that dramatic concessions were avoided in the screenplay – even though this is not a very good attitude when you think of a film as a product to be sold.
—Bielinsky to Amadeo Lukas (Lukas 2009)

Fabián Bielinsky's career was brief, but incandescent, yet his moment in the public eye came after years of hard work and apprenticeship. Born on the 3 February 1959 in Buenos Aires, Bielinsky became obsessed with cinema during childhood and, by the age of 13, began making films while studying at the Colegio Nacional de Buenos Aires – one of which was the short film *Continuidad de los Parques* (1971), based on a short story by Julio Cortázar. After graduating from high school, Bielinsky suddenly decided to pursue studies in psychology, but soon abandoned this to enter the Centro de Experimentación y Realización Cinematografia (also known as Escuela Nacional de Experimentación y Realización Cinematográfica or ENERC) where he directed another short film – *La Espera* (*The Wait*, 1983), from a story by Jorge Luis Borges – which also attracted favorable attention, winning first prize at the International Festival of Huesco in Spain (Moviefone 2013). This led to a plethora of work as an assistant director and, before his debut as a feature director with *Nine Queens* in 1998, Bielinsky drove himself into the ground working on roughly 400 television commercials along with, in the words of one biographer,

---

* I thank Arso Risteski for his translation of Spanish-language sources. A version of this chapter was first published in 2013 by *Film International* (online) as "The Disquieting Aura of Fabián Bielinsky" (29 April): http://filmint.nu/?p=7610.

Figure 5. Fabián Bielinsky on the set of *The Aura*.
Source: Image courtesy of Photofest.

several high-profile feature films including Marco Bechis' *Alambrado*, Mario Levin's *Sotto Voce*, and Carlos Sorin's *Eterna Sonrise de New Jersey*. Bielinsky then worked his way up the ladder, climbing up to the tier of co-screenwriter and second director on two projects for filmmaker Fernando Spiner: *Bajamar, la Costa del Silencio* and *La Sonámbula*. Bielinsky's graduation to director happened somewhat capriciously; he won first prize in a filmmaking contest sponsored by Patagonik Film Group, Kodak, Cinecolor, JZ y Associados and FX Sound – a cash prize that gave him the funds to shoot his debut feature. This effort, 1998's *Nine Queens*, [won] awards around the globe, including Best Film, Best Director, Best Screenplay, and seven other accolades at the 2001 Argentinean Film Critics' Association Awards; Best Argentinean Film of the Year by FIPRESCI 2001; and the Audience Award and Best Director prizes at the 2001 Lleida Latin-American Film Festival. The picture, a labyrinthine crime thriller sans the comic overtones of *Pulp Fiction* and *True Romance* that had become *en vogue* at the time, deals with two small-time con artists, Juan (Gastón Pauls) and Marcos (Ricardo Darín), who partner up for a hotel-centered scam that involves a philatelic forgery. (Moviefone 2013)

Indeed, the film was a worldwide hit and even spawned a tepid American remake – *Criminal* (Gregory Jacobs, 2004), with John C. Reilly, Diego Luna and Maggie Gyllenhaal. Diplomatically, Bielinsky refused to discuss *Criminal*, telling Jorge Letelier that, "I promised not to talk about it. Let everyone draw their own conclusions. What do I know? It has very good actors" (Letelier 2006). In the meantime, *Nine Queens* unexpectedly "typed" Bielinsky as an expert in "caper comedies," something that he hadn't fully appreciated when the film was first released. But, even with *Nine Queens* – which is nothing more or less than a blinding series of double and triple crosses coupled with "slamming door" farce dealing with inopportune and/or staged exits and entrances – Bielinsky was trying mightily to break out beyond the barriers of convention. Fluent in both Spanish and English, Bielinsky was courted by the World Press and gave a series of valedictory press junket interviews on the film, telling the BBC's Tom Dawson that

> people told me that they wanted to make something more commercial. Before *Nine Queens*, in Argentina if you wanted to make money with your film, you had to do a stupid comedy with television actors. *Nine Queens* proved that you could make a personal film, without big stars, which wasn't a comedy, and that it could still make a load of money and get good reviews. (Dawson 2002)

But, of course, this really isn't the case; *Nine Queens* is resolutely commercial from start to finish and is seemingly designed to both dazzle and confuse audiences in the most nonthreatening fashion possible. One can hardly blame Bielinsky, though, for trying so ferociously to work his way out of the world of 60-second television spots and assistant director jobs with his first feature, for which he also wrote the screenplay. As Andrew L. Urban noted while conducting an interview with Bielinsky shortly after the film's release,

> Bielinsky has the odd phone call from those producers who had been offered the script but [rejected it]. "Some never called me again, but a few called and said, 'What can I say, I was wrong, I'm an [asshole] […] everybody's telling me I'm an [asshole] and they're right' […] but believe me, it's nothing like revenge for me because I did end up with the right producers and I'm glad I didn't make the film with those that knocked me back. Fate led me to the right place […] I've had a lot of phone calls – something like 15 different production companies from all over the world, but mainly Americans – have approached the production company to buy the script and do an English language remake. But not only American […] there were also people from England and France

interested. When there was vague talk of me directing a remake, I said absolutely not. I'm not going to make my first and second film the same. That's a crazy idea. [Instead, I'm working on] a psychological thriller – or something like that [...] about a decent man who is tempted by crime. I'd like to [...] you know, make it a small, warm film and keep full control. But the most amazing thing that happened to me with *Nine Queens* is that everybody from all over the world is calling me and they want to work with me and they offer me production and everything. All these doors are wide open waiting for me. But I'm trying not to think about all that [...] just thinking of the script and to finish that first." (Urban 2002)

Of course, in refusing to try to repeat himself, Bielinsky almost guaranteed diminishing returns – not to mention limited his future creative options for the rest of his career. But Bielinsky was already moving on, even disavowing the film that had put him on the map to a degree by refusing to categorize it as a comedy; rather, he called it a "personal film." Yes, it was a film over which Bielinsky had total creative control, but if he had followed in the ill-advised footsteps of such directors as Géla Babluani, whose slavishly uninspired 2010 American remake of his brilliant *13 Tzameti* (2005, titled simply *13*) pretty much finished his career, or George Sluizer, whose watered-down and fatally compromised 1993 American remake of his 1988 hit *Spoorloos* (*The Vanishing*) also caused a major career setback, he probably would have suffered much the same fate. As he told Urban of the proposed American remake, even at that early stage, the entire idea was inherently ridiculous: "You as director and the crew and the producers who made the film with you, we all agree that the film was perfect. Everybody loved the film, and it went great at the box office and we won all these accolades and awards and everybody liked the film [...] so, let's do it again" (Urban 2002).

No – that would *not* happen to Fabián Bielinsky. Even though, as Stuart Klawans would point out after Bielinsky's death, Bielinsky received "no [financial] windfall from *Nine Queens*, having signed away the film's rights to the [organizers of the competition that provided the financing]" (Klawans 2006, 348), making *Nine Queens* as his debut feature was still an exceptionally shrewd move. As Klawans notes, *Nine Queens* outgrossed Ridley Scott's *Gladiator* in Argentinian cinemas, but such outsize success comes with a definite price. As the press junket for *Nine Queens* wore on and on – even into 2002 – Bielinsky

[began] to sound apologetic. Because of *Nine Queens*, "I'm in a privileged situation," he [said] in March 2002 to Anthony Kaufman, an American reporter for *IndieWire*. "I have international connections and European

and American production companies contacting me to see what I want to do next. But filmmaking here is still very hard. I may be okay, but some of my friends are not, and the rest of the country is not, so it's not exactly a happy feeling" [...] To the world at large, [Bielinsky] embodie[d] the New Argentine Cinema; but to [...] critics and festival programmers who support them, Bielinsky is more like a Hollywood director with a Porteño accent. They see that the intricate, money-driven plot and quick pace of *Nine Queens* might easily be translated into an American re-make [...] [m]eanwhile, the upsurge of New Argentine Cinema is producing films that can't be categorized, translated or easily financed: Lucrecia Martel's brooding, atmospheric examination of middle class rot, *La Ciénaga*; Adrián Caetano's neo-realist portrait of an immigrant laborer, *Bolivia*; Diego Lerman's lesbian punk road movie, *Tan de repente*; Carlos Sorin's rueful and funny portrayal of small lives in large Patagonian spaces, *Historias minimas*. (Klawans 2006, 347)

And money, as it always is, remains the real stumbling block to creating anything of lasting value and worth in the cinema: give the public what they want and you'll probably make a least a modest profit, even if you don't hit the jackpot; try something riskier and you're in unchartered territory. As Klawans put it,

Bielinsky was not an impractical man. He chose to put forward *Nine Queens*, rather than another screenplay on hand, because it was playful in spirit, full of trickery and imposture. So ingeniously constructed was this mechanical toy that it might have belonged to a fairytale Emperor of China. So smoothly did the device amuse its actual owners – the ticket-buying masses – that audiences could accept it as if it were a conventional product. Bielinsky started out by giving the people something he knew they'd want: a yarn about an inexperienced young con artist, a swaggering older one, a primly beautiful woman, and an allegedly valuable sheet of postage stamps. [...] Stylistically self-contradictory and precedent-defying yet instantly accessible, *Nine Queens* belonged to no category except the biggest of them all: the movies. The generic thrill that Bielinsky offered his audience, and shared with them, was that of a Saturday matinée. "I felt the pleasure as a spectator all my life," he told an American interviewer, Pam Grady, around the time *Nine Queens* was released in the United States. "A teenage feeling. Oh, two hours of movies! To see the Metro lion and the Twentieth Century Fox searchlight and the Warner Bros. WB [...] It's like somebody telling you that you're going to have a good time." (Klawans 2000, 348–9)

Except that something terrible happened in the interim: Argentina's financial structure, always somewhat perilous, spiraled into near total collapse. As Anthony Kaufman reported,

> On December 19 [2001], mass protests erupted in Argentina over an economic crisis that was only getting worse. After riots in Buenos Aires resulted in a reported seven deaths, the economic minister and the president resigned, and what was South America's second largest economy (after Brazil) lay in ruin. Subsequently, the country has had several interim presidents and seems to be on the road to recovery, but as Campanella says, "No one knows exactly what's going to happen. It's even more complicated than Enron." At the 2002 Rotterdam Film Festival, several attending Argentine filmmakers issued a statement expressing their collective concerns. "Due to the lack of honesty and talent of the governing class," it said, "a richly endowed country was brought down at the very same moment that the Argentine cinema started to bear the fruits of the changes in the industry." (Kaufman 2002)

In this atmosphere of free fall, Bielinsky stood out as a commercial director in both senses of the word – he not only directed feature films that were resolutely commercial, as evidenced by *Nine Queens*, but also directed actual commercials for television, relying upon his skill in the medium to support his family while driving himself harder and harder. He was, in short, successful in the midst of catastrophe. Chain smoking, eating heavy foods, living on coffee and nerves, Bielinsky was soon diagnosed with hypertension brought on by both overwork and overweight, but he could see no way out of his situation. To repeat himself would be both artistic and career suicide; he could see that clearly. What, then, to do other than to continue on with his hectic lifestyle, living hand to mouth directing commercials, desperately trying to patch together funding for the project that would emerge as his last feature film, *The Aura* (2005)?

The roots of *The Aura* go way back in Bielinsky's childhood to a screening of John Boorman's *Deliverance* (1972), which so mesmerized the young cineaste that he refused to leave his seat until the management gave him a poster of the film as a souvenir (Harley 2006). Over the years, *Deliverance* occupied almost the entire space of the young director's mind; it's worth noting that, even as he suggested that after the success of *Nine Queens* he might next like to try his hand at "a psychological thriller," the first draft of the script for *The Aura* was written in 1983, the year he directed the short film *La Espera* and graduated from the national film school (Harley 2006). The film was in every way darker and more fatalistic than *Nine Queens*; as he declared from the outset of the film's production, *The Aura* was designed to please no one but its maker.

As Bielinsky told Jorge Letelier in the film journal *Mabuse*, "the [film's] theme is crime, but its structure allows for more discussions because [...] I decided to accept a series of brutal and dangerous breaks in the structure, because in a genre film audiences expect a certain type of structure and rhythm according to the rules of the genre in question. I opted to go on breaking those rules, so that things wouldn't happen when they were supposed to happen" (Letelier 2006). And this, indeed, is precisely what sets *The Aura* apart from more traditional crime "thrillers": it is, at its heart, a study in psychological penetration, gesturing back to the director's early studies in psychology and his examination of the ethos of *machismo* in Latin American society.

And it's clear that, as an omnivorous moviegoer, Bielinsky knew much better than most of the people who interviewed him that *Nine Queens* had been a work of precise calculation – every bit the same sleight-of-hand trick that the film itself celebrated. Make *The Aura* first? Not likely. Make a crowd pleaser first, designed to appeal to the widest possible audience, and *then*, if you were lucky and worked hard, you just *might* get a shot at a script that had been kicking around in your file drawers since your 24th birthday – a work so dark, so uncompromising, so willfully designed *not* to please that it might as well have been Godard's *Le Petit Soldat* or *Les Carabiniers* (both 1963), films which represented an outright assault on their respective audiences. And, when an unsuspecting critic suggested that someone like David Mamet might have been an influence on Bielinsky's work, the director was quick to disabuse them of *that* mistaken notion. When David Edwards ventured that Mamet might perhaps have been "a particular influence," Bielinsky good naturedly, but firmly, put Edwards in his place, saying:

> [Well], you know I was writing ideas like this before I even knew David Mamet existed! Of course, it's flattering to be compared to him because he's such a great scriptwriter and playwright. But, you know, Mamet didn't invent this. There's a whole history of con man movies before he came on the scene. I mean, I think about films like *The Sting, Paper Moon, The Flim Flam Man, House of Games*, the films of Fellini and other Italian films I saw when I was a teenager. (Edwards 2002)

So, the roots of both *Nine Queens* and *The Aura* run deep – not only into Bielinsky's past, but into the past of cinema as a whole. And now, with the immense success of his first film and the American remake racking up acceptable grosses, producers who were formerly unwilling to take a chance on Bielinsky's pet project agreed to participate. True, he had to cobble together financing from a variety of sources – and, especially in the wake of Argentina's financial collapse, *everything*, not just filmmaking, was a daily struggle – but, at length, all was in place and Bielinsky was allowed to embark upon the dark journey of *The Aura* – which, though he did not know it at the time, would be his last testament as a filmmaker. If *Nine Queens* presents the picture of a world becoming undone – a film that, in the words of Michael Chanan, "presents the picture of a corrupt society, where everyone is conning everyone else, a metaphor for a dangerous political situation on the verge of coming to a head, with a closing scene – as a bank puts up its shutters and depositors clamor for their money – that is nothing short of prophetic" (Chanan 2006) – then *The Aura* shows the aftermath of that society's collapse – now no longer a joking matter, but rather a deadly serious fight for survival.

The Aura's central plot – in contrast to that of *Nine Queens*, though equally complex – takes on a much more sinister hue from the film's first moments. When we first meet *The Aura*'s protagonist, an epileptic loner named Esteban Espinoza (Ricardo Darín again, in a superb performance), it is in a vertiginous overhead crane shot as he regains consciousness after passing out at an ATM in the deserted lobby of a Buenos Aires bank with no one around to help him. From the opening of *The Aura*, Esteban's isolation from society is complete; afflicted with blackouts he can't control, alienated from the world and utterly alone, Esteban is the epitome of the modern man – solitary, hopeless, friendless. Pulling himself together, Esteban marches his way back to his house where he works on some stuffed animals for a museum display while listening to Vivaldi's *Sinfonia alla rustica* on his radio.

From the next room, his wife pounds on the translucent glass door to Esteban's workroom, but Esteban ignores her and turns up the radio to drown out her voice, continuing with his work in a calm, unconcerned manner. It's clear that whatever relationship they might have had is over. And, indeed, we never really see his wife – just her shadow as she tries to get his attention with shouts and threats, none of which touch Esteban in the slightest; he's in his own world, bringing the dead "back to life" with artificial eyes, fur and other totemic aspects of existence, even if this imitation of life is utterly superficial and phantasmal.

At the museum, Esteban meets a fellow taxidermist who is also bringing along some dead animals for display, but, though the two men "know" each other, one could hardly call them friends. Sontag (Alejandro Awada) is a gruff, brutal man, utterly lacking in compassion or humanity and both men readily admit that they're trying to palm off some inferior goods on the museum – recycled trophies that they've previously used in other dioramas. Wandering through the museum while they wait for the display director to decide what he'll buy from them, Esteban and Sontag walk through the halls of the decaying building, commenting on how rundown the place has become.

When Esteban gently touches one of the stuffed animals on display, its antlers immediately fall off; everything is appearance and fragile appearance at that. A few minutes later in the payroll office of the museum, however, as Esteban and Sontag line up for their checks, the film's central narrative kicks in: Esteban's fantasy life as a master criminal. In a superbly executed "fantasy projection" sequence, Esteban describes to Sontag just how he would rob the payroll office with a group of imaginary accomplices. As Bielinsky shows us the entire robbery in detail in a blur of activity, Esteban and Sontag remain in the center of the commotion, unaffected by the events around them. None of this is "really" happening, of course. It's all in Esteban's mind and his calm detachment as he narrates the details of the crime to Sontag – a crime we are "witnessing" – is in stark contrast to the sleek efficiency of the phantom criminals, who pull off the "robbery" without a hitch and vanish down a secret catwalk to make good their escape.

This is the most visceral scene in the film up to this point in the narrative; it's clear that Esteban lives more fully in his imagination than he does in real life. Sontag has heard all this before, in various other scenarios – how Esteban would pull off the "perfect" robbery in any number of locations – but he is still amazed by Esteban's photographic memory. Without looking twice, Esteban is able to instantly memorize the serial numbers on the bags of money carried by the payroll guards; perhaps this is a side effect of his epilepsy – of the "aura" that envelopes him with inexorable inevitability just before each attack. But with the fantasy robbery "complete" in Esteban's imagination, Bielinsky returns us to the quotidian drabness of the payroll office and the dull certainty of everyday life. It's just a dream, after all – though we sense that Esteban, if given the chance, might just follow through on such a scenario.

Returning home, Esteban discovers that his wife has left him, leaving just a cursory note that we never see. When Sontag suggests that the two men take a vacation to do some hunting, they eventually arrive at the forest lodge of Carlos Dietrich (Manual Rodal), a mysterious figure who keeps a secret hunting lodge deep in the woods and, as eventually becomes clear, is involved in preparations for an elaborate payroll robbery. However, we don't meet Dietrich at this point in the narrative; he is out on a hunting trip, leaving his abused wife, Diana (Dolores Fonzi), in charge of the lodge. In the meantime, Sontag becomes disgusted with Esteban's inability to effectively stalk and kill the very same animals that he stuffs for a living and, after a quarrel, the two men separate, with Sontag essentially abandoning Esteban at Dietrich's remote hunting lodge. Alone, unsure of what to do next, Esteban ventures deep into the forest, determined at last to hunt and kill a deer to prove, in some fashion, that he has the *cojones* to take a life.

But, just as he is about to pull the trigger and bring down a magnificent stag that seems unaware of his presence, Esteban suffers another epileptic seizure – which Bielinsky signals with a series of sweeping tracking shots as the world seems to collapse around Esteban, obliterating his conscious existence. When, at length, Esteban wakes up, not knowing how long he's been unconscious, he instinctively grabs his rifle and aims at the first thing that moves. Unfortunately, this turns out to be Dietrich; Esteban, in the first genuinely violent act of the film, kills him with a single shot to the head. This is the first time we've seen Dietrich and it's also the last; a figure viewed in distance, his living presence in the film is confined to a matter of seconds. The corpse of Dietrich is a different matter altogether, however. It reveals, upon examination, a host of information about Dietrich's planned payroll job and a key to the cabin in the woods where Dietrich secretly made his plans. With Dietrich's death, Esteban is also "adopted" by Dietrich's dog – a massive animal with one blue eye and one brown eye who seemingly transfers his loyalty from his dead master to Esteban and serves as Esteban's erstwhile guide into Dietrich's dark domain. Entering Dietrich's cabin, Esteban discovers the complete plan for the robbery and, with his photographic memory, absorbs every detail of the plan.

Returning to the lodge, Esteban is confronted by two of Dietrich's criminal associates – Sosa (Pablo Cedron) and Montero (Walter Reyno) – and passes himself off as Dietrich's partner in the proposed payroll robbery, explaining that Dietrich had to leave suddenly on business. Dietrich's wife, Diana, is completely unaware of her late husband's plans, although she knows that something is in the works. But, at the same time, the much younger Diana – who bears the scars of Dietrich's savage beatings on her back – is really more a prisoner of Dietrich's lodge than anything else; it's clear that she long ago ceased to care for her husband.

As Esteban, Sosa and Montero proceed with their plans for the robbery, Diana keeps her distance even as she befriends Esteban, recognizing that there's some good in him. The robbery, for Esteban, is more of an adventure than a criminal enterprise – for once in his life, Esteban would like to see one of his schemes played out for real, but he doesn't really understand the potential consequences of what he's doing. Esteban is a dreamer, not a hardened criminal; by contrast, Sosa and Montero are utterly ruthless, willing to kill at a moment's notice. As the plan picks up speed and starts to unfold, Esteban finds himself utterly alone in a hostile world of greed, violence and brutality far more vicious than anything he could ever have imagined. "Perfect" crimes happen only in daydreams; in the real world, with everyone out for themselves, things unfold in a decidedly different manner.

I will leave the rest of the narrative to the viewer to discover; indeed, all I have sketched is the first thirty or so minutes of the film, which then embarks on a series of spectacular double crosses and deceptions reminiscent of *Nine*

Queens, but far more sinister in both their implications and their consequences. Through it all, Esteban sleepwalks through the steps of Dietrich's plan as if lost in a dream in which reality and fantasy are impossible to separate. The music for the film – a stunningly hypnotic drone score composed by Lucio Godoy – suitably amplifies this "disconnect" from society. Even though he is "part" of Dietrich's scheme, Esteban is still in the dark about many of the twists and turns in the plan and is left to discover, often to his detriment, numerous aspects of the scheme that aren't readily apparent.

Indeed, Esteban seems almost more like a spectator than a participant in the film's action – he's along for the ride, but he has no real idea of how things will eventually turn out. During one memorable sequence midway through the film, as Esteban is tracking the various ancillary characters in Dietrich's scheme, he witnesses a payroll robbery at a manufacturing plant from his car across the street, not more than 100 feet away from a scene of violence and mayhem. As the robbery unfolds – viewed exclusively from Esteban's point of view in a series of long shots – Esteban leaves his car and wanders across the street right into the thick of a vicious gun battle between the thieves and the police, seemingly oblivious to the risk he's taking. And, indeed, he *is* oblivious; none of this is real to him. His entire life is a dream. Indeed, all of the events in *The Aura* may well be entirely imaginary – is any of this really happening at all?

As Bielinsky's friend, Diego Lerer, noted after the director's death,

> In the world of Fabián Bielinsky, behind every corner there was darkness. The unexpected, the impossible, the surreal could come up at every turn. In *El aura*, his second and, sadly, last film, the main character walks in the woods, surrounded by shadows and fog, with only flashes of light illuminating the tall trees. The light is out there – the world, the possibility of happiness – but he can't see it. His mind is somewhere else: planning the next step of an elaborate robbery, stealing the identity of the man he just killed. Obsessive to the point of memorizing every number, every face, every step he had to walk to get out of the woods, the protagonist cannot, finally, control everything that's around him. Because real life, real things, can't be controlled, processed, written down on a piece of paper and handled as if it were a map, where space and time are fixed and easy to follow. His mind controls him, but can't control the world [...]
>
> [Like Esteban, Bielinsky's] mind was always somewhere else, maybe a few steps ahead of yours, like a great chess player that has the entire game in his mind before even moving the first piece [...] He would shoot and reshoot every scene until it looked exactly the way he had conceived it in his mind. He fought to maintain a very long cut of *El aura* (at the expense of a tighter editing that would have given the film a better and

longer commercial run) because he believed that was the only way the audience could get into the mind of the protagonist. He also made the entire film from the main character's point-of-view, forcing the audience to be outside the main action during long sequences. But he had a vision of what he wanted. And he stuck to that, with great results. *El aura* was also a great step to show his qualities as a filmmaker [...]

[Bielinsky] was able to show a strong command of storytelling in *Nine Queens*. But that film was – still is – basically a great script, shot in a very classical, unobtrusive way, helped by a career-making performance by Darín. No wonder it was compared to the films of David Mamet, another great storyteller not particularly famous for his visual skills. *El aura* was a different thing altogether. Standing apart from the precise logic of *Nine Queens*, Bielinsky dared to abandon the big city and go to the woods in Patagonia, when time, space and events are harder to predict. The wildlife, the guns, the mysterious animals, the traps were not as easy to handle as they had been when the main character [...] was in Buenos Aires working as a taxidermist. These animals, these people, these guns were real, and they could turn things around at any given time.

Even the shooting of the film ended up being more difficult than the production company had predicted: they couldn't control the weather, the light, the hundreds of things that can go wrong when you are out in the wilderness. With *El aura* came a different approach in terms of screenwriting, a decision to let things more open to interpretation, to avoid closing all the doors to the audience for a satisfying and conclusive ending. With that, also came a more lyrical approach to filmmaking. Longer takes, moody atmosphere, a visual palette that's closer to a painting created by a disturbed mind (the mind of the protagonist), and a filmic style you can compare to David Lynch's *Twin Peaks* or Sam Raimi's *A Simple Plan*. (Lerer 2006)

Bielinsky's achievement in *The Aura*, then, is one of transcendence – of escape from the real into the zone of imagination, which then doubles back up on itself to encompass actuality. It's also worth noting in passing that this idea of a "sleepwalking" protagonist was not new to Bielinsky, who scripted the equally dreamlike *The Sleep Walker* (*La Sonámbula*) for director Fernando Spiner in 1998 and, when working in commercials, assisted none other than Wim Wenders in the shooting of a Renault Mégane commercial (the Mégane is a small family car manufactured by Renault) in Argentina, which had a similarly surrealistic bent (Chanan 2006). As Esteban tells Diana Dietrich in *The Aura*, he lives his life in a state of perpetual uncertainty – never knowing when an attack will come on, simultaneously dreading each episode and yet anticipating it, as if his hold on reality remains very slight indeed; as he describes it, "there's a moment, a shift [...] things suddenly change [...] The fit is coming, and there's nothing you can do to stop it. Nothing. It's horrible [...] and it's perfect. Because during those few seconds, you're free. There's no choice. No alternative. Nothing for you to decide."

And yet, for all of its sophistication – or rather, precisely because of it – *The Aura* failed to duplicate the commercial success of *Nine Queens*; then again, Bielinsky made it manifestly clear going into the project that he more or less expected a lukewarm public reception. Never mind; he would keep directing commercials until a new project presented itself. Though not a box-office smash, *The Aura* had been an overwhelming critical success and that was all that mattered. But it was not to be. As Vince Keenan notes,

> *El aura* did not achieve *Neuve Reinas*'s level of exposure in the United States. It was distributed via the Independent Film Channel's First Take series, released on demand and in theaters simultaneously. This approach makes films available to a wider audience [...] but at the expense of publicity. Even being named one of 2006's best films by the *New York Times*'s A. O. Scott didn't garner *El aura* additional attention. On June 26, 2006, *El aura* swept Argentina's film awards, taking home prizes for best picture, Bielinsky's script and direction, and Darín's performance among others. Two days later, in a hotel room in São Paulo, Brazil where he was casting a TV commercial, Fabián Bielinsky died of a heart attack at age 47, leaving behind a wife and a young son. (Keenan 2009)

In one of his last interviews, conducted on 21 April 2006 by Mariano Colalongo and Alvaro Fuentes at Bielinsky's home in La Plata, Buenos Aires – "a comfortable and bright house with a home theater, with DVD shelves of some 400 classic American films" (Colalongo and Fuentes 2006) – Bielinsky told his two listeners that, with regard to *The Aura*,

> I am glad to have done what I did in terms of the whole work. I was convinced I wanted to open the picture to other completely different spaces, to precisely my own decisions [...] *The Aura* is a more personal film, from a different place, linked to certain obsessions or fantasies or thoughts that are mine [...] [at the premiere of the film] I remember [Ricardo] Darín [saying], "It's you that you see on the screen – it's you." [...] Yes, the truth is that there is a personal component in terms of atmosphere, climate, a level of obsession [...] (Colalongo and Fuentes 2006)

But who is it that Darín saw on the screen? As Megan Ratner noted,

> Despite their tight narratives, Bielinsky's films pose questions about the suppositions and assumptions most film viewers make, even about the very act of viewing itself. The taxidermist especially is remote, unable to be in life except as a kind of fill-in. Even in the midst of a shoot-out, he seems invisible to those taking part, protected by his semi-existence. Later in the film, deep into a heist, one of his unwilling associates accosts him: "Who are you? Where do you come from?" as if unable to imagine this man is flesh and blood. What he responds to is the taxidermist's lack of affect, the profound uninvolvement that allows him to watch even a gunfight as if at a screening. Though his plotting and techniques drew largely on traditions of Wilder and other established masters, Bielinsky set challenges as far-reaching as Michael Haneke's in *Code Unknown* and *Caché* about our roles as actors and witnesses and about the soothing passivity so easily abetted by standing by and watching, watching, watching. (Ratner 2007)

Thus, Bielinsky – the obsessive moviegoer, the perpetual spectator, the creator of hundreds of television commercials that sold a lifestyle that never existed – seems in the end to have had a similarly disassociated view of life itself. *Nine Queens* was a commercial entertainment that put him on the map, but in *The Aura*, he reveals what's behind all the duplicity, greed and violence: emptiness. Esteban's greatest moments of clarity – by his own admission – come right before the seizures that render him unconscious; in the real world, he observes, but doesn't really interact. It's only when he accidentally stumbles into someone else's fantasy projection that he actually embraces his existence – and then, only because he's caught up in the excitement and intricacy of Dietrich's scheme.

It's telling that the only time we see Dietrich is for the split second before Esteban accidentally shoots him. Although there's no actual communication between the two men, Dietrich does leave behind his master plan – his own dream of a life beyond the insulation of a remote hunting lodge, located at the outmost margins of society, catering to a clientele of losers, misfits and violent outcasts. It is very much like the world of *Deliverance* – Dietrich's hunting camp can only exist beyond the boundaries of conventional society, in an outlaw zone where the only law is the rule of brutality and greed. In this phantom zone, people cease to exist as we know them; they become only the manifestations of their primal designs – to hunt, to kill, to steal, to break all the rules and somehow get away with it. The question is really apt: "Who are you? Where do you come from?" No one knows and there really is no answer.

In the end, the genre trappings of *The Aura* fade into insignificance; the film is more concerned with the human condition than any quotidian criminal enterprise. That and the uncertainty and ephemerality of existence – the unknowable interior of each person's individual being. "Who are you? Where do you come from?" – there will *never* be an answer to these questions, not for Esteban or Bielinsky or for any of us. The triumph of *The Aura*, then, is to make the mystery of our being a question that perpetually hovers over every other aspect of the film. We can't know ourselves or each other or even the motives that drive us towards certain specific actions and away from others.

For me, at least, the career of Fabián Bielinsky had just begun and his death has robbed us of one of cinema's most original and deeply penetrating talents. What he might have accomplished had he lived is, of course, a matter of utter conjecture, but there can be no doubt that, in his brief time on earth, Bielinsky was moving toward a meditational cinema that extended beyond the boundaries of the known – both in life and in art – and far beyond the vicissitudes of daily life, toward larger questions of metaphysical existence and philosophical contemplation – a journey he had only just begun.

Part II
HISTORY

Chapter 6

FAST WORKER: THE FILMS OF SAM NEWFIELD*

Newfield is hard, that's a hard one, you can't do too much of that.
—Martin Scorsese (22 March 1991)

Sam Newfield is, in all probability, the most prolific director in American sound-film history, but very little archival material survives on his career. The director of more than 250 feature films, as well as numerous shorts and television series' episodes, in a career that spanned four decades (from 1923 to 1958) Newfield leaves behind him only his work on the set; next to nothing is known of his personal life. However, using conversations with Sigmund Neufeld, Jr. and Stanley Neufeld – the sons of Sam Newfield's (born Neufeld) brother Sigmund Neufeld (all quotes from them in this essay are from these interviews) – as well as materials from the Margaret Herrick Library of the Academy of Motion Picture Arts and Sciences in Los Angeles, I was able to piece together a rough sketch of the man behind such a torrential output of work.

Comedies, musicals, Westerns, horror films, jungle pictures, crime dramas, espionage thrillers – Sam Newfield did them all, often on budgets of fewer than $20,000 per feature and shooting schedules of as little as three days. But, as Martin Scorsese notes, watching Newfield's work *is* hard because he often seems absolutely detached from the images that appear on the screen, as if he is an observer rather than a participant. Then, too, the conditions of extreme economy that Newfield labored under created a pressure-cooker environment in which the ultimate goal of all his films was simply to get them done on time and under budget. Nevertheless, as arguably the most prolific auteur in American motion picture history, Newfield deserves mention and brief examination as one of the key "second rung" directors of 1940s Hollywood, Newfield's most productive era.

---

* A version of this chapter was first published in 2007 by *Senses of Cinema* (online) as "Fast Worker: The Films of Sam Newfield" (issue 45): http://sensesofcinema.com/2007/feature-articles/sam-newfield/.

Figure 6. Bert Sternbach, Sam Newfield, Sigmund Neufeld, Jack Greenhalgh.
Source: Author's collection.

Born on 6 December 1899 in a cold water flat in the Bronx to immigrant parents from Budapest, Sam Neufeld was one of four children. His older brother, Sigmund Neufeld, Sr., was born in 1896 and, with the premature death of his father, Simon Neufeld, Sigmund rapidly became the family's sole source of income. Sam and Sigmund's other brother, Murray, became an electrician, while their sister, Sadie, eventually married a "grip" in the 1920s and settled down to life as a housewife and mother. But all of this was well in the future when Sigmund was forced to drop out of school in the sixth grade after his father's sudden death. At the age of 11, he got a job delivering beer to New York saloons with a horse and wagon. Other jobs rapidly followed in succession and Sigmund learned to hustle to support his indigent family.

Sigmund's father, Simon, had been a "picker" in the fur business, taking scraps of fur left over from bigger jobs and preparing them to be sewn together in cheaper fur coats. However, endlessly toiling in poorly ventilated workshops left Simon susceptible to a variety of ailments and his early death from pneumonia made Sigmund wary of following in his father's footsteps. Instead, while Sigmund's mother eked out a meager living washing floors of the cold water tenements in the building where they lived, young Sigmund developed a reputation as an aggressive entrepreneur, who saw early on that he would have to take chances in order to survive and advance.

Fired from his beer delivery route, Sigmund delivered newspapers, sold fruit on street corners and finally got a job as a delivery boy for a local tailor and dry cleaner. One day, Sigmund was sent to drop off some clothes for the head of Universal Pictures' New York office and was immediately entranced by the hum of creative activity. Sigmund refused to deliver the clothing to anyone other than the head of the company and, as a reward for his persistence, was hired in 1914 as a go-fer, runner and general assistant; from there, he rapidly advanced to the cutting room. The job for the tailor was immediately forgotten; Sigmund Neufeld had found his life's work.

Sigmund's driving ambition inspired his brother, Sam, to try his luck in the film business as well – although, for the moment, Sigmund remained the family's chief breadwinner. By the late teens, Sigmund was asked to go out to California to Universal's studios there and supervise the editing of two-reel comedies made by the Stern Brothers' production company, but released through Universal. By now an experienced editor, Sigmund saw that there was considerable wastage in the shooting of the comedies and impressed his bosses when he managed to put together a "new" two-reel film from outtakes and unused scenes of two or three comedies, creating more product and profit for his employers.

For each "extra" comedy Sigmund manufactured for the Stern Brothers, he would get a modest bonus; on one occasion, he got a diamond ring for his efforts, now worn by his son Sigmund Neufeld, Jr. But the young Sigmund Neufeld noticed that, while he might get a little something extra for his efforts, his bosses pocketed a cool $10,000 for each "instant" comedy Sigmund stitched together. Thus it was that, after a few desultory stabs at directing, Sigmund decided to make a move to production so that he could reap the full benefits of his labor.

Sigmund was still the main source of support for his mother, two brothers and sister, sending money back home to New York at regular intervals to keep his family solvent. One by one, his family members joined him in Los Angeles. The first to follow his brother west was Sam, who changed his name to "Newfeld" and later "Newfield" as he climbed up through the studio hierarchy on his way to the director's chair. Starting off in the industry in 1919 as a runner, set assistant and occasional actor – as his brother had – Sam soon found that he had a knack with actors and enjoyed working on the studio floor – much more so than Sigmund, who was increasingly drawn to the business and production end of the industry.

Rapidly moving up through the ranks at the Stern Brothers Company thanks to his brother's influence with the front office, Sam Newfield directed his first silent film in 1923. Later silent films included *Which is Which?* (1926) as part of the *Excuse Makers* series and comedy entries in the popular *Let George Do It*, *What Happened to Jane* and *Buster Brown* series. For the *Jane* series, Newfield directed *Jane's Predicament* (1926), *Jane's Engagement Party* (1926), *Jane's Sleuth* (1927) and other titles; his *Let George Do It* entries included *Sailor George* (1928), *George's School Daze* (1928), *George's False Alarm* (1928) and many others; and, for the *Buster Brown* series, Newfield's films included *Buster Trims Up* (1928), *Buster Minds the Baby* (1928), *Busting Buster* (1928) and numerous other comedies.

In all, between 1926 and 1930, Newfield directed more than 50 two-reel comedies, learning the ropes as he went along. This in itself would be enough for mention in any comprehensive film history, but, as it turned out, Sam Newfield was just getting warmed up. Making these films on very rapid schedules and tight budgets, Newfield consolidated his reputation as a fast and conscientious craftsman – he was so busy, in fact, that he began freelancing for the bottom rung outfit, Educational Pictures, on additional two-reel shorts while still working full-time for the Stern Brothers at Universal. However, the landscape of the industry was changing. By 1930, sound had definitively arrived in Hollywood and, while Sam made the switch to talkies with relative ease, the market for shorts was beginning to stagnate. The Stern Brothers Company was absorbed by Universal, but Universal saw no reason to promote either Sam or Sigmund out of its two-reel comedy unit, which was arguably the lowest rung of the studio production ladder.

With no opportunities for advancement, Sigmund struck out on his own as an independent producer. At first, the going was tough and Sigmund had to scrimp and economize to produce his early programmers, such as *The Red Haired Alibi* (1932, directed by Christy Cabanne) and *Red Blood of Courage* (1935, directed by John "Jack" English, who would later become a prolific co-director of action serials for Republic Pictures, working with the gifted William Witney for most of his career). Sam Newfield, oddly enough, didn't work for his brother in his new producer capacity during this period and he struggled to get his first feature assignment, *Reform Girl*, followed by *The Important Witness* and *Under Secret Orders*, all shot in 1933. But the films were successful and Sam pressed on. In 1934, he directed four independent features: *Big Time or Bust*, *Marrying Widows*, *Beggar's Holiday* and *African Incident*, all modest but successful program pictures. By 1935, Sam had established himself as a reliable second rung director and brother Sigmund had partnered with Maurice Conn to create Ambassador Pictures, a small production company specializing in Westerns and outdoor action fare. For Ambassador, Newfield directed *Northern Frontier*, *Code of the Mounted* and *Trail of the Wild*, all in 1935, and it seemed as if the partnership between the two brothers might extend profitably in the future.

But, for the next few years, while Sigmund produced a slate of routine Westerns, Sam went over to Republic to grind out Johnny Mack Brown and Bob Steele Westerns on an assembly line basis; he then switched to Sam Katzman's tiny Victory Studios in 1939 to create a similar series of Tim McCoy Westerns, all made on modest budgets. Sam clearly liked Westerns more than almost any other genre and, while the production values of many of these programmers were obviously threadbare, all of the films returned a tidy profit. However, events would soon conspire to bring the two brothers together under the roof of the same studio, Producers Releasing Corporation, where, for better or worse, they embarked on the most productive – some might say notorious – period of their long careers.

PRC itself came about through the collapse of Producers Distribution Corporation, or PDC, which was originally set up by Poverty Row producer Ben Judell. Working with Sigmund Neufeld as his co-producer and Sam Newfield as the director, PDC produced a relatively ambitious anti-Nazi film: *Hitler: Beast of Berlin* (1939), featuring, in a bit part, a very young Alan Ladd. The film was topical, reasonably budgeted in the $100,000 range, but it ran afoul of the German American Bund, then quite active in isolationist pre–World War II America. The Bund members broke into the PDC lot and destroyed the film's sets almost entirely. They were rebuilt, but then local censorship boards refused to pass the film for exhibition because of its "anti-German" slant. With many distribution possibilities blocked, production bills began to pile up. With six additional features in production, Judell was seriously overextended and PDC collapsed in a hail of debts.

Sigmund Neufeld, however, sensed an opportunity and, working with Robert S. Benjamin – an attorney for Pathé Film Laboratory, one of PDC's chief creditors – he forestalled payment of a $90,000 debt to Pathé in return for a stake in the reorganized PRC (Backstreet 2007). Judell was out, Sigmund Neufeld was in, and he lost no time in signing up his brother, Sam, as PRC's house director. Newfield would single-handedly helm the majority of the company's feature output from 1940 up until the demise of PRC in 1947. Indeed, he was so prolific that he became something of an embarrassment to the fledgling studio and, on the advice of his brother, Newfield adopted two aliases (Sherman Scott and Peter Stewart) to cover his tracks.

Sigmund Neufeld, Jr. told me that, while these pseudonyms are now fairly common knowledge, at the time of their implementation, they were a closely guarded secret. PRC's New York office, in fact, called Sigmund in for a meeting, telling him that, while Sam's work was good and Sherman Scott's work was also acceptable, Peter Stewart was the real "find" for the studio and that Sigmund should use him more often in the future. Sigmund cheerfully complied with this directive and Sherman Scott's output declined, while Peter Stewart's escalated (Neufeld 2007).

It has been written that Newfield used these aliases on a "genre" basis – using "Newfield" for Westerns, "Scott" for crime films and "Stewart" for more serious dramas – but there seems to be little foundation for this. "Scott," for example, directed *Billy the Kid's Fighting Pals* (1941), while "Stewart" directed *Billy the Kid in Texas* (1940) and Newfield directed *The Lone Rider Fights Back* (1941) under his own name. Further, Newfield abandoned this "triple threat" strategy early in 1943 with only one exception (1946's *The Flying Serpent*, which he directed as Sherman Scott) until PRC itself collapsed and Newfield began the final phase of his career freelancing for William Pine and William Thomas (known as "The Dollar Bills" for their unflagging production economy) at Paramount and producer Maurice Conn at Twentieth Century Fox, one of Newfield's few brushes with a major studio. In these films, Newfield alternated between his alter egos with seeming impunity until, in 1950, working for Robert Lippert's cost-conscious production company, Newfield abandoned the practice altogether and was billed solely as Sam Newfield from 1950 to 1958, when he directed his final films.

All this was in the distant future when Newfield assumed the key directorial reins at the newly minted PRC and began turning out product at a torrid pace. Obviously, Newfield wasn't the only director on the PRC lot. Edgar G. Ulmer, whose films have since been recognized as some of the most interesting and influential genre films of the 1940s, was PRC's "prestige" director. Ulmer himself referred to his position with the company as being "the Capra of PRC" (Bogdanovich, 397), and such films as *Detour* (1946), *Bluebeard* (1944), *Strange Illusion* (1946) and *Her Sister's Secret* (1946) have long since developed a cult status among aficionados of 1940s Hollywood cinema. Even so, Ulmer had minimal resources to work with: a strict schedule of five or six days per feature, a 2 to 1 shooting ratio and an average of 60 or more camera setups a day.

Indeed, Ulmer adopted a style of shooting the close-ups in his films for PRC against a neutral grey background to disguise the fact that they were shot back-to-back for all the day's scenes, with one setup in the final hour of shooting every day. Ulmer would direct the actors to look "camera right" or "camera left" as they read off dialogue from all the day's sequences and put his hand over the lens to separate the takes. (Bogdanovich, 397). Such draconian economy did not come naturally to Ulmer, who had been used to the relative production luxury of such films as Universal's *The Black Cat* (1934) earlier in his career. For Sam Newfield, such tactics were an everyday occurrence.

This, of course, is the most problematic factor of Newfield's films for PRC; with so little time and money at his disposal and the bottom line always strictly enforced, Newfield had no time for delicate touches in his work. Newfield's many Westerns are straightforward and violent, with a minimum of character development; his big city dramas, such as *Queen of Broadway* (1943) and his horror films – in particular. *Dead Men Walk* (1943) and *The Flying Serpent* (1946) – are grimly procedural, moving with inexorable assurance towards their generically predestined ends. *The Black Raven* (1943), a crime drama set in a rundown inn, is unrelentingly bleak and fatalistic; *I Accuse My Parents* (1944), an early juvenile delinquency film foreshadowing Nicholas Ray's later *Rebel Without a Cause* (1955), offers a similarly grim view of wartime absentee parenthood and its social consequences. *Swing Hostess* (1944) is a typically cheerless PRC musical, simultaneously tacky and tawdry, while *Murder Is My Business* (1946) is a grimy crime thriller that embraces its shoddy world with world-weary certainty.

The pace of production was unrelenting. In 1943 alone, Newfield directed no fewer than 18 feature films; in 1945, 12 films; and, in 1946, 15 full-length features. On the set, Newfield preferred to shoot long master takes with few close-ups, making his master shots the key coverage of his scenes. Close-ups were reserved for detailed action – a door opening, a gun firing, a safe being cracked – and thus Newfield's films have an air of hermetic finality in their execution which is, for better or worse, his alone. One gets the feeling that Newfield's actors do not so much appear in his films as they are trapped in them, entombed in their frames for cinematic eternity, consigned to low-budget limbo, inhabiting a shadow zone of hastily constructed sets and borrowed narratives. Indeed, one of Newfield's most controversial projects is his "riff" on Billy Wilder's *Double Indemnity* (1944), which he directed as *Apology for Murder* (1945); the original title of the project, amazingly enough, was *Single Indemnity*. Paramount, Wilder's home studio, wasn't fooled by the title change and slapped an injunction on the finished film that remains in force to this day. Although it is an interesting and often effective thriller, *Apology for Murder* survives only in private collections and on bootleg DVDs and is seldom, if ever, screened in public.

For all the pressures put on Newfield and his cast and crew, however, those who witnessed him at work on the set recall a director who was patient with actors, genuinely enjoyed working with them and who kept the mood light no matter how somber the subject matter. Sigmund Neufeld's son, a teenager in the 1940s, often went to the PRC sound stages on Saturdays to watch Sam at work and later went into the business as a director himself. Despite the rapid pace of shooting, Sigmund Neufeld, Jr. recalled that Sam would take his time to get the right effect from an actor and do his best to bring out the desired emotion in a scene. As he told me during an interview,

> I watched him work with some kids a few times when he needed them to cry, and he was very good in talking to them and getting out of them

what he wanted. He would just have a conversation with them until he got them right in the right mood and then he'd wave his hand, say "Let's roll" and the kid'd be there crying throughout the dialogue. And I thought, "That's pretty darn good." (Neufeld 2007)

At the same time, Newfield was an inveterate gambler whose gaming habit eventually got the better of him. Even in his early PRC days, he would get a crap game going during breaks or in the studio bus on the way to Iverson's Ranch to shoot one of his Westerns or at the end of the day as production wound down. Newfield loved any sort of wagering and, in one case, matter-of-factly informed the cast and crew on one of his films that, whatever happened, he had to finish the day's shooting by 3 o'clock so he could get to the Santa Anita racetrack in time to see a heavily favored horse – whom he had backed to the hilt – run in the day's final race.

Sadly, it was this affliction more than anything else that marked Newfield's personal decline in his last years. Estranged from his wife – the former Violet McComas, whom he had met as a script supervisor on one of his films – Newfield lost custody of his children, Joel and Jacqueline, in a bitter divorce case and never really recovered from the aftermath of the affair. These events, mercifully, would be confined to his final days; for the moment, in the early 1940s, Newfield was at the top of his game, the purveyor of the cinematic Blue Plate Special in genre-driven Hollywood.

For someone who made so many films, it's both interesting and intriguing that Newfield kept no scrapbooks, photo albums or other mementos of his career and that today there are only two known photos of Newfield in existence – an astounding fact for the most prolific director in the history of the American sound cinema. While gregarious, Newfield never sought out publicity and was happiest on the set, working on one project after another, taking each new script as a fresh challenge. As he consolidated his hold on PRC's top directorial spot, Newfield gathered around him a crew of skilled technicians whom he could rely upon to knock out the day's work with speed and efficiency.

In one of two known photographs of Newfield, he appears with his brother and the two key members of his crew at a formal studio dinner at PRC in the early 1940s. From left to right: Bert Sternbach, the studio's ace production manager, staring at the camera, is flanked by Newfield himself, his eyes confronting the viewer with an inscrutable and impassive gaze, next to his brother, Sigmund, every bit the hard-edged businessman and Jack Greenhalgh, a rough-and-tumble cameraman of legendary speed and efficiency.

My first reaction upon seeing this photograph (which was also my first view of Newfield himself) was a sense of shock; here, unmistakably, was

Hollywood's working class, completely aware that they were creating genre entertainment for mass audiences at a price and utterly unapologetic about their films or their production methods. Unlike many directors, Sam Newfield felt most comfortable making straightforward films for audiences eager for 60 to 70 minutes of cheerfully brutal entertainment. Newfield and his crew were, as the photo attests, tough customers, uninterested in theorizing or pushing back the limits of genre filmmaking. At the same time, because of the inherent hardscrabble desperation implicit in all PRC films, Newfield and his colleagues ultimately presented a truer picture of 1940s America than many of his slicker compatriots at the major studios.

At PRC, it was a constant fight to find story material, hire actors at cut rates, recycle sets from existing flats and then push through 40 to 50 setups a day to get the finished film in the can. PRC was involved in a continual struggle for mere survival on an everyday basis, much like the rest of the country during World War II. Sam Newfield and his crew were populist filmmakers, who never condescended to their audiences and yet never stretched the limits of genre filmmaking either. Life in the 1940s was hard; life at PRC was hard. Unlike studio life at the majors – from MGM on down, where luxury and privilege were a way of life for many of the studio's most valuable players – at PRC, everyone from the top down *worked* for their living. As Sigmund Neufeld, Jr. told me, "I think they were happy where they were. My dad and Sam both realized that they were doing what they were really good at" (Neufeld 2007). In short, at PRC, the quotidian struggle for survival was real, both on and off the screen.

PRC was, in the truest sense of the word, a "mom and pop" operation; between them, Sigmund and Sam pretty much ran the studio, although Leon Fromkess, a former accountant from New York with a degree from Columbia University, was the titular head of the organization. Before Fromkess, until 1944, O. Henry Briggs served as PRC's financial head, but he ultimately clashed with Sigmund Neufeld and resigned. The division of labor was fairly straightforward: Sigmund, always more of a "roll up your shirtsleeves" type, kept an eye on daily production, supervising the activity on PRC's eight sound stages throughout the day. Fromkess supervised finance and kept the distributors and film exchanges from interfering too much in production. Indeed, shortly before PRC dissolved, Fromkess left the company to join Samuel Goldwyn's much more prestigious organization, working with Goldwyn on William Wyler's *The Best Years of Our Lives* (1946) and Henry Koster's *The Bishop's Wife* (1947). But, as we'll see, Fromkess was soon restless at the Goldwyn studios and left to set up his own production company, where his path would again cross with Sam Newfield on a number of projects.

Another aspect of PRC's studio identity was the fact that, during the run up to World War II, both Sigmund and Sam felt strongly that Hollywood had to oppose the Nazi regime in Germany, as evidenced by their first project, *Hitler: Beast of Berlin* (*Goose Step* in re-releases). In their rejection of Nazism, PRC was ahead of the curve in Hollywood, as the major studios still sought to appease Hitler and thus avoid the loss of film rentals in the lucrative German market. Only Warner Bros. – arguably the most socially conscious studio in the 1930s and early 1940s – followed PRC's lead with the production of Anatole Litvak's *Confessions of a Nazi Spy* (1939) when the rest of the majors advised Warner's to avoid the subject.

But PRC served another function in the battle against Hitler. Though neither Sam nor Sigmund were particularly religious, the studio soon became an informal haven for many gifted Jewish artists escaping from the Nazis, such as Edgar G. Ulmer, Franz Wysbar (who "anglicized" his name to "Frank Wisbar") and the brilliant cameraman Eugen Schüfftan. And yet, like most of the minor studios, what most defined PRC was a strong work ethic, shooting from dawn to dusk six days a week to get the film in the can on time.

Salaries were very tight. Newfield received only $500 to direct *Secrets of a Model* in 1940, but rose to $1,250 for *Prairie Rustlers* in 1945, while cameraman Jack Greenhalgh was paid a mere $200 for shooting *Secrets of a Model* and only broke through to the $1,000 range in the late 1940s. And yet, despite the frantic pace, PRC was a close-knit "family operation," according to Sigmund Neufeld, Jr.: "We were all friends, and we used to have weekend parties, dances, stuff like that. They worked so much together that they all knew each other really well, and almost everyone got along" (Neufeld 2007).

There was another factor to consider: unlike the major studios, PRC never sold its films on a percentage basis to theaters, but rather as straight rentals. Most PRC films played the bottom half of double bills. If a PRC film was an unexpected box-office hit, the theater owners, not PRC, reaped the benefits. All PRC ever got for their films was a flat rental rate, no matter how well or poorly the film performed with audiences. (PRC owned a few theaters where they got a better break on their product, but the number of screens – about 10 at most – was so small, this had little impact on the company's bottom line.) Thus, the margin of profit was very slim. PRC films cost so much and they made so little; on some of the Westerns, PRC's actual profit after all the production, exploitation and distribution expenses was as low as $1,000. Because of this, PRC was never really able to expand or move on to more ambitious pictures. Budgets and profits were both strictly limited.

For all the penury of PRC's financial situation, Sam Newfield lived well during the 1940s with his two children in a house on the beach in Malibu. But warning signs were evident. Sam never exercised and smoked cigarettes incessantly. While he never drank, gambling became an overwhelming addiction for him and, by 1950, his wife, children and PRC had all vanished from his life. In 1947, PRC was completely absorbed by the newly formed Eagle Lion Pictures, which Sigmund and Sam both viewed as a serious mistake. Eagle Lion, which was eventually folded into United Artists in February of 1951 (Flynn and McCarthy 1975a, 41), started out with an ambitious slate of productions – such as Ulmer's *Ruthless* (1949) and a series of atmospheric noirs directed by a young Anthony Mann – but soon became overextended. As Sigmund Neufeld, Jr. remembers:

> My dad [Sigmund], Sam and all their friends left the studio, because Eagle Lion had goals of making bigger and better movies. And my dad said, "You're making a mistake to change the formula – what we're doing is very successful." But the new people who came in wanted to change to "prestige films," and they did. But they didn't last very long. (Neufeld 2007)

With PRC's demise, Sam Newfield and Sigmund Neufeld felt as if the ground had been cut out from under them. By 1950, Newfield's home life was just a memory and yet the director soldiered on through a slate of films for a variety of smaller American companies, such as Lippert, Film Classics and even two films for Eagle Lion (*Lady at Midnight* and *The Strange Mrs. Crane*, both made in 1948) before accepting an assignment with Britain's Hammer Films under producer Anthony Hinds to direct two films for the young company, *Scotland Yard Inspector* (aka *Lady in the Fog*) with Cesar Romero and *The Gambler and the Lady*, starring Dane Clark, both completed in 1952. Robert Lippert was just the right sort of producer for Sam Newfield: cost-conscious and aggressive. As Sigmund Neufeld, Jr. told me:

> Bob Lippert owned three or four hundred theaters up in the Bay area. The reason he got into producing was because he was having trouble buying the pictures from the major studios. He had fights with them and he couldn't get the shows he wanted. So he got really mad and said, "Okay, I'm coming to Hollywood and produce my own movies," which he had never done. So he came to Los Angeles and my dad [Sigmund] ended up working with him to do a lot of his movies. But Sam's attitude towards his work never changed over time. I think he would have probably kept on working 'til he dropped, if he could have. But the old way of doing business was definitely coming to an end; Lippert was the last of the low, low budget independent producers.

It was also during this period that Newfield tackled one of his most ambitious projects: Lippert's science fiction themed *Lost Continent* (1951), which featured stop-motion dinosaurs reminiscent of Willis O'Brien's work in *King Kong* (1933) and an unusually luxurious shooting schedule and budget. Sigmund Neufeld, Jr. was on the set of *Lost Continent* and remembers that the film

> was shot at the Sam Goldwyn Studios on the biggest stage that they had there, because they actually built that mountain on the stage. When they designed it, Sam was a part of the process, because he had to shoot it all. They designed it so that they could work their way around the mountain, going higher and higher as they shot the film. The damn thing went almost to the top of the stage. They designed it so they could just work their way around it without having to change the lighting throughout the shoot, and it worked very well. (Neufeld 2007)

Jack Greenhalgh shot the film for Newfield, one of his last assignments in a career that began in 1935, ended in 1953, and spanned more than 200 films as director of cinematography. Stanley Neufeld worked on the film as an assistant director and remembers that much of the second part of the film was shot at the Santa Anita Botanical Gardens, where, much later, exteriors for the American teleseries *Fantasy Island* were also photographed (Neufeld 2007).

Despite the challenge of making *Lost Continent* with a larger than average budget, a solid cast and an unheard of 18 days to complete principal photography, Sam Newfield was growing bored with his profession. With hundreds of films to his credit, Newfield was in the odd and uncomfortable position of having to work harder than ever just to keep up; for a lifetime of work, he had put nothing aside for his retirement. In addition, surprisingly for someone who had been in the business for so long, he simply didn't know how to market his talent. Notes Stanley Neufeld,

> Sam was good making films but didn't know how to present himself, in today's market or even back in the '50s, of being proud of what he was doing, or publicizing it.
>
> He just did his work, and didn't care about publicity or anything like that. And it hurt him, because he never had an agent, never held out for a better deal. He just liked to work more than anything else. He just accepted doing all these program pictures and he never got a real break to do anything better. In the film industry, you get typed. And so working at PRC insulated him from many of the realities of the business, because Sig always handled the business end. On the films he made, if you didn't do 50 setups a day, you were fired, no matter if you were the assistant director or the director. So, Sam really didn't have the time to be worried. He had to keep working simply to survive. (Neufeld 2007)

In his final years, Newfield predictably moved over to television, working with his brother, Sigmund, and Leon Fromkess to create the violently colonialist and racist television series *Ramar of the Jungle*, starring Jon Hall as a white doctor bringing "civilization" to African tribal culture. Comprised for the most part of stock footage, with hastily staged sequences on a few sparse sets, *Ramar* was a surprise hit of the 1953–54 American television season and remained in reruns for many years after; some 44 episodes of the series are now available on DVD.

Working at a rapid clip, Newfield directed roughly a third of the series' episodes, completing each half-hour segment in an astonishing *one and 2/3 days* before moving on to direct episodes of *Captain Gallant of the Foreign Legion*, another 1950s American children's television show, starring Buster Crabbe, at a similarly rapid pace. By the mid-1950s, however, both Sam and Sigmund were out of step with the industry, clinging to past generic conventions to complete four routine Westerns in 1956 for Sigmund's newly formed Associated Film Releasing Corporation, which folded in 1957.

Newfield accepted a final assignment in Canada, becoming one of the first American directors to produce films there because of the cost incentives. In 1956, he directed 37 episodes of the syndicated television series *Hawkeye* and *The Last of the Mohicans*. His last theatrical feature productions were *Wolf Dog* and *Flaming Frontier* (both 1958), which he shot back-to-back for Regal Films Canada, a subsidiary of Robert L. Lippert's United States and UK production entities. Both films, shot in RegalScope – a CinemaScope-like widescreen process – were given routine distribution on the bottom half of double bills by Twentieth Century Fox. With them, Newfield's directorial career came to a close.

Newfield still wanted to work. He needed to work. But, as Stanley Neufeld told me:

> I think that the type of films he was doing sort of died out at that point. And so it was hard, very hard getting a job. And he never took care of himself or anything. He never stopped gambling either, which didn't help the situation. So he ran up like big gambling debts, and my dad [Sigmund] would have to bail him out. He gambled on anything at all. He loved Las Vegas. He loved gambling on sports. It became an addiction. It ruined him. He just couldn't get work. So he lost a lot of connections. His health was okay until probably the last six months of his life. But he couldn't get work. And then he got diagnosed with liver cancer. So that was the end of that. (Neufeld 2007)

Sam Newfield died on 10 November 1964, at the relatively young age of 64. In his last years, he lived in a small apartment two blocks away from Grauman's

Chinese Theatre, supported in large part by his brother Sigmund. Though retired from the business, Sigmund had managed to save enough and invest wisely so that his last years were comfortable; he died on 21 March 1979. Sam Newfield's daughter, Jackie, married the owner of a large swimming pool company, Blue Haven Pools, while his son, Joel, became a graphic artist for the *Los Angeles Times*. Sigmund Neufeld's sons both entered the business. Stanley worked his way up through the ranks and became an executive producer on such films as *Come Back, Charleston Blue* (1972) and *Popi* (1978), before retiring in 2006. Sigmund, Jr. had a long career directing episodic television, including episodes of *Simon and Simon*, *Buck Rogers in the 25th Century* and *Scarecrow and Mrs. King*; he retired in 1989 and now lives in Las Vegas.

In the end, Sam Newfield's accomplishments as a director are both ephemeral and yet somehow quite solid. When PRC went out of business, the negatives for the entire PRC catalogue were sold to a television syndicator for a flat $1,750 each and, in the early days of the medium, when the majors shunned television as a threat to their hegemony, Newfield's films were ubiquitous. In time, the copyrights on all the PRC films lapsed when no one bothered to renew them and the films entered the public domain, available for anyone to screen, copy or sell to the public. With the advent of DVDs, Alpha Video, a small American video distributor specializing in copyright-free material, began releasing nearly all of Newfield's work in cheap, five dollar editions.

So, for better or worse, Newfield's work is everywhere. With the coming of the worldwide web, downloads of Newfield's more popular films are now readily available for free – for use on cell phones and video iPods – from a number of archival websites. Perhaps surprisingly, many viewers have a great affection for Newfield's films precisely because of their compromised origins. Films such as *Dead Men Walk* (1943) retain a certain sinister appeal in the grim certainty of their visual execution, while Newfield's many slapdash Westerns are favored by aficionados of the genre for their utter disregard of narrative or character motivation; with Newfield, action always comes first. And yet, at the center of all this activity, Newfield himself remains a remote personality – jocular with his crew, eager to please his employers, yet essentially indecipherable as both a man and the most prolific director in the history of the American sound film. Despite all the films he left behind, Newfield himself is something of an enigma.

What drove him to create so much work so quickly? Money, certainly, but there's more to it than that. Perhaps Sam Newfield was comfortable with himself only on the set and would rather keep working on anything rather than endure enforced idleness. One could argue that Newfield existed only in his films and that his addiction to gambling was an outlet for his uneasiness with life outside the sound stage. On the set, Sam Newfield knew exactly what he wanted and got it. Off-screen, it seems Newfield searched restlessly for personal satisfaction – which in the end, sadly, remained elusive. What little now survives of his personal life is little more than a few newspaper clippings and two photographs; for the rest, he leaves behind more than 250 feature films. In this, Newfield, one might argue, is the true phantom of the cinema.

Chapter 7

THE POWER OF RESISTANCE: *LES DAMES DU BOIS DE BOULOGNE**

Destiny is tragic. But I prefer one of our own making to one that is forced upon us.
—Agnès (Elina Labourdette in *Les Dames du Bois de Boulogne*)

As I wrote of *Les Dames du Bois de Boulogne* in a review of the film,

> One of Robert Bresson's most incandescent works, this early film also marks the teaming of two of France's most personal and idiosyncratic artists: Robert Bresson and Jean Cocteau. Cocteau, whose 1949 film *Orpheus* (*Orphée*) mesmerized post-World War II audiences in addition to his numerous other accomplishments, wrote the dialogue for *Les Dames du Bois de Boulogne*, loosely based on Denis Diderot's short story *Jacques le Fataliste et Son Maître*. Elina Labourdette plays Agnès, a young woman who has been forced into a life of prostitution in wartime Vichy, France, in order to support herself and her ailing mother (Lucienne Bogaert). At the same time, Hélène (the serpentine Maria Casarès) is breaking up with her longtime lover, Jean (Paul Bernard), and, feeling jilted by him, concocts an elaborate plot for revenge. Contacting Agnès and her mother, Hélène offers to take over their debts, move them out of the brothel they call home, and set them up in a sleek, modern apartment, with no strings attached. We discover too late Hélène's true motives; she is doing all of this so that Jean will "accidentally" meet Agnès, fall in love with her, marry her, and then become the subject of public ridicule because of Agnès' past. All of this goes off with clockwork precision, but Jean, when confronted with the monstrousness of Hélène's treachery, shakes off his bourgeois prudishness, embraces Agnès despite her fall from grace, and the film ends on a note of hope and Bressonian redemption. (Dixon 1999)

---

* A version of this chapter was first published in 2008 by *Senses of Cinema* (online) as "The Power of Resistance: *Les Dames du Bois de Boulogne*" (issue 46): http://sensesofcinema.com/2008/feature-articles/dames-du-bois-de-boulogne/.

Figure 7. *Les Dames du Bois de Boulogne.*
Source: Author's collection.

This unique collaboration between Cocteau and Bresson would be a one-off in every sense of the term. Bresson's later "stripped down" style, so brilliantly presented in such films as *Un Condamné à mort s'est échappé ou le vent souffle où il veut* (*A Man Escaped or: The Wind Bloweth Where it Listeth*, 1956), *Pickpocket* (1959), *Mouchette* (1967) and his other mature films was directly at odds with the studied artificiality of Cocteau's brittle, yet transcendent vision. As Daniel Millar points out in his perceptive essay on *Les Dames*, Bresson's signature late films are marked by, among other notable characteristics,

> drab clothes and stark, bare settings, filmed strictly on location, with little or no studio work; a low-key, muted, realistic photographic style [...] a sense of ritual, either overtly religious or apparently secular, emphasized sparingly by music; a reticently indirect treatment of sex and of emotion generally; [and] a predominance of non-professional actors. (Millar 1970, 33)

In *Les Dames*, we can see many of these later stylistic tendencies beginning to blossom – albeit under the auspices of professional actors, whom Bresson would henceforth do away with entirely. This rigorously sparse *mise en scène* is diametrically opposed to the dark-hued celestial paradise presented by Cocteau in his second film, *Le Sang d'un Poète* (1930) – a world of camera trickery, overt homoerotic symbolism, ornate sets and autobiographical self-promotion. Where Bresson sought to efface himself in his films, Cocteau's public personality is the centerpiece of not only *Le Sang* but also *Orphée* and his 1946 fairy tale for adults, *La Belle et la bête*. Yet, one could certainly conversely argue that, in his later stark, sparse visual style, Bresson is equally "present" in his films; the empty spaces, downcast glances, monotonal dialogue delivery and deliberate absence of spectacle make Bresson's style at once unique and also offer a direct link to his persona as a filmmaker. And yet, as Richard Roud commented in a 1959 essay in *Film Culture*, it is precisely this clash of methodologies that gives *Les Dames* much of its richness as a text. For Roud, it is the contestation between Cocteau's distanced representationalism and Bresson's severe moralism that forms the stylistic and thematic core of the film. As Roud wrote,

> [the] most extraordinary thing about *Les Dames* is the way the different levels of abstraction are constantly brought into play [...] The dialogue written by Cocteau is itself a stylization or an abstraction of the speech of today. Furthermore, the dialogue never describes the actions of the characters but always counterpoints them. For example, in the scene where Hélène tells Jean that he has married a whore, she is standing at the window of his car. Over her highly stylized words – "Vous avez epouse une grue [...] On dirait que vous ne savez pas ce que c'est qu'une femme qui se venge" ("You've married a tramp [...] You don't seem to realize what a vengeful woman is capable of") – we hear the sound of the windshield wipers moving back and forth. [sic] Dialogue and sound, action and character are all; [...] there is an interaction of one mode of reality and another [...]. (Roud 1968, 36)

Bresson found working with professional actors both trying and ultimately unnecessary as his career progressed, but even in this most theatrical of his films – with the possible exception of his early farce, *Les Affaires Publiques* (1934), and the dark moral fable, *Les Anges du péché* (1943) – Bresson still effectively managed to bend his performers to the demands of his austere vision. Maria Casarès, a favorite of Cocteau's as an actor for her "fire and ice" emotionalism, originally tackled the role of Hélène in *Les Dames* with the same sense of theatrical bravado, which soon led to a clash of will between Casarès and Bresson. But, as Bresson told interviewer Charles Thomas Samuels during an interview conducted in English in Paris on 2 September 1970 – many years after the completion of the film – the director soon devised a method to counteract her somewhat theatrical approach. As Bresson recalled:

> A friend told me that in Julien Green's *South* she had to appear on the stage saying, "it's raining"; in French, *il pleut*. Despite the simplicity of these words, her tragedian's temperament made her shout emphatically: "*Il ... Il ... pleut!*" [...] To get courage, she used to drink a little glass of cognac before acting. When I chanced to discover this, I asked her to take a sedative instead, which she willingly did. Then things started to go better. (Samuels 1970)

In doing this, Bresson prefigured his late style of direction, in which his protagonists would be subjected to intensive rehearsal periods during which they would be obliged to repeat their dialogue over and over until nearly all emotion was stripped from its on-camera delivery. By drugging Casarès, Bresson tamped down the actor's inherent emotionalism and forced her to become an instrument to recite, as dispassionately as possible, Cocteau's dialogue. It is one of the great performances of the screen, as Casarès dispassionately arranges for the destruction of all who oppose her. As Doug Cummings documented, "Years later, Casarès described Bresson as 'a sweet tyrant' who forced his actors to abandon their personal wills in order to offer 'a body, hands, and a voice that he had chosen.'" (Cummings 2004). Perhaps no better description of Bresson's attitude towards professional actors exists; in these few words, Casarès perfectly distills both the strength of Bresson's will and his studied detachment.

When one recalls that Cocteau often described, as in the prefatory titles of *Le Sang d'un Poète*, his ideal cinema as consisting of "a realistic document of unreal events," the direct contrast to Bresson's own cinematic approach becomes immediately apparent. Again speaking to Charles Thomas Samuels, Bresson emphasized that, for him,

> filmmaking is combining images and sounds of *real* things in an order that makes them effective. What I disapprove of is photographing with that extraordinary instrument – the camera – things that are not real. Sets and actors are not real [...] My first film was made with professional actors, and when we had our first rehearsal I said, "If you go on acting and speaking like this, I am leaving." [...] I think that, in other films, actors speak as if they were onstage. As a result, the audience is used to theatrical inflections [...] I want the essence of my films to be not the words my people say or even the gestures they perform, but what these words and gestures provoke in them [...] We are too clever, and our cleverness plays us false.

We should trust mainly our feelings and those senses that never lie to us.
Our intelligence disturbs our proper vision of things. (Samuels 1970)

Yet, it is this "cleverness" – this flirtation with the "false" or theatrical – that remains the hallmark of Cocteau's work as a novelist, scenarist and playwright – a complicit acknowledgment of the inherent artificiality of all fictive presentation. Conversely, what Bresson was seeking – seemingly from his first films – was a minimalist approach to his, for, in his words, "cinema is the art of showing nothing" (Samuels 1970). For Cocteau, the realm of the cinema belonged to the magical, the inherently unreal. As always, Cocteau wanted to "astonish" his viewers; Bresson wanted to force them to concentrate on an inner struggle that lies beneath the surface of his carefully composed images.

So what, then, brought these two disparate artists together? The answer is simple: the Occupation of France during World War II by the Nazis and their puppet Vichy government. In his moving appreciation of Resistance cinema, *André Bazin, the Occupation, and I*, François Truffaut argues persuasively that, for all of the restrictions placed on artists during this grim period in France's history, the cinema flowered under the yoke of the Occupation precisely because of the moral imperative to make films that defied the ruling order – films that criticized the dominant regime in the time-honored disguise of genre and thus managed to slip under the radar of the Occupation's censors. While agreeing that

> there was no place for subversion or protest in the films of this period; the sanctions imposed would have gone beyond those of the Commission de Censure [… and thus] it is therefore understandable that cinema took refuge in historical films and films of fantasy and enchantment […].
> (Truffaut 1981, 18)

Truffaut noted that, in comparison to the years directly following the war:

> Whereas twenty-five new directors had […] the opportunity to make their debuts during the four years of the Occupation – among them [Jacques] Becker, Bresson, and [Henri-Georges] Clouzot – in the fourteen years between 1945 and 1959 (the beginning of the New Wave) the only new names were René Clément, Jacques Tati, Jean-Pierre Melville, Roger Leenhardt, Yves Ciampi, Alexandre Astruc, and Marcel Camus. The numerical disproportion is obvious. (Truffaut 1981, 20)

Thus, adversity created an atmosphere – a hothouse, pressurized zone of creation – in which divergent artists gathered together to create works in defiance of a common enemy whose tyranny they were dedicated to abolish.

In my essay "'How Will I Get My Opium?': Jean Cocteau and the Treachery of Friendship," I noted that, while many French cinéastes and other artists fled Paris during the Occupation, Cocteau elected to stay behind and play a dangerous double game, retaining his place in the spotlight (always an important consideration for Cocteau, to whom publicity was as essential as oxygen) while clandestinely fighting for the concerns of his countrymen and still managing to stay in the good graces of the Vichy authorities (Dixon 2004, 127–41). Cocteau was, during the Occupation, certainly a much more recognized artist than Bresson – who, at this point in his career, had only one short film (*Les Affaires Publiques*, which the director never really cared for) to his credit before his 1943 drama *Les Anges du péché*, with dialogue by Jean Giraudoux, brought him to initial public attention. (See Erik Ulman's insightful essay on *Les Anges du péché* for more details; in many respects, the film is an equally dark companion piece to *Les Dames*.) But Cocteau during this period was overcoming a crippling addiction to opium and had essentially been idle as a filmmaker since *Le Sang d'un Poète*.

It was only through the intervention of his lover, Jean Marais, that Cocteau reentered the cinema with a script for Serge de Poligny's *Le Baron Fantôme* in 1942 (Cocteau also served as narrator for the film and made a brief cameo appearance) and then the scenario for Jean Dellanoy's updated version of *Tristan and Isolde*, *L'Eternel retour* (1943). This set the stage for Cocteau's participation in *Les Dames*, which began shooting on the 24th of April 1944 – during the last days of the Occupation – under the working title "L'Opinion Publique," (Roud, 35), an ironic title in view of the film's initial reception. Due to a variety of production difficulties, the film was begun, stopped and then begun again under circumstances of direst financial concern, eventually bankrupting the film's producer, Raoul Ploquin, and opening to initial public indifference after the liberation of France in 1945.

Indeed, during the film's production – which lasted until February 1945 – the production of the film was halted for nearly six months due to electrical shortages and a severely limited supply of raw film stock. The film was almost scrapped until Cocteau's connections prevailed and shooting resumed (Reader 2000, 20). In short, the film almost vanished before it even had a chance to exist and, although it is readily available on DVD today, for many years before the advent of video, it was a "phantom text," intermittently available in 16mm film from a variety of small distributors before dropping out of sight almost entirely in the mid-1970s. The ephemerality of the project is thus apparent from the outset; here is a film made in spite of, rather than because of, circumstance.

In addition to the differing temperaments of the film's two key auteurs, one must factor in the knowledge that, while Cocteau treated Paris during the war as an extended salon for his creative efforts, managing to remain on good terms with both the members of the Resistance and the occupying authorities, Bresson himself had direct contact with the war; he was taken prisoner by the Germans in 1939 and held for 18 months in a prison camp. These events in part influenced Bresson's postwar film, *Un Condamné à mort s'est échappé* (1956), a historical drama set during this period of the Resistance. This imprisonment, in many senses, marked Bresson for life and made him simultaneously suspicious and fearful of capricious external authority. Taught by circumstance to internalize his emotions during this period by his captors, Bresson's own approach to the war became that of a direct combatant while, for Cocteau, the Occupation merely served as the backdrop for his work as an artist.

The narrative of *Les Dames*, described in brief thumbnail form in the opening paragraphs of this essay, is thus a jumping-off point for two competing, yet incontestably real visions of the French wartime milieu. Cocteau, the boulevardier, never strayed far from the public's attention no matter what else he did while Bresson, a much more interior personage, sought to express himself only through a series of screens – or baffles – deflecting attention from himself. And yet, for all the luxury of its surroundings, *Les Dames* exists in a world of privation and emotional starvation. In the film's opening moments, Hélène is returning from an evening at the theater with a gentleman friend who knows of her tortured relationship with Jean and warns Hélène that, "There's no love there, only tokens of love." For all this, Hélène remains infatuated with Jean – despite the fact that, in the next scene, it is apparent that he has forgotten the anniversary of their initial meeting. Hélène presents Jean with a gold cigarette case – which Jean describes as "warm, cold, light, dark, incorruptible" – but Jean himself has nothing to offer but regrets and, subsequently, the "shocking" revelation that he is no longer in love with her.

But even this moment of honesty must be extracted from Jean; he gives nothing, but in his weakness wants everything immediately and without discussion. Hélène speaks first of the gradual breakdown of their relationship and only then does Jean admit that he too feels a diminution of passion between them and wants to terminate their affair. Although she struggles to retain her composure, it is clear that Hélène is stunned by Jean's rejection. It is one thing for Hélène to break off their relationship, but quite another for Jean to admit that his own ardor has cooled. Hiding her outrage and surprise, Hélène shows Jean to the door in wordless silence and then collapses on her bed, idly playing with her pet dog. As the camera tracks in on her face slowly and impassively, Hélène utters the words that will set the film's entire plot in motion: "I'll be revenged." Thus, Jean's fate is sealed and the rest of the film documents Hélène's campaign against him.

In nearly every – if not every – critical account of *Les Dames*, Paul Bernard's performance as Jean comes in for rather harsh criticism, often mentioned as the one "weak spot" (Roud 1968, 37), as being "lackluster" (Reader 2000, 23) or even as being "a [...] unanimously accepted [...] failure" (Millar 1970, 33). It seems to me that this is far from the case; Jean is a fool, as Agnès bluntly says in the film. He is interested only in the surfaces of people, not in their interior selves. Bernard's weak, pliant, falsely earnest performance is in many ways the perfect contrast to Casarès' barely controlled ferocity; he is the ultimate dupe, absolutely unaware of the web that Hélène spins for him. He is unconscious of having gravely offended Hélène during their breakup and supposes her to be his "friend" in some curious regard; in this, he could not be more mistaken. By contrast, Agnès is almost immediately suspicious of Hélène when she comes into her life, sensing sinister motives behind Hélène's seemingly reassuring smiles.

The film is composed of a series of visually dazzling, almost sensual set pieces despite the somewhat desperate circumstances of its construction. Hélène's apartment is like a museum, lit from above with a series of coldly efficient "pin spots," and Jean-Jacques Grünenwald's relentlessly romantic score suffuses the film with a sense of both grandeur and tragedy. When Hélène decides upon revenge in the opening scene, Bresson uses a sound bridge of music and percussive accompaniment to transport us with a dissolve to the precincts of a shabby café where Agnès dances for a group of bored, indifferent sophisticates, many of whom will try to force their attentions on her later that evening. Alone at a table, Hélène – appearing as if by magic – watches her with cool circumspection.

Only 22 at the time of the film's production, Casarès makes Hélène a creature of menace and destruction as she coolly observes Agnès' dance routine in a series of even tighter close-ups, her cloak covering her head like the hood of a coiled cobra, her face wreathed in cigarette smoke. As Agnès (who has, in the film, a serious heart condition) dances for the crowd, Hélène regards her simply as a means to an end without any regard for Agnès' free will or even her life. It isn't hard to make the connection between Hélène and the occupying Nazi forces here; it is absolutely explicit. Hélène's rapacious pursuit of her plans against Jean will threaten to destroy all who oppose her and Hélène's wealth and social position (particularly in wartime, for *Les Dames* is firmly, I would argue, situated in the world of occupied Paris) will always protect her from reprisals.

Agnès completes her pathetic cabaret performance with a falsely confident smile and leaves the stage pursued by a horde of young men all seeking her sexual favors. It is clear that economic circumstances caused by the war have brought ruin to Agnès and her mother and that even cabaret dancing is not enough to support their increasingly tenuous lifestyle. Agnès, it is clearly implied, has drifted into prostitution, with her mother as her apparently willing enabler. The young men pursue Agnès back to her apartment where her mother – a simple, yet morally ambiguous figure – seems quite content to almost literally pimp her daughter to the admirers in exchange for endless bouquets of flowers, money, chocolate and other false tokens of affection. Even at the start of the film, Agnès is disgusted with her situation and reproaches her mother for accepting the vases of flowers; as she puts it, "Behind every flower, there's the face of a man."

In return, the young men treat Agnès as little more than a tramp, blowing smoke in her face while she is dancing and tormenting her with their unwanted advances. At length, while dancing with a particularly insolent suitor, Agnès reacts to his "smoke in the face" gesture of contempt by grabbing his lit cigarette and stubbing it out on his cheek. He immediately slaps Agnès in response and she pushes him back into an end table, knocking both him and the table over and spilling champagne and an ice bucket on the floor of the room. As always, Agnès' mother reacts by trying to restore a sense of order to this utterly amoral social universe, obediently rushing to pick up the champagne while Agnès regards her with ill-disguised disgust. Hélène, who has followed Agnès and her mother to their apartment, watches this degrading scene with a smile of satisfaction and then moves in for the kill.

Confronting Agnès' mother in a side room, Hélène feigns sympathy for the mother and daughter's desperate situation and offers to set them up in a luxury apartment, settle their debts and restore them to society, seemingly with no strings attached. Agnès is immediately suspicious, but goes along to keep her mother happy. And yet, the airy, spacious apartment seems strangely barren and claustrophobic. Whenever Agnès dances around the rooms and opens the windows in an attempt to take "possession" of the space, her mother closes the windows that let in light and air with protests that Agnès should not exert herself in view of her weak heart, trapping Agnès further within the décor of the apartment and Hélène's machinations. Indeed, Agnès collapses after one brief attempt at pirouetting through the apartment and it becomes clear to her that Hélène's entire scheme is simply a trap for Agnès and her mother.

But it is also a trap for Jean after Hélène arranges an "accidental" meeting between Jean and Agnès at the park near the Bois de Boulogne. Immediately smitten with Agnès – in a sequence staged in a series of sensuously interlocking reciprocal dissolves – Jean demands to know Agnès' address and begins pursuing her with manic, childish intensity. He knows nothing of Agnès' interior torments or her past life, but is attracted by her physical presence alone. Hélène, shrewdly judging this infatuation as a dream state from which Jean refuses to awaken, devises various means to keep Jean and Agnès apart while gradually divulging more and more information about their supposedly "secret" apartment. At length, Jean's pursuit results in a proposal of marriage, which Agnès eventually acquiesces to and immediately regrets. She composes a letter to Jean telling him of her past, but he refuses to read it and, in a detailed and resonantly Catholic ceremony, the couple is wed.

Her triumph complete, Hélène doesn't even wait for the wedding to conclude; as she works her way down the receiving line, Hélène whispers in Jean's ear that she has made a "terrible mistake" about Agnès' pedigree. "Make inquiries," she urges and, when Jean demands clarification, Hélène coolly tells him that he's married "a tramp" and that this is the revenge she has exacted for his "betrayal" of their love. Jean, speechless, flees the scene of the wedding as Agnès collapses on her bed, the victim of another heart attack. At length, ashen, Jean returns and, in the film's final moments, begs Agnès to "stay" with him and not to die. Agnès' last words in the film – "I'll stay" – signal that, despite all of Hélène's elaborate plans and despite Jean's essential human weakness and the general condemnation of society, the couple will make a go of it. More importantly, Jean has finally begun to look behind the surface of both people and things, and values Agnès as a wife and partner in his life. Hélène, ultimately, has failed. It is not so much love, but rather faith, that has triumphed.

Cocteau, ever the expert manipulator of both people and things, saw to it that the film opened at the Rex Theatre in Paris, the largest cinema in the city. Despite the subsequent cool reception, director Jacques Becker – who was present at the premiere – later wrote that, "the public has understood Bresson, I know, and I had the proof of this in a large Boulevard cinema in which some three thousand spectators followed the film in attentive silence" (Reader 2000, 22). Thus, the well-known story of the film's immediate failure should be qualified by Becker's account of this initial success, even though Cocteau himself noted that the film ultimately "won its case in the appeals court" of subsequent critical opinion, particularly with the *Cahiers du Cinéma* crowd (Euker 2007).

But most contemporary critics and audiences misunderstood or disliked the film, perhaps because it reminded them of the recent Vichy past and, for many, their collaborationist share in it. Bresson's future as a director hung in the balance for a time, while Cocteau immediately skipped along to his next project. Another factor that militated against the film's reception was Bresson's relative disinterest in dealing effectively with the critics. As he himself later noted,

> I hate publicity. One should be known for what he does, not for what he is. Nowadays a painter paints a bad painting, but he talks about it

until it becomes famous. He paints for five minutes and talks about it on television for five years. (Samuels 1970)

This is a sentiment that Cocteau, who always cultivated public opinion in his favor, would never have understood. As a result of these and other factors, Bresson never worked with Cocteau again. The two dissimilar artists were moving in decisively different directions in their respective careers – Bresson gravitating towards asceticism, while Cocteau was drawn to a world of fantasy and ornate spectacle. Thus, the intensely romantic vision afforded by Bresson's meticulous direction, Max Douy's sumptuous decors (Douy would later work for Jean Renoir on his equally transcendent romance, *French Cancan*, 1954, as well as Jules Dassin's *Topkapi*, 1964 and, amazingly enough, on Lewis Gilbert's *Moonraker*, 1979, along with numerous other films), Grünenwald's passionate musical core and Philippe Agostini's sharp-as-a-knife cinematography became a curiosity in both Bresson and Cocteau's respective careers.

Bresson would not make a film again until 1950, when his *Journal d'un curé de campagne* (*Diary of a Country Priest*), emerged as the first of a series of austere, sculptural films that completely rejected the theatricality of conventional screen performance, editing, camera movement and musical cues to create nothing less than an utterly unique and distinctive language that Bresson made entirely his own for the rest of his long, but not prolific, career. For Cocteau, *Les Dames* remains a triumph of polished, cynical upper-crust dialogue on par with his masterful 1929 play of love betrayed, *La Voix humaine*, which was eventually filmed by Roberto Rossellini in 1948 (titled "Una voce umana" and part of *L'Amore*). But Cocteau had his own vision as a director to pursue on-screen and made a triumphant return as an auteur with his *La Belle et la bête* (shot in 1945, shortly after the liberation of Paris) – a film as far removed from Bresson's spare, sculptural style as one could possibly imagine.

Yet, their collaboration in *Les Dames* – one might even call it a clash of wills, both intent on the same object, but approaching it through different means – remains a key text in understanding the work of both artists. In the precise choreographing of movements, gestures and screen space, one can already see the beginnings of Bresson's later style. Composed of a series of precise, individuated movements and edited with an air of inexorable inevitability rather than kinetic excitement, Bresson's deconstruction of time and motion is both mathematically precise and laden with meaning (the champagne and table fall, the mother mops up – momentary violence is followed by order restored). Cocteau's script is almost a catalogue of aphorisms; at one point, when Agnès has gone missing in an attempt to evade Jean's ever more intensive advances, Hélène professes ignorance of Agnès' whereabouts, saying, "Wherever she is, she's doing something sublime; in short, ruining herself." And so, *Les Dames* can correctly be seen as a romance – a drama of revenge and its consequences, a window into France under the Nazi Occupation and even, in a bizarre way, as a seriocomic melodrama on the vicissitudes of friendship and maternal attachments.

But, in the final analysis, *Les Dames* remains – as François Truffaut and André Bazin both suggested – a film of resistance, in which a group of talented men and women joined forces to create a parable of one's need for personal responsibility and the consequences of evading it. Reductive though it might be, on at least one level, *Les Dames* is an attack on the "caretakers" of the Vichy regime, who implicitly promised Parisians – and, by extension, all of France – that nothing would change under their rule except perhaps the loss of a few personal liberties and the disappearance of much of France's Jewish population. As Truffaut pointed out in 1975, Marcel Ophüls' epic examination of French culpability during the Occupation, *Le Chagrin et la Pitié* (*The Sorrow and the Pity*, 1970), placed the era of the Vichy regime into much sharper focus; he is quick to acknowledge that more than a few French cinéastes – especially Lucien Rebatet (who often wrote under the pseudonym François Vinneuil) – willingly cooperated with the Nazis in creating an atmosphere of anti-Semitism in French cultural life with, as he put it, a very "heavy hand" (Truffaut 1981, 13).

To place the production of *Les Dames* in its proper context, Truffaut quotes from a text written in April 1941 by Rebatet/Vinneuil under the title "Les Tribus du Cinéma et du Théâtre" (the tribes of the cinema and the theatre), in which the author categorically lays out the future of French cinema in a world ruled by the Nazis:

> Sooner or later, our soil will have to be cleared of several hundred thousand Jews, beginning with Jews without regular papers, those who are not naturalized, those who have most recently arrived, those whose political and financial malfeasance is most obvious – in other words, all the Jews working in cinema. Before this is done, we will pick out those for whom exile would be too benign a punishment and who will have to pay their debt with prison terms at least. In the meantime, the entire French film industry, from the production to the printing of films to the management of the smallest theater, will have to be inexorably and definitively closed to Jews without distinction of either class or origin. (Truffaut 1981, 13)

What does one do in such an untenable situation? One either fights or flees. Now, from the perspective of more than fifty years, the struggle for the mind and souls of France during World War II seems simultaneously remote and difficult to quantify; we look back from the standpoint of those who have vanquished evil (at least in this case), as if victory was always assured. But it was not. Life in France during the Occupation was a constant battle – a series of opportunities for resistance and obligations to one's conscience that were either heeded or ignored. In *Les Dames*, Cocteau and Bresson created a parable that still resonates today – in a time when governments fail to heed the will of their citizens and engage in violence to extract both information and the subjugation of all opposing voices.

If you give up your freedom, you give up your ability to alter your situation. To fight against such tyranny is not only the right thing to do, Bresson and Cocteau argue – in the final resolve, it is the *only* thing to do. What will be the "resistance" films of today, in a time of war that seems to stretch endlessly before us? No doubt, they masquerade as genre entertainments – romances, action films, other escapist fare – in order to stay off the radar screen of the ruling culture. But they exist, as *Les Dames* exists, and offer examples of strength and courage in a time of extreme adversity. Ultimately, *Les Dames*' lasting power derives from the brilliance of its execution, the sophistication of its dialogue and the message of faith, hope and struggle contained within its narrative. Such was the work of the Resistance cinema – and all "resistance" cinema – and such is the achievement of *Les Dames du Bois de Boulogne*.

Chapter 8

BEYOND CHARACTERIZATION: PERFORMANCE IN 1960s EXPERIMENTAL CINEMA*

The New American Cinema of the 1960s differed from conventional models of filmmaking in many ways: embracing chance, roughness of physical execution, an impoverishment of technical and financial facilities, but also freeing the filmmakers to create personal films that reflected their lives, their sexuality and their social beliefs. The "actors" in these films were really performing themselves, even if they were following a script; "performance" in experimental films of the 1960s was really an extension of each actor's personality and, often, actors were left to their own devices without traditional direction during the production of a film. This essay discusses some of the key films of the era, along with the directors and performers who created them.

Acting and performance styles in experimental films are many and varied, but all rely to some degree on the force of individual personality to relate to the film's intended audience. The nomad bikers in Kenneth Anger's *Scorpio Rising* (USA, 1963), for example, are essentially performing themselves for the camera as part of the normal daily catalogue of ritualized behavior. Gerard Malanga as Victor, however – the Victor in Andy Warhol's *Vinyl* (USA, 1965) – working from Ron Tavel's script, delivers an exaggerated, over-the-top "declamatory" performance that was partly the result of Warhol's refusal to let the actors rehearse; Malanga was forced to read much of the script from enormous cue cards during the filming, essentially reading the scenario for the first time. Since all acting contains a certain element of theatricality, the strategy in experimental cinema depends either on complete improvisation (as in the case of Taylor Mead in Ron Rice's free form feature film *The Flower*

---

* A version of this chapter was first published in 2010 by *Screening the Past* (online) as "Beyond Characterization: Performance in 1960s Experimental Cinema" (number 29): http://tlweb.latrobe.edu.au/humanities/screeningthepast/29/performance-in-1960s-experimental-cinema.html.

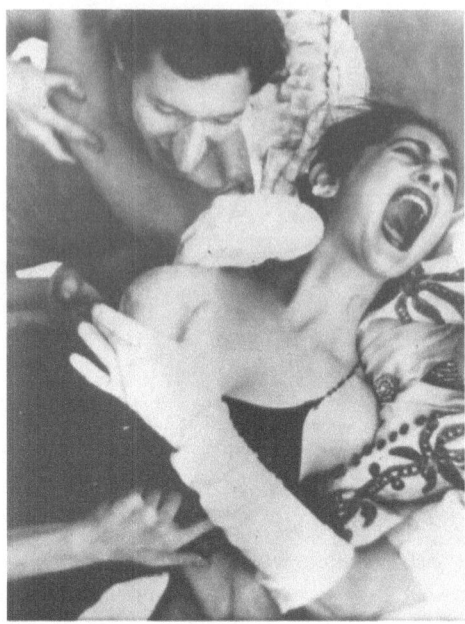

Figure 8. *Flaming Creatures.*
Source: Author's collection.

Thief (USA, 1960)), or else upon a stylized sensibility that seems to bring to the forefront the essential artificiality, or performative nature, of acting.

Often, actors in experimental films are friends of the director, or else stage actors working on the fringe of performance arts and so there is a strong sense of exploration and uncertainty in experimental filmic acting styles; in many cases, the film is a combined voyage of discovery for both the performer and the director alike. Using examples from the works of such artists as Andy Warhol, Ron Rice, Jack Smith, Gunvor Nelson, Gerard Malanga and others, I'll attempt to examine the question of what defines "performance" in the world of experimental cinema and the many ways in which it manifests itself in some signature works of this multifaceted genre.

In the early 1960s, before the specter of AIDS consciousness closed off the body into a site of dis/ease, American experimental filmmakers were more intent on exploring the limits of their physical/mental existence than on more formalist questions of filmic structure and syntax, which would dominate the American avant-garde in the 1970s and '80s. All of these filmmakers shared one thing in common: a highly personal and deeply-felt vision of a new and anarchic way of looking at film and video, fueled by the inexhaustible romanticism of the era and the fact that film and video were both very "cheap" mediums with which to work during the 1960s.

The Flower Thief is a good example of the essence of performativity as content and as the informing structure for creating a finished cinematic work. Produced to final, optical sound print for considerably less than $1,000 on outdated black-and-white film stock – specifically, leftover aerial gunnery film in 50-foot cartridges from World War II, donated at the last minute, curiously, by the notoriously cost-conscious Hollywood producer Sam Katzman – the film follows Taylor Mead, the Chaplin of the 1960s underground, on a series of picaresque adventures in and around San Francisco. The film has little plot and needs none; the title derives from a random incident in which Mead steals a flower from a street vendor, then fantasizes that the police are about to arrest him for his crime. Escaping down the steep San Francisco streets in a Radio Flyer child's wagon, desperately clutching his much-abused teddy bear, Mead is at once pathetic and endearing, projecting an image of holy foolishness on the screen.

As the film progresses through its 75-minute running time, Taylor Mead interacts with groups of roving beatniks, school children, jazz musicians and North Beach hustlers to create a portrait of a man unfettered by the constraints of society. The film's construction is equally anarchic, incorporating as it does light flares, punch holes, mere fragments of film edited together to form a semi-coherent whole and, at times, entire 50-foot reels of film unedited, straight from the camera. The soundtrack for *The Flower Thief* is, appropriately enough, a mixture of scratchy old records and Beat poetry; no attempt at image/sound synchronization is made. The soundtrack is every bit as rough in its execution as are the images; it is simply the gathering of Mead's acts of performance that interests Rice above all other formalist concerns. Considered perhaps the most uncompromising and genuinely avant-garde feature film of the very early 1960s, *The Flower Thief* is a paean to the plight of the common man in a world that is both unresponsive and unyielding.

This motivated extravagance extended to Rice's other films – most notably *Chumlum* (USA, 1964), which starred Mario Montez, Gerard Malanga and Jack Smith (more on these widely variant personalities later) in what René Micha in *Les Temps Modernes* described as "an infinite spectacle, superimposing bodies swinging in hammocks, back and forth through gossamer draperies that slow the movements, and suspend them on the edge of the abyss" (Filmmakers' Cooperative 1967, 125). Shot in ravishing color, the film is an indolent spectacle of pleasure run rampant, existing in a world in which the only pursuits are desire and temptation. In sharp contrast to the "rough-and-ready" look of *The Flower Thief*, *Chumlum* is quietly seductive for its brief 26-minute running time, aided considerably by Angus MacLise's trance-like musical accompaniment. In this film, performance consists almost exclusively of a series of poses; inaction becomes action and passivity, enticement. It is enough to drift through the world of *Chumlum* with its protagonists; Rice has created a pansexual dream world in *Chumlum* that is both intoxicating and mesmerizing.

Ron Rice himself died of bronchial pneumonia in Acapulco, Mexico in 1964, not long after making *Chumlum*; his excessive lifestyle and his insistence on putting the cost of film production before all other considerations (food, rent and other more mundane expenses) seemingly ensured his early death from spectacular, performative self-neglect. In the late 1990s, looking back on the career of what he described as "the greatest director I ever worked with," Mead described the genesis of *The Flower Thief* and how the film represented for him – and for Ron Rice – a departure from the conventional cinema as it was then being practiced, even at the margins of production:

> The philosophies of the '50s "Beat" writers came to cinematic fruition [...] in the film *Pull My Daisy* (USA, 1959) by Robert Frank and Alfred Leslie. I attended this film with Ron Rice, and we both picked up on how interesting and easy it was to respond to our surroundings in real life and even transfer to cinema. Though the "professionalism" and cost of *Pull My Daisy* was even beyond our financial and mentally competent or inclined disposition. We thought we could make a "worse" film, and it would cost a fraction of the well-lit and correlated *Pull My Daisy*. What I think we bought especially was the philosophy within the film of Allen, Gregory, and Peter, and their friends – that this was the new way to do things, including live. And, in film, Ron Rice's basic advice to filmmakers was "Push the button." Unfortunately he carried "living" to its ultimate at the early age of 28 [...]. (Mead 1998, 2)

In Taylor Mead's other performative films of the 1960s – *Passion in a Seaside Slum* and *The Hobo and the Circus* (both directed by Bob Chatterton; USA, 1961) and *Lemon Hearts* (directed by Vernon Zimmerman; USA, 1960) – Mead retains his childlike innocence in a world that continually seeks, without success, to corrupt him with the desire for conventional material rewards. *Lemon Hearts*, a 16mm 30-minute black-and-white film with an optical soundtrack, was financed by the actor Richard Kiley and produced in its entirety on an amazingly low budget of $50 (Sargeant 1997, 88). Mead plays *eleven* different roles in the film as he drifts aimlessly through the ruins of a series of soon-to-be-demolished Victorian houses, sometimes appearing in drag, sometimes in blue jeans and a sweatshirt.

The soundtrack is once again pirated from jazz records, interspersed with Mead's own Beat poetry ("Oh God, oh God, oh God, my feet smell [...] I pissed on Jane Wyman's picture"). In his lackadaisical avoidance of conventional plot and characterization in those films he appeared in, Taylor Mead – in concert with the filmmakers he worked with – created a cinema in which his performing body was the central focus of the camera's gaze. Whenever he is off the screen in *The Flower Thief* or *Lemon Hearts*, the audience grows restless. Taylor Mead creates – with his gracefully languid nymph-like body and his blissfully blank expression – the perfect picture of absolute innocence in a hopelessly corrupt universe.

I knew Mead during the Warhol era in the late 1960s and found him to be a fascinating, deeply innocent and vastly talented performer. Once, at Warhol's 33 Union Square West Factory, I spontaneously began filming Mead with my Bolex absolutely without warning and was stunned when he immediately improvised what he later termed "The Dance of the Ruptured Swan," making up the choreography for the piece entirely on the spot. From a series of graceful pirouettes, Mead suddenly fell to the floor in mock agony, clutching his genitals, screaming, "I've been castrated!" while still attempting to carry on with his dance performance with a flurry of vigorous leg thrusts and extravagant arm gestures as he did so.

What amazed me even more was that, as my spring-wound Bolex ended each 15 foot burst and needed rewinding, Mead would pause and wait for me to quickly rewind the camera. When we continued, Mead resumed the sequence without a gap. I shot two 100-foot reels of Mead in this fashion, without a word spoken between us, and when I had exhausted my supply of film, I simply gestured towards him and remarked, "That was brilliant. Thank you." With characteristic modesty, Mead, now in his nonperformance persona, brushed off my praise with a wave of his hand and I left the Factory with the very real sense that I'd just been in the presence of an authentic performing genius.

The other aspect that struck me as remarkable was that Mead had *instinctively* responded to the whir of my camera, reflexively kicking into performance mode without missing a beat. Further, I could make no claim for "directing" the footage I had just shot; Mead had created the whole thing from the start of filming. Nor did he inquire what I wanted, what I intended to do with the footage or even who I was (we were relative strangers at the time). Simply put, Mead was the auteur of the sequence much more than I was; I was simply recording his performance on film.

In short, Taylor Mead was an ideal actor for a "hands off" director like Andy Warhol or Ron Rice; given literally no direction, he transfixed the gaze of the camera with his consummate skill as a performer. But, then again, this skill served Mead best in experimental cinema; although he has made a few forays into semi-commercial cinema, such as Jim Jarmusch's portmanteau film *Coffee and Cigarettes* (USA, 2004), when bound to a script, Mead seems tied down. A perennial free spirit, Mead is best left to his own devices.

In a similar vein, Mario Montez (born René Rivera in 1935 in Puerto Rico) was another distinctive performer, although his work was in a somewhat narrower vein – adopting the drag persona of a 1940s movie siren, patterned after the iconic Maria Montez, the "Queen of Technicolor," in such films as Robert Siodmak's *Cobra Woman* (USA, 1944). With her premature death at age 33 of a heart attack, Montez became the patron saint of gay "underground" actors and directors and René Rivera, a New York City postal worker, adopted Montez's name and extravagant attitude, bursting forth from the screen in a series of experimental epics beginning with Jack Smith's notorious *Flaming Creatures* (USA, 1963), in which he was billed as Dolores Flores ("Zagria"). *Flaming Creatures*, a parody of the Arabian Nights costume pictures both Smith and Montez were so fond of, climaxed in a transvestite orgy coupled with an earthquake. The film was an instant *succès de scandale* and the object of numerous obscenity busts, but it became Smith's signature work and launched Montez into a sort of twilight stardom.

Subsequently, in *Mario Banana No. 1* (USA, 1964), Montez solidified his screen persona by seductively fellating a banana for four minutes in lavish, explosive color – just the sort of *mise en scène* that Maria Montez herself would have appreciated in form, if not content. Shot in the style of Warhol's "screen test" series – 100-foot rolls of film run through a Bolex camera with an electric motor to capture all the action in one take – *Mario Banana* is at once an homage to '40s camp and effectively queers the entire costume drama genre with its shimmeringly aggressive shot composition. Framed in a tight, glamorous close-up, Montez regards the camera as a potential suitor, an object to be seduced, even as she/he eagerly consumes the banana for the spectator's implied pleasure.

Montez then appeared in Warhol's *Screen Test Number 2* (USA, 1965), as well as Warhol's *Harlot* (USA, 1965), loosely based on the cult of Jean Harlow, and *Hedy (The Shoplifter*, USA, 1965), a spoof of Hedy Lamarr's Hollywood career. Her final appearance in a Warhol film was a brief cameo in *Chelsea Girls* (USA, 1966), in which Warhol pushed her in front of the camera to sing "They Say Falling In Love is Wonderful," while two men engage in a sexual liaison on a sloppily made bed. Montez's performance has a double-edged verisimilitude; one is conscious of the drag aspect of his onscreen persona, but at the same time, Montez embraces his alter ego with such fervent devotion that the masquerade becomes almost transparent. He is what he presents himself to be: a transgendered figure of androgynous desire, upon whom the audience can project either a male or female gender identity.

As Montez says forthrightly, "I learned my acting basically from watching old movies," and so his performances form a link not only between masculine and feminine performance styles, but also classical Hollywood and the New

American cinema of the 1960s, which discarded many of the "rules of the game" by which the cinema had previously operated. Not that he made much money at it; "With Warhol, everyone was forced to sign releases before you did anything. We were all naïve and we signed away [...] I was working [in] the daytime as a clerical worker and I had to squeeze in time to do things for Warhol, [as well as theatrical performance artist] Charles Ludlam. I don't know how I did it" (Martorell 2010). Eventually, Montez decided that New York was too inhospitable a climate and, in the late 1970s, moved to Florida, more or less abandoning his performing career – although he is, from time to time, lured out of retirement at benefit screenings for Warhol's films or those of Jack Smith.

Gerard Malanga, once Andy Warhol's right-hand man and now a full-time photographer and archivist, created a series of deeply romantic films in which his own persona of "the young poet" was foregrounded in each frame. In contrast to the gaze of Warhol's detached, somnolent Auricon camera – loaded with 35 minutes (1200 feet) of 16mm film at a clip to record the happenings staged by Warhol's Factory regulars – Malanga's films, shot almost entirely with a handheld Bolex, present a world in which all is celebration, beauty and sacrifice of the self for art. While such early Warhol films as *Camp* (USA, 1965) – a shoddily improvised "variety show" featuring Paul Swan, Baby Jane Holzer, Jack Smith, Mario Montez and Tosh Carillo – also present the human body as the sole point of interest to the gaze of the camera, Warhol's informing strategy in such films as *Horse* (USA, 1965), *The Life of Juanita Castro* (USA, 1965), *Vinyl* (USA, 1965), *Poor Little Rich Girl* (USA, 1965) and his magnum opus *The Chelsea Girls* (USA, 1966) is to confront the performer (and spectator) with the documented image of the performing body.

Malanga's handheld, restlessly moving camera interprets the actions he records; with *In Search of the Miraculous* (USA/Italy, 1967), Malanga creates an emotional, vivid poem of adoration for his then-fiancée, Benedetta Barzini. Other early Malanga films also put the performer center stage within the filmmaker's lens – which once again *extends* rather than *contains* the performances it records. *Mary for Mary* (USA, 1966) is a portrait of the actor Mary Woronov; *Donovan Meets Gerard* (USA, 1966) documents a performative meeting between Malanga and the folk singer, Donovan, at Warhol's studio, which is obviously staged for the recording camera. One of Malanga's most ambitious works, the 60-minute, split screen, two-projector, stereo sound *Pre-Raphaelite Dream* (USA, 1968), documents the filmmaker's friends and extended family in Cambridge, Massachusetts, as they perform their lives for the camera. In *The Recording Zone Operator* (Italy, 1968), shot on location in Rome in 35mm Techniscope/Technicolor, Malanga worked with Tony Kinna, Anita Pallenberg and members of the Living Theatre to improvise a 40-minute performance piece in which a group of gay "angels" accost passersby in a local park, leading to an orgy in a nearby apartment.

The almost forgotten Kip Coburn created a series of sensuous personal films, working entirely in standard 8mm reversal color with sound-on-tape accompaniment. Such films as *Cocain* [*sic*], *Flesh*, *Hitchhiker*, *Johns Doll* [*sic*], *Trips*, *Stoned* and *Colors* (all USA, all undated) document an internal odyssey in which the filmmaker is at one with the world he creates, presenting himself as the ritualized performer in a drama of the artist's quest for life beyond the boundaries of normative experience. Similarly, Storm de Hirsch's *Divinations* (USA, 1964), *Peyote Queen* (USA, 1965) and *Shaman: A Tapestry for Sorcerers* (USA, 1966) extend the filmmaker's body into the performance space of the film frame, as de Hirsch photographs herself, nude, through a variety of prismatic lenses and diffusion filters, presenting her body as the site of ritualistic display to her audience. Stan Brakhage was another filmmaker who celebrated the human body in many of his films, especially such early works as *Window Water Baby Moving* (1962), his epic feature film *Dog Star Man* (1964) and perhaps his most direct and controversial film, *Lovemaking* (1968), a forty-minute film that depicted numerous couples – both straight and gay – photographed with unflinching honesty, locked in ecstatic embrace.

Ed Emshwiller's *Dance Chromatic* (USA, 1959), *Lifelines* (USA, 1960) and *Thanatopsis* (USA, 1962) center on the body in motion – particularly on dance as a location of celebration of the human instinct for physical pleasure and self-expression. Arnold Gassan's *Marsyas* (USA, 1963) follows the plight of an African-American who seeks to escape, metaphorically, the suffocating domination of the White world around him. Fleeing from the city into the woods, he is symbolically castrated and then, in the final images of the film, confronts himself as a negative-imaged ghost in his bathroom mirror. Disturbing and powerful, *Marsyas* offers us a performative vision of the loss of human identity through the twin exigencies of social alienation and racial marginalization and focuses on only one character, Don Crawford (as Marsyas), throughout its 12-minute running time.

Gunvor Nelson, working with Dorothy Wiley, created the groundbreaking film *Schmeerguntz* (USA, 1966), which deals almost exclusively with the traditionally non-documented physical aspects of childbirth and child rearing: nausea and vomiting, cleaning dirty diapers, morning sickness and the general chores that one must accomplish when one gives birth to a child. Intercut with clips from 1930s beauty pageant films and other images of the "idealized" feminine corpus, as well as clips from the Jack LaLanne exercise program ("Merrily we exercise!" Jack sings, as Nelson and Wiley, in their ninth month of pregnancy, struggle simply to navigate the length of their cramped apartment), *Schmeerguntz* is a 15-minute expression of anger, disgust and protest against a society which artificially sanitizes and erases images of the reproductive body from the mainstream media.

In a much more celebratory vein, the late Barbara Rubin's *Christmas on Earth* (USA, 1963) – astonishingly created when the filmmaker was only 18 – is a 30-minute 16mm double-projection film in which two separate reels of images of the human body engaged in sexual intercourse, straight and gay, are superimposed to create a landscape of desire and corporeal performance which remains one of the most audacious cultural statements of the 1960s. Rubin photographed the images for the film in a freeform, documentary manner, then cut the developed reels of film into short strips, threw them into a basket and drew the individual shots out one by one, splicing them together in random order. As Daniel Belasco notes of the making of the film,

> In June 1963, [Rubin] corralled five friends into the Ludlow Street crash pad rented by musicians John Cale and Tony Conrad and instigated a night of playful debauchery. "Barbara held us hostage for 24 hours, from early evening to the next day. It was very Cocteau-ish. We were locked in and hermeticized in this apartment, it was a very freewheeling situation," recalled Gerard Malanga, one of the performers in the film [in a telephone interview with Belasco]. (Belasco 2007)

This free-associational approach to the shooting and editing of *Christmas On Earth* extended to the film's presentation, as well. After extended consideration, Rubin cut the finished film into two separate reels, screening the images on two projectors simultaneously to create another layering of imagery within the work. While requesting that one projector's image fill the entire screen and the second projector's image be "approximately 1/3 smaller, [filling] only the middle of the screen," Rubin was very much interested in enlisting the projectionist of her film as a co-creator of the work, as evidenced by these remarks to the projectionist, found on a sheet of paper enclosed in the film can:

> It doesn't matter which reel is on which projector. During the screening, the projectionist is asked to play with color changes by holding colored filters in front of the lens of one or the other projector, or both. Moreover, the film has neither head nor tail – it can be projected either way. (Filmmakers' Cooperative 1967, 129)

Rubin's vision of the human body as a performative site of pleasure, desire, mystery and ritual role play is certainly one of the most direct to come out of the 1960s American experimental cinema and one of the most unashamed.

By holding up the human body (male and female) to the careful scrutiny of the camera lens, Barbara Rubin, in a single film, managed to reclaim the sexualized body from the zone of pornographic representation it inhabits in the Dominant Cinema – as a location of fear and prurient desire. Instead, the Edenic images Rubin offers the viewer in *Christmas On Earth* remind us of our own genesis – our life and breath – and our concomitant mortality.

Ben Van Meter, a West Coast filmmaker most active in the 1960s, created a gorgeous series of films that celebrate the human body in such works as *The Poon-Tang Trilogy* (USA, 1964), *Colorfilm* (USA, 1964–65), *Olds-Mo-Bile* (USA, 1965) and his epic *Acid Mantra: Re-Birth of a Nation* (USA, 1966–68), a 47-minute color and black-and-white work of such propulsive energy and intensity that viewing it is almost an exhausting experience. Starting with footage of various rock bands in concert – including the Velvet Underground and the Grateful Dead – the film superimposes as many as ten different layers of images simultaneously to engulf the viewer in a cornucopia of sight and sound, all leading up to a climactic orgy during a summer picnic at a party in the Bay Area countryside.

Men, women and children are seen frolicking about nude, unashamed before Van Meter's camera: swimming, playing Frisbee, lounging on the grass in the late afternoon sunlight. As the film enters its final third, the men and women participate in a celebratory group sex experience, which we barely glimpse through a haze of filters, quasi fabrics and competing imagistic material. As the couples engage in ecstatic sexual performative role play, Van Meter drips blobs of colored paint directly on the film, as if to suggest the intensity of the energy that is being released by this performance. As the film ends, we see family units once again engaged in relaxed outdoor activities still in the nude, playing various sports, relaxing or walking in the tall grass with their children.

Carolee Schneemann created the beautiful film *Fuses* (USA, 1964–68), a 22-minute meditation on the act of lovemaking, which Schneemann photographed with her partner during the act of intercourse. Unlike the stratified images of sexual activity removed from any human context, Carolee Schneemann, throughout the film, allows her camera to film the family cat disinterestedly watching them or window curtains blowing in the afternoon breeze. Schneemann also created a number of performance pieces during the 1960s and '70s that involved the use of her body as a site of performative ritualistic display; sometimes these events were documented, but often they remained merely as memories in the minds of those in the audience. José Rodriguez-Soltero's *Jerovi* (USA, 1965) and Naomi Levine's *Jaremelu* (USA, 1964) celebrated the act of masturbation as a rite of sexual performance and self-actualization in a way in which even censors of the period found unsettling. *Jerovi* and *Jaremelu* were both denied admission to the 1965

Ann Arbor Film Festival on the grounds that they were "pornographic," as the late Gregory Markopoulos reported in an essay on the festival:

> [...] I learned that certain films had not been admitted to the festival because Mr. Manupelli's selection committee thought them unworthy of inclusion. Among these were Naomi Levine's lovely *Jaremelu* and José Soltero's *Jerovi*, another film on masturbation like [Nathanael Dorsky's] *Ingreen* (USA, 1964) but more direct. A part of the selection committee ran *Jerovi* and they were visibly shaken. One young woman immediately proclaimed it "pornographic." "What's pornographic about it?" I asked. No reply [...] (Filmmakers' Cooperative 1967, 128)

Warren Sonbert began his filmmaking career with *Amphetamine* (USA, 1966), a student film Sonbert shot in February of that year featuring his friends and roommates shooting up amphetamine on camera, then engaging in passionate gay sexual displays of performative lovemaking. The film was stunning both in its apparent artlessness as well as its unashamed embrace of both the drug culture and the performative act of homosexual lovemaking, performed directly in front of Sonbert's camera. Shot in 16mm black-and-white and scored to the beat of '60s rock and roll, *Amphetamine* was hailed as one of the clearest and most direct films of the 1960s, receiving an ecstatic review from critic James Stoller.

> [...] *Amphetamine* is especially symptomatic as in its intimation that the filmmaker has not performed enough *work* for this to be art. But I would suggest that the work has indeed been done, although principally in an unaccustomed direction: the direction of freeing the imagination first so that a statement could be made for which, in its transparency and unpretentiousness, there was no comfortably precedent. The result is beautiful and pure: behind the bald surface we feel, first, that many inessentials have been cleared away, and then, that the need for them has been cleared away. (Filmmakers' Cooperative 1967, 141)

One of the most compelling images in the film, indeed, is the result of an accident. As Sonbert told me in 1969, he was shooting another film about the denizens of 42nd Street in Manhattan – then, a notorious zone of drugs and debauchery – when the film in his camera lost its loop, resulting in a (supposedly) completely unusable image. When the footage came back from the lab, he was advised to simply throw the material away. But Sonbert saw the value in embracing this mistake, much as Marcel Duchamp would have done, and cut sections of the light, fluttering material into *Amphetamine* to create what

Stoller referred to an "exquisite blur," right before a "shock cut" to two young men locked in a passionate embrace while Sonbert's camera swoops around them in an ecstatic dance of communal abandon.

Sonbert went on to a long and riveting career as a filmmaker; while his later works are much more formalist, starting with the structuralist film *Carriage Trade* (USA, 1971), his early films, such as *Where Did Our Love Go?* (USA, 1966), *Hall of Mirrors* (USA, 1966) and *The Bad and the Beautiful* (USA, 1967) belong to the classical period of American experimental cinema, and document the lives and loves of his large circle of friends and colleagues – often scored to rock and roll soundtracks to create an indelible, ineffably romantic portrait of life in New York City during what was arguably its greatest period as an artistic breeding ground for all the arts, not just film.

In similar fashion, Jud Yalkut's *Kusama's Self Obliteration* (USA, 1967) offers us a vision of the Japanese performance artist, Yayoi Kusama, engaged in a "self-obliteration" ritual in which she paints dots of color on leaves, animals, various other objects and finally on a group of people ecstatically copulating in one of Kusama's endlessly mirrored "Infinity Chambers" who carry on making love, seemingly oblivious to Kusama's painterly brushstrokes being applied to their naked skin. By linking nature in the form of trees, flowers, grass and animal to the human experience of performative re/production, Kusama demonstrates that the physical fact of "individuality" is mediated by the performative act of "self-obliteration," in which individuality is subsumed into the larger fabric of shared existence. Kusama – whose work as a performance artist, painter and sculptor is now undergoing a major renaissance – was one of the first artists in the 1960s to incorporate performativity into her work, which was presented with or without the apparatus of documentation. It is only because Jud Yalkut was present with his camera that we have the record of Kusama's performance work in her *Self Obliteration* piece; many of her performance works were documented only with stills or not at all.

Sara Kathryn Arledge, a pioneering feminist filmmaker who began making 16mm color films in 1941, produced a series of meditations on human sexuality and ritual body display in such films as *Introspection* (USA, 1941–46), *What Is A Man?* (USA, 1958), *Tender Images* (USA, 1978) and others, which celebrated the union between masculine and feminine with a directness of address that still strikes the viewer as being fresh and original. Arledge was a pioneer in this area, making films that were uncompromising in their graphic specificity for the era, depicting sexuality as a performative human act rather than inhabiting the pornographic zone of the forbidden. As Judith Butler notes, with filmic pornography, "'construction' is not simply the doing of the act [...] but *the depiction* of that doing" (Butler 1995, 221), depicting the act of sexual intercourse in a manner which can be construed as degrading and/or dehumanizing. Arledge's work directly tackles the issues of filmic sexual performativity and transcends the mere documentation of human sexuality through the mediation of her humanist gaze. In similar fashion, wife and husband Marie Menken and Willard Maas collaborated on the precedent shattering film *Geography of the Body* (USA, 1943), which reviewed the human body in extreme close-up with the aid of magnifying lenses and specially designed filters.

All of these films retain their power to impress audiences today, if only because of their inherent innocence and lack of shame – a visual and sexual freedom that arose out of an era of pre-viral consciousness. We will never see the likes of the performative "body work" films of the 1960s again. It would be impossible and inauthentic to attempt to recreate them. These performative films of human sexuality and ritualized body display were a response to the repressive atmosphere of the 1950s and a breaking down of then-established rules of gender, sex roles and social taboos. In the films discussed in this essay, the viewer can see the human body as the site of ritualized displays within a social context of imagistic and sexual self-actualization, a revolutionary act that altered the course of the cinema both in its explicitness and honesty. The legacy that these films bequeath to us today is a terrible vision of the beauty of the human body as a performative locus of both fear and desire, the domain of the spirit made visible and tangible.

In all experimental cinema, "performance" is a value that is very much in flux – both during the production and viewing of the film. Straight viewers get one set of responses; gay viewers another; lesbian and transgendered spectators yet another series of insights; and bisexual viewers receive still another series of takeaway impressions. Gender performance is one of the central concerns of classic experimental cinema, but added to that, such artists as Warhol (and his scenarist, the late Ronald Tavel) purposefully set out to investigate the limits of filmic narrative and question what passes for a "performance" in a film. In conventional, mainstream cinema, foreign or domestic, the role of the actor is clearly defined as a person who can learn lines, hit marks and seemingly "become" the character they are playing, shedding their own personality as part of the performative process. Experimental films largely rely on their protagonists to bring *themselves*, rather than a set of inherently artificial and mimetic skills, to the set; thus, in a very real sense, the individuality and intensely personal approach one sees in the films discussed in this article represents arguably a more genuine connection to the "real" than any scripted performance. There is a genuine element of risk and spontaneity in these films that is often absent from mainstream cinema, with its all-too-often predictable story arcs, twist endings and recycled plot lines.

Experimental cinema, by contrast, puts the heart on trial, as it exposes the fears and ambitions of its protagonists, performing for the love of the art rather than any conventional critical acclaim. In the end, then, experimental films almost by definition interrogate the very process of traditional screen acting and find it innately superficial and often lacking in real human resonance. Not everyone is willing to open himself or herself up to the scrutiny of such a naked gaze; those who are gesture towards a re-evaluation of theatrical and cinematic standards of performance and, in the process, bring us closer to ourselves.

Chapter 9

VANISHING POINT: THE LAST DAYS OF FILM*

There can be no doubt that the digitization of the moving image has radically and irrevocably altered the phenomenon which we call the cinema and that the characteristics of this transformation leave open an entirely new field of visual figuration. For those who live and work in the post-filmic era – that is, those who have come to consciousness in the past twenty years – the digital world is not only an accomplished fact, but also the dominant medium of visual discourse. Many of my students remark that the liberation of the moving image from the tyranny of the "imperfect" medium of film is a technical shift that is not only inevitable, but also desirable.

For younger viewers, the scratch-free, grain-free, glossily perfect contours of the digital image hold a pristine allure that the relative roughness of the filmic image lacks. Indeed, by doing away with film, many of my students persuasively argue that we are witnessing the next step in what will be a continual evolution of moving image recording – which, in turn, will be followed by newer mediums of image capture now unknown to us. For others, those of my age, the filmic medium is a separate and sacrosanct domain and the "coldness" of the digital image – stripped of any of the inherent qualities of light, plastics and colored dyes – betrays a lack of emotion, a disconnect from the real in the classical Bazinian sense. DVDs are easy to use and cheap to produce, but can't afford the visual depth and resonance of a projected 35mm filmic image. It seems to me that both arguments have valid points and are equally worthy of serious consideration.

Yet the problem, ultimately, with such considerations is that, in the end, there is no "right" answer – no clearly superior medium, no set of values that emerges as the clear winner in any disputation that must, of necessity, be based on personal aesthetics, as well as practical and financial consideration.

---

* A version of this chapter was first published in 2007 by *Senses of Cinema* (online) as "Vanishing Point: The Last Days of Film" (issue 43): http://sensesofcinema.com/2007/feature-articles/last-days-film/.

Figure 9. Film suffering neglect.
Source: Author's collection.

16mm, we might as well face it, is dead and I mourn its passing as much as anyone. Indeed, I run 16mm prints in my classes as much as I possibly can and revel in the pictorial values and warmth of the film image during my analytical student screenings of classic films. But, in my home, I no longer have a 16mm projection setup, which I had for many years in the 1960s through to the early 1980s; DVDs have replaced the hundreds of 16mm prints I used to own and have since sold or donated to various archives. When screened on a 50-inch plasma monitor in the proper aspect ratio, DVDs offer a very satisfactory viewing experience – even if what emerges is, at least in my view, a copy of a copy.

It is important to note that the majority of viewers – and I include many of the new generation of academics here – make no such distinction. Watching Alfred Hitchcock's *The Birds* (1963) on DVD, for example, twenty-first century viewers realize that they are watching (optimally) a 35mm negative transferred to digital memory and then downloaded to a DVD for home use and that the final image they watch "copies" the filmic nature of the original image, but, at the same time, gives only the "impression" of its original source material. But, given this *a priori* assumption, twenty-first century viewers quickly move past this empirical certainty to embrace this newly digitized image as the simulacrum of a twentieth-century medium. There is no sadness in this and no betrayal of the maker's original intent; it is merely a translation from one image capture medium to another.

Certainly it can be argued that this is an oversimplification of a rather knotty problem; film comes with one set of values inherently present in the stock itself (a tendency towards warmth in color for some film stocks, or towards cooler hues in others, as well as characteristics of grain, depth and definition which are unique to each individual film matrix), while the digital video image offers another entirely different set of characteristics, verging on a hyperreal glossiness that seems to shimmer on the screen. To achieve a reconsideration of the basic states of representationalism inherent in any comparison of these two mediums is a difficult task, calling into question more than a century of cinematic practice and a host of assumptions shared by practitioners and viewers alike. Insofar as the moving image is concerned, it might well be termed what Friedrich Nietzsche cited in *Ecce Homo* as the re-evaluation of all values — or "the old truth coming to an end" (Nietzsche 1992, 86) – opening up a series of questions, claims and counterclaims that instantaneously obliterate almost all of our preconceptions of the nature of the moving image.

This is hard work and, yet, it is work that must be attempted critically and theoretically because, paradoxically, it has already been accomplished as a physical fact – the film image is about to become the sarcophagus of memory while a new medium of moving image recording takes center stage for the moment, *its* moment, bringing with it a whole new host of aesthetic and practical issues, such as archiving, distribution and audience reception; how different is it to view these images primarily in the privacy or isolation of one's own home, as opposed to the communal nature of traditional filmic projection in an auditorium of strangers?

As Paolo Cherchi Usai notes:

> I won't shed tears over the death of cinema. This might be its first real chance to be taken seriously. It is estimated that about one and a half billion viewing hours of moving images were produced in the year 1999, twice the number made just a decade before. If that rate of growth continues, three billion viewing hours of moving images will be made in 2006, and six billion in 2011. By the year 2025 there will be some one hundred billion hours of these images to be seen. In 1895, the ratio was just above forty minutes, and most of it is now preserved. The meaning is clear. One and a half billion hours is already well beyond the capacity of any single human: it translates into more than 171,000 viewing years of moving pictures in a calendar year. (Usai 2001, 111)

In short, cinema history is so vast that it can never be encompassed – no matter how assiduously one might try – and images are disintegrating or being erased faster than we can possibly archive them. Jean Cocteau was right when he observed in 1943 that "a cinema studio is a factory for making ghosts. The cinema is a ghost language that has to be learned" (Cocteau 2001, 131). But such a language, despite having widespread currency, is also a language that is inherently ephemeral, leaving a series of impressions that have more tangible currency than the fragile film stock on which they are fixed. The twenty-first century has given us a new "ghost language" with its own rules, ciphers and grammar.

Such twentieth-century fetish films as Peter Delpeut's *Lyrical Nitrate* (1991) and *The Forbidden Quest* (1993) document the evanescent ebbing and fading of the filmic image in its last stages of existence – as its hold on physical existence threatens to expire from moment to moment, finding a tragic beauty in the ineluctable decay of the film image. But the digital image is also given to similar displays of spectacular mortality, dissolving at a moment's notice in a whorl of pixels, image rips, rolling sync bars and video grain. For contemporary moving image production, the line between film and digital has crossed this boundary, as well; in each instance, the image is only temporarily fixed, as mortal as we are ourselves. Geoffrey O'Brien once posited that the act of viewing a film plunges the spectator into a world of endless self-references and permutations, in which one inhabits a world populated by, among other things,

> [*The Battleship*] *Potemkin* (Eisenstein, 1925), Charlie Chaplin in drag, Filipino horror movies about mad surgeons, animated maps tracking the pincer movements of [Field Marshal] Rommel's Panzer divisions, Egyptian soap operas in which insanely jealous husbands weep for what seems like hours at a stretch, made-for-TV stories about hitchhikers and serial killers, a long row of seventy-minute cavalry Westerns, Russian science fiction intercut with nude scenes shot on Long Island, the best of the Bowery Boys, an amateur bondage cassette filmed on location in a dentist's office in Ronkonkoma, *They Drive by Night* [Raoul Walsh, 1940], *All This, and Heaven Too* [Anatole Litvak, 1940], *The Barkleys of Broadway* [Charles Waters, 1949], Hindi religious musicals, Japanese gangster movies, countless adaptations of the works of William Shakespeare, Charles Dickens, and the Brontë sisters, *L'Avventura* [Michelangelo Antonioni, 1960], *The Gene Krupa Story* [Don Weis, 1959], *La Noche del terror ciego* [*Tombs of the Blind Dead*, Amando de Ossorio, 1972], Betty Boop cartoons with color added, touristic documentation of Calcutta and Isfahan, a Bulgarian punk band captured live, and the

complete photoplays of Louise Brooks, Greta Garbo, and Veronica Lake. (O'Brien 1995, 24)

For O'Brien, viewing these images accomplishes one thing above all others: it provides "minimal proof that you were not dead" (O'Brien 1995, 27). But these images – now accessible to you primarily through the scan lines of a flatscreen television, on DVD or Blu-Ray DVD – exist at a distance, separated from the faces and places that created their phantom existence. A digital copy is a copy of a copy, transformed into another medium and yet more concrete than the presence of the original negative of the film itself, stored in a different vault miles below the surface of the Earth, indifferently awaiting revival, retrieval, transfer or oblivion. Gerard Malanga, Andy Warhol's right-hand man during his most prolific period in the early-to-mid 1960s, noted of his own cinematographic work in 1989 – long after Warhol's Factory had vanished – that the most mundane images often held unexpected resonance for him; he noted that, in the archival process, "I discovered images I would not have seriously considered at the time of having made them. But I truly believe photographs have [an] innate and unique ability to take on new significance with age" (Maddow 2000, 123).

And yet, as Usai argues, even as he venerates the images that informed the interior landscape of his youth, "nostalgia in any form gives me the creeps. Brooding over the past bores me to death" (Usai 2001, 113), a paradoxical stance to take when he simultaneously admits that "an archive for moving images will end as a kind of museum – in the sense we currently give that term of an asylum for cultural artifacts" (Usai 2001, 115–16). As a medium, the cinema – whether digital or filmic – has always thrived on and actively sought out agencies of dramatic and transformative change. Paper film gave way to cellulose nitrate and then to "safety film"; black-and-white has fallen to color film, silence has given way to multidimensional stereophonic sound, digitally recorded for Dolby playback. Yet, it seems at each juncture in this evolutionary parade that it is the critics and theoreticians of the medium that are most resistant to change – as when Rouben Mamoulian's *Becky Sharp* premiered in three-step Technicolor in 1935 to one critic's comment that

> the total impression is one of a brass band in color rather than a well-modulated symphony [...] As long as color in film has the quality of a gaudy calendar lithograph, there is no future for it, artistically, except in the embellishment of [...] the animated cartoon.

while producer Walter Wanger enthused, "color is just as inevitable as speech. I don't believe that one black-and-white picture will be produced four years hence," while Samuel Goldwyn announced that all his new pictures would be made in Technicolor, predicting that "black-and-whites soon would be as rare as silent films" (Jonas and Nissenson 1994, 20).

VCRs, along with a host of other factors, eventually killed drive-ins by making it possible to view a film at home with ease and convenience; DVDs wiped the VHS format out of existence a few years after their introduction. In the same fashion, second-run theaters were also killed off by the burgeoning DVD market, as the window between VHS and the theatrical release of a film and its appearance on DVD dwindled into nonexistence. And yet, as the public audience for twentieth-century cinema film becomes increasingly specialized and narrowly segmented to the point that American Blockbuster stores no longer even bother with a token "classics" section – even such reliable standbys as Michael Curtiz's *Casablanca* (1942) are ignored in most of the chain's stores – for those who embrace the past, a wider range of films has become available. Often these DVDs go out of print in a matter of months, so one must purchase them immediately upon their release as fetish objects that also have a temporal existence of their own and a thriving bootleg "industry" exists as well, making copies of all but the most fugitive films available to the private collector.

In 2001, I wrote an essay entitled "Twenty-Five Reasons Why It's All Over," which argued that the cinema as we had grown up with it had been altered so drastically so as to be a different medium altogether – as the combined result of the collapse of theatrical distribution as an across-the-board "given" for all 35mm films, the ever-rising bottom line, the tyranny of teen audiences and hyperconglomerates driven to satisfy the greatest number of viewers with the least amount of risk, the "lock out" of foreign films from US audiences except in a few major cities and numerous other factors. While all of this is demonstrably true, it now strikes me as profoundly beside the point. The digital reinvention of the cinema is every bit as revolutionary as the dawn of cinema itself and it comes with an entirely new set of rules and expectations. While James Cameron and George Lucas may embrace these new tools for more superficial ends and the medium will never be any more democratic than it has been historically, newer works continue to pop up on the margins of moving image discourse, created by filmmakers who simply do not care if their images are captured on film, digital tape or a hard drive, so long as their phantom vision reaches the screen – the screen of your plasma television, the screen of your local multiplex, the screen of your cell phone.

Just as a generation in the 1960s celebrated the inherent "funkiness" of the 16mm image – especially when blown up to 35mm – as being somehow more "raw" and "real" than its slicker cinematographic counterpart, the digital generation is comfortable with the roughness of low-end digital video and hails the "water marks" of cell phone footage and YouTube downloads as artistic cultural artifacts. In addition, a South Korean company has developed a miniature laser video projector that can fit into mobile phones and digital cameras. In April 2006, the Iljin Display Company publicly demonstrated various prototypes of a number of mini-size video projectors built directly into mobile phones. Using this technology, consumers can screen photos and video images on the wall from the built-in projector, making movies truly portable, downloaded through one's phone and projected at a moment's notice. Who needs to go to the movies anymore when you can simply carry them with you? This is yet another example of cross-platforming, which demonstrates that the theatrical film experience is being faced with numerous alternative delivery systems (Jin-seo 2006).

As A. O. Scott and David Denby noted in two separate articles that appeared almost simultaneously in, respectively, the *New York Times* and the *New Yorker*, young viewers today are, in Scott's words, "platform agnostic, perfectly happy to consume moving pictures wherever they pop up – in the living room, on the laptop, in the car, on the cell phone – without assigning priority among the various forms" (Scott 2007). While Scott is, in his own words, an "unapologetic adherent" (Scott 2007) to standard theatrical presentation as the preferred medium of choice for movie-going, his children have opened up for him an entirely new way of seeing films, whether mainstream contemporary films or canonical classics. With a house full of DVDs, Scott's son and daughter (then aged 10 and 7) mix the past and the present with impunity, cross-platforming between Turner Classic Movies, iPod downloads, DVDs and trips to revival houses to see older films on the big screen. As Scott noted of the experience of taking his children to see an older film,

"Why is he purple?" my daughter asked in the middle of *West Side Story* [Robert Wise, 1961], noticing the effects of an aging Technicolor print on Tony's face. In *The Man Who Shot Liberty Valance* [John Ford, 1961] the tint would periodically switch from sepia to silver and back again. My son, noting each shift, wanted to know why it was happening: a question about aesthetics that I could only answer with a whispered lecture about chemistry. Most of the old movies he had seen were delivered by means of new technology; this one was old in the physical as well as the cultural sense.

What he made of it I don't know. (He was amused that Lee Marvin, as the titular villain, calls Jimmy Stewart's character "dude.") But he watched with an unusual intentness, the same quality of attention he brought to *Monty Python and the Holy Grail* [Terry Gilliam and Terry Jones,

1975], *Oliver!* [Carol Reed, 1968] and *Samurai Rebellion* (*Jôi-uchi: Hairyô tsuma shimatsu*) [Masaki Kobayashi, 1967], some of the other stops on our haphazard tour of movie history. I'm convinced that these films' beguiling strangeness was magnified by the experience of seeing them away from home and its distractions, with the whir of the projector faintly audible in the background and motes of dust suspended in the path from projector to screen. (Scott 2007)

And yet, Scott's son would never have had this experience if his father hadn't bothered to take him to the cinema; even as an older teen, he probably would be more likely to seek out the latest *Indiana Jones* sequel over a 1962 black-and-white film by John Ford. For the generation of students who now are involved in cinema as both a critical and/or active pursuit, the digitization of the cinema is an accomplished fact. Some younger artists seemingly side with Scott in his preference for conventional filmic projection, a "museum format" if ever there was one. As Melissa Gronlund comments of some of these new image-makers:

> Hollywood pictures, newsreels and documentaries, film stock, cameras and projectors and the auditorium space itself have become the focal point for several artists' works – particularly since celluloid has come under threat from digital technology. The collaborative Al and Al are using their residency at FACT in Liverpool to transform a defunct train station into a blue screen studio. In *Kodak* (2006) Tacita Dean filmed the last standard 16-millimeter film factory in France on the final five rolls of stock the factory produced. At Cerith Wyn Evans' show at London's ICA in 2005 a bulky 35-[mm] film projector screened a blank film, tracking the deterioration of the celluloid to create a changing abstraction of scratches and tears. (Gronlund 2007, 29)

Such an act memorializes the past of cinema, even as the industry itself rushes to become a part of the new digital domain. Barry Meyer, the chairman and CEO of Warner Brothers, sums the current situation up in two sentences: "Digital distribution is easy, ubiquitous, and inexpensive. We have to adapt, or we'll become dinosaurs" (Denby 2007, 56). John Fithian, president of NATO (the National Association of Theater Owners), is even more direct, noting,

> we're competing with the high-tech entertainment crowd, and we're using technology in theaters that's a hundred years old. We need to modernize existing theaters, and tear down old ones at the same rate [...] In ten years, I doubt there will be any more film. (Denby 2007, 62)

Critics Nathan Lee, Kent Jones and Paul Arthur concur, noting that *Superman Returns* (Bryan Singer), *Apocalypto* (Mel Gibson), *A Prairie Home Companion* (Robert Altman), *Flyboys* (Tony Bill), *Miami Vice* (Michael Mann) and *Click* (Frank Coraci), all released in 2006,

> have one thing in common: they were all shot in high-def [digital video]. And no one blinked. All the huffing and puffing about the purity of 35mm now feels very 2003 [...] all things considered, [2006] may have been the year when film and video became indistinguishable. (Lee, Jones and Arthur 2007, 39)

It's true that all these films were transferred from digital high-definition video to 35mm for conventional theatrical release, but that's simply a holdover from the past. Soon high-definition movies will be projected in theaters worldwide in their original production format and conventional film production will become, for better or worse, a thing of the past – a museum format.

There is another new development in the area of theatrical moving image exhibition related to our discussion here, which shoots off in new and interesting directions. In Madrid, Spain, theater owners are discovering that conventional films, no matter what their format (digital or film) or genre, are failing to attract all-important younger viewers. Thus, a new theater, Cinegames, has opened in Madrid, offering theater-screen-size video gaming for a predominantly male audience. "Forget the pathetic speakers of a PC or television!" exhorts one advertisement for the new facility. "Come feel the sound that puts you at the center of the action!" For a mere 3 euros – or about $4, much cheaper than a conventional movie admission – audience participants engage in spirited group contests of *World of Warcraft* and other popular video games projected on a giant cinema screen (Carvajal 2007). As described by one observer, the resulting environment is "a hybrid movie theater with all the digital fire and fury of a video game: fog, black light, flashing green lasers, high-definition digital projectors, vibrating seats, game pads, and dozens of 17-inch screens attached to individual chairs" (Carvajal 2007) to monitor each person's game play while the combined contest plays out on a huge screen in the front of the auditorium. "We're trying this concept because there are so many theaters in Spain, and admissions are down. We have to offer new products," notes Enrique Martinez, proprietor of Cinegames. "We see the future with multiplexes with five screens, one for the traditional Hollywood spectaculars and the others for screens for video halls and 3D. That's the next step" (Carvajal 2007). Similar facilities throughout Europe and North America are scheduled to open in the future and the model seems to be working quite well, although it skews the audience almost entirely to "young men in their late teens and 20s," while "a few [...] female supporters [...] paid 1 Euro each to watch the action," but not to participate (Carvajal 2007).

Whether or not this will become a major new audience model remains to be seen. Big screen video gaming may go the way of 3D movies and Cinerama, or it may become a solid niche market appealing to a younger audience. But while the "platform" of film may vanish, I would argue that, for most audiences, the "films" themselves will remain and audiences, now adjusted to viewing moving images in a variety of different ways, will still want to see their dreams and desires projected on a large screen for the visceral thrill of the spectacle as well as the communal aspect inherent in any public performance. *Film* is indeed disappearing, but *movies* are not. If anything, they are more robust than ever and are shot in a multiplicity of formats that boggle the mind; analogue video, digital video, conventional film, high-definition video, on cell phones and pocket-size, hard-drive, fixed-focus, auto-exposure cameras, in 16mm, 35mm, 70mm and a host of other platforms now just emerging from the workshop of image making.

For those of us who see the cinema as a vast tapestry of films and filmmakers covering more than 100 years of cinema from all over the world, the use of digital technology is a plus because it allows us to access the images of the past with ease and efficiency. For those who know only the cinema of the present – pure Hollywood product for the most part – it nevertheless puts the tools of production into the hands of the rawest enthusiast – anyone capable of shooting a video and downloading it on YouTube or Current TV. The literally hundreds of thousands of clips now on the web at Google, Yahoo and other sites (many of them lifted from existing films and television programs) present an inchoate glut of imagery that resembles a new forest of the imagination. This thicket of conflicting images, both home brew and borrowed, reminds me of the British filmmaker Anthony Scott's conceptual feature film, *The Longest Most Meaningless Movie in the Whole Wide World* (1969), which represented a similar cacophony of images to its viewers nearly forty years ago, entirely prefiguring our current image overload. As described by David Curtis, the film

> consist[ed] [...] of adverts, complete and incomplete sequences from feature films, out-takes, sound-only film, home-movie material and so on. Often a shot or a whole sequence will repeat *ad nauseam*, sometimes whole lengths of film appear upside down and running backwards [...] By rearranging familiar material into new and often absurd relationships, the viewer's traditional dependence on continuity is rudely interrupted, and in that disturbed state, some kind of re-evaluation of the material shown (either to its advantage or to its detriment) is inevitable. (Curtis 1971, 145)

This same sort of "re-evaluation of the material shown" is now taking place on a much larger scale, larger than nearly anyone could have conceived of even five years ago. Film is disappearing, but in its place a new platform has emerged which can comfortably support all previously existing formats. As with all such previous technological shifts in moving image study and production, a host of new aesthetic and practical considerations thus sweep to the fore. Is a digital copy of a film still a film? It is and it isn't. Is the digital image preferable to the filmic image or the other way around? It's clearly a matter of personal opinion.

The archival concerns raised by the digital shift are many and varied, but as Val Lewton observed in the 1940s of his own work in film, making movies "is like writing on water" (Dixon and Foster 2011, 20). Some images will survive, others will not. I would argue that the digitization of our visual culture will lead to the further preservation of its filmic source materials rather than the other way around. With a whole new market opening up for these films of the past, the master negatives are being taken out of the vault and digitally transferred for popular conservation with one especially desirable side effect: newer audiences now know of the film's *existence*. Entombed in 16mm and 35mm frames for projection equipment that is becoming less and less prevalent (especially in the case of 16mm), these films might otherwise never reach a twenty-first-century audience. Perhaps film isn't disappearing after all. Perhaps it is coming back to life.

Part III
INTERVIEWS

Chapter 10

"LET THE SLEEPERS SLEEP AND THE HATERS HATE": AN INTERVIEW WITH DALE "RAGE" RESTEGHINI*

On a plane coming back from a research trip in Los Angeles, I fell into a conversation with one of my seatmates, who turned out to be Dale Resteghini, one of the most prolific music video directors of the contemporary music scene. As it happened, he was on his way to Omaha to shoot a music video the next day. We swapped contact information and this interview is the result. Rage, as he is professionally known, directs two to three videos a month and, by his own estimation, has created at least 400 music videos in the course of his career. At one time, these videos were a staple of programming on MTV, VH1 and BET, but as these outlets turned to longer-form programming, the music video has become something of a luxury for many performers. Yet the market for Rage's services remains unabated. There are many interesting aspects to Rage's work, but one of his chief attributes is his versatility. Rather than favoring one musical genre, his videos swing all the way from heavy metal to hip hop with numerous stops in between, on budgets that range from several thousand dollars to large, complex productions with significant price tags. Nothing seems to faze him; as he told me when we first met, "I function best in absolute chaos, when everything seems to be falling apart. Everybody else is losing it, but I see the opportunities that arise. That's the time I come up with some of my best ideas." His production company, Raging Nation Films, is a joint effort between Rage and his wife Kim, who handles the business end of things.

Some of the artists he's worked with since he broke into directing in 2003 include Anthrax, Busta Rhymes, Cypress Hill, P. Diddy, Fall Out Boy, Guns N'

---

* A version of this chapter was first published in 2012 by Taylor & Francis as "'Let the Sleepers Sleep, and the Haters Hate': An Interview with Dale Resteghini," *Quarterly Review of Film and Video* 29 (1): 1–11.

Figure 10. Dale Resteghini on the set.
Source: Image courtesy of Kristen Glaze.

Roses, Ice Cube, Lil Wayne, Method Man, Redman, Cam'ron and numerous others across the musical spectrum, usually wrapping up a video in a day or two of hectic shooting. Rage is something of a paradox: a tough customer who, by his own admission, was involved in more than a few brushes with the law during his youth, he is nevertheless an artist with a definite visual signature to his work which keeps him in constant demand as the "go to" guy for sharp, compelling concepts and cost-conscious execution. While he's completely at home in the digital era, Rage still prefers to shoot 35mm film rather than high-definition video and, at this point in his career, is poised to make the jump to features. Forthright, direct and honest, Rage is a self-taught director whose street smart attitude allows him to create work that is commercially viable, while at the same time retains an edge that sets him apart from the rest of his peers. He's an "up from the streets" auteur, which is what makes his work that much more real. This conversation took place by phone on 29–30 March 2011, with some additional questions answered by e-mail. I also want to thank Kristen Glaze for the photos of Rage on the set that accompany this interview.

WHEELER WINSTON DIXON: Dale, you were born in Boston, Massachusetts, on 28 August 1968. What can you tell me about your childhood, your early upbringing and your mother and your father? How would you describe your life when you were growing up?

DALE RESTEGHINI: I was born and raised in a blue collar section of Massachusetts. My dad was a fireman and construction worker. We lived in Framingham, which has a largely Italian population. That was my home community. I grew up there and learned all about life, work, blood, sweat and tears, an honest day's pay for an honest day's work, playing soccer, hockey and baseball, going to see the Boston Red Sox, the Boston Bruins and the Boston Celtics.

DIXON: Was your mother a housewife or did she have a job outside the house?

RESTEGHINI: My mom was a housewife, but she also worked in the school library and was constantly turning me on to books, making sure I read a lot, from elementary school to middle school to high school.

DIXON: How did you get interested in film and when? Was there anyone in your family who pushed you to be creative?

RESTEGHINI: Actually, nobody pushed me to be creative at all. I wasn't actually encouraged to do anything in the arts and I was never – unlike my brother and my sisters – gifted in academics. I was sometimes a C, sometimes B student, but I always excelled in arts. I could paint, draw and sketch. I was inspired by cartoons and things like that and so I pursued that in high school with courses in commercial art. It was my parents' perception if you weren't an A student, then you might as well give up any thoughts of college and become a blue collar worker or join the military, which I did for a little bit as well. I found my way back to Massachusetts after pursuing two years in the Navy when I was 18, 19. I heard an audition at a local dance troupe called The Male Encounter, which is somewhat similar to the Chippendales. I went on that audition and it kind of opened up my eyes to the possibility of performing, being a model, how to present yourself for the camera – all these aspects of performance.

DIXON: At this point, had you had any exposure to film whatsoever?

RESTEGHINI: Well, I used to go to the movies when I was 6, 7, 8 years old to see films like [Don Siegel's] *Escape from Alcatraz* [1979] or even [Hal Needham's] *Hooper* [1978] or *Smokey and the Bandit* [1977] and then guess – believe it or not – what the opening weekend would be. How much money it would make. And, as I look at it now, it's such an odd way to start. At that age, I had no concept of what directing was, much less of directing anything myself. I just would want to see if I knew what the opening weekend would be for one film against the other. So here we are, all these years later, I'm a film director and it's truer now than ever. Today, everyone puts the emphasis on what the opening weekend for a film will be, just as a lot of weight is also put on the opening first week for bands, for music, for how many units you sell, how many downloads, how many people buy tickets to your concerts. When I was growing up, it was much more primitive, but there was a section in the Sunday paper, in the middle, that always had the top ten. And I was usually right on the money with my predictions.

DIXON: Yet you must have been paying some attention to the visuals, to story construction and directorial styles. You told me on the plane that directors as varied as Robert Aldrich, Ridley Scott, Orson Welles, Steven Spielberg, Anthony Mann and John Huston have an influence on your work.

RESTEGHINI: Yes, that's true.

DIXON: Because you're talking here, so far, only about the commercial aspect of film. So where do Tony Mann, John Huston and people like that come in?

RESTEGHINI: Well, growing up, I watched a lot of old movies on TV with my father and he pointed things out to me and I began to look at the credits. I suddenly realized that a film made by one person looked very different from a film, even in the same genre, made by somebody else. And that was when I began to think, "Hey, there's somebody back there behind the camera figuring this stuff out." So that's when the director consciousness began to kick in. After I got involved in dancing and modeling that opened me up to wanting to do more in the creative end of the business. And then things started to click for me.

In Boston, at that point in time, one of the biggest pop groups was New Kids on the Block. Their producer was Maurice Starr, a fantastic producer and songwriter with a real knack for business. He put the group together in 1984 after he split up with New Edition, a band he'd been working with before that. At that point in time, I was doing extra work on films like [Carroll Ballard's] *Wind* [1992], which Francis Ford Coppola produced, and [Frank Oz's] *Housesitter* [1992], with Steve Martin and Goldie Hawn. At first I was just doing background stuff, but then I got my Screen Actors Guild card and started to do a lot of extra work. I ended up working on a lot of films shot in Boston, like Gus Van Sant's *Good Will Hunting* [1997]. But another interesting aspect of my life during all of this is that I was arrested about fifty times –

Dixon: Fifty times?
Resteghini: Fifty times.
Dixon: For what?
Resteghini: Oh, everything from stealing or hustling or credit card fraud. I got arrested one time for possession of marijuana because it was in my car. Even though I never drank or did any kind of drugs in my entire life, I just was always catching all these different bad breaks. This was from 1985 to 1993 or so – just about the time I was getting into the business. Mind you, all that stuff happened inside of a short period, but during that time I did a lot of dumb things, like driving without a license or with a suspended license and I'd get arrested and go to jail. That happened a couple of times. But the last time it happened, I was tossed in jail for eight months and that was a real wakeup call. And then, in the jailhouse library, I found this book called *The Kid Stays in the Picture* by Robert Evans, the guy who produced [Roman Polanski's] *Chinatown* [1974], and it opened up my eyes to what could happen if you just kept working at it and didn't give up. It's a great book, almost a game plan for how to get into the business.

In *The Kid Stays in the Picture*, Evans talks about a lot of different people he dealt with in business – certain films and filmmakers – and how he'd work with them. It was inspirational. I'm not an advocate for a lot of the self-help stuff out there, but because I was in a situation where all I could do was read a book or two, I read Napoleon Hill's *Think and Grow Rich*, which is a classic in the genre. It was written in 1937, right in the middle of the Depression, but they keep updating it and I read one of the later editions. And it had some really good tools to put in one's hands, to help them get through a situation or achieve a goal. And that was it, achieving a goal. So I decided that I was through with all of this stuff and, when I got out, I was going to move on with my life. And get back into film with a vengeance.

Dixon: What genre appeals to you the most?
Resteghini: Action/adventure, without question.
Dixon: What about noir?
Resteghini: I love noir. But the kind of films I hope to direct are the ones that can gross 100 million dollars or more and open big on their first weekend. Obviously, it's action/adventure that does that and not so much noir. But that genre does appeal to me. Orson Welles's *Touch of Evil* [1958] is a fantastic film; the long shadows, the costumes, the framing, the lighting and Orson Welles's

performance in the film – incredible stuff. But if you're going to try that today and you don't have the right kind of cast, crew and visual style right across the board, it simply doesn't work. Noir is more '40s and '50s; this is 2011. It's the age of escapism, action and keeping people entertained.

DIXON: So you're coming up, you've had all these life experiences, you've worked as a model and a dancer, now you're working as an extra and you're watching these directors work, right?

RESTEGHINI: Right.

DIXON: Is this when you begin to get the idea that you want to move behind the camera and direct?

RESTEGHINI: The last time I was incarcerated, I had a lot of time on my hands and, in addition to reading, I wrote my first screenplay based on a relationship I was having, which became my first film, *Colorz of Rage* [1999], which I shot for $26,000 in 16mm.

DIXON: How did you raise the $26,000?

RESTEGHINI: I put it together piece by piece by piece. Little bits of money, one chunk at a time. $1,000, $2,000, $3,000. It was a long haul. I shot it in 1997, it came out in 1999 and it's a full feature. There were some people in the industry that encouraged me to do it, but there was one particular person who said, "No, make it into a short." At that point, I'm 32, in a relationship with a professional woman –

DIXON: Kim?

RESTEGHINI: Yes, Kim. *Colorz of Rage* is about an interracial couple who moves to New York and how reality hits them in the face in ways they didn't expect. It's based on my relationship with Kim – although, of course, it's part fiction, part fact. I believed that I was talented enough to make a film that would make its money back. So I refused to make it into a short. I couldn't let Kim down. There's just no money in short films; you know that.

DIXON: Right.

RESTEGHINI: When I got out of jail, I had that screenplay in my hand and I was motivated to bang on every door I could to get it made. At that point, I had never directed anything. So I wanted to get someone else to do it and I never thought about directing it myself. But I had every Tom, Dick and Harry telling me, "No, no, no." So out of frustration, I said, "Okay, I'm going to do it myself." So I started hustling up funds and equipment to do it and I was able to get some film gear from Camera Service Center in New York for free, donated for two months.

DIXON: That's amazing. Who was your cinematographer?
RESTEGHINI: It started off being one guy who was working for free, but I had to fire him because, even though he came with his own camera and sound gear, he showed up late twice and he called in sick on another day when I had cast and crew and everybody waiting to film. So I ended up shutting down for two or three weeks. And, usually, when independent productions with zero dollars shut down, that's the end of it. But I was able to find a superb cinematographer from Sweden, Martin Ahlgren. He shoots commercials, music videos and now he's moving into features. His work is fantastic. So he finished the film for me as DP. Sabine Hoffman, who is an incredible editor, cut the film. Sabine was, at that point in time, known for cutting Morgan J. Freeman's *Hurricane* [1997] and now she cuts all of Rebecca Miller's films [the daughter of playwright Arthur Miller and photographer Inge Morath].

Colorz of Rage came out and looked good – much better than anything you could make for $26,000 – and made its money back. Sabine was trying to get me to stay in New York City and be a part of what I call a "blue blooded," elitist sort of film community run by Gary Winick, who is now a feature film director, and John Sloss, who's a producer. But that was absolutely not my scene. I couldn't even – I wouldn't even want to fake that being my scene. I told her, "[Listen], this isn't me and I can't do it. I'm going to follow in the footsteps of people like Brett Ratner and Steve Carr, who both went on from being video directors to getting their shot at features."

I should point out, though, that the path from videos to features is now dead. One of my music video brethren, a producer in the business, said, "Dale, I think you are the last one of us to actually go from music videos to feature films." And right then, the bridge collapsed. Because, now, nobody watches MTV or BET and there are so many outlets for so many videos that the only people who watch videos are fans of that particular artist. It used to be when you had your name credited on the end titles of a music video as the director, everybody saw it. This would give you a shot, but we're talking 15, 20 years ago. Now it's dead.

DIXON: Then you did a micro-budgeted film called *Da Hip Hop Witch* [2000], which is a spoof of [Daniel Myrick and Eduardo Sánchez's] *The Blair Witch Project* [1999]. But what a cast: Eminem, Ja Rule, Pras, Vanilla Ice, Mobb Deep and lots of

	other A-list talent in it. How did you fall in with these people? What drew you to hip hop and rap?
RESTEGHINI:	Well, I moved to New York City from Boston in '94 or '95. And at that point in time, New York City, the music industry, was all about hip hop. Rock was nonexistent. New York had the biggest rappers. The scene was exploding; Puff Daddy, Biggie Smalls, Busta Rhymes, the Fugees, the Wu-Tang Clan; everyone was there. So, if you were looking to get into music videos, that was the scene to be in and I was right there. A lot of the extra work I was doing at the time was for TV shows like *New York Undercover*, a cop show that aired on the Fox network from 1994 to 1998 which had all those rappers in it. I knew one of the biggest recording studio engineers in New York City, John Kiehl, who earlier had a place called Soundtrack Studios in Boston. John moved to New York City and so I had a connection in the studio at a time when hip hop was reigning. I was trying like hell to get something off the ground.
	Finally, in 2000, I heard that there was a tour starting called "Tattoo the Earth" that was taking on the world's heaviest bands like Slipknot and Metallica and everyone else on the scene, so I took a job with the tour because it was interesting and I met a lot of people who I ended up working with three years later. So, there it was: the world of rock and metal videos. And once I finally crashed through the door of rock and metal videos, I just took off like crazy and ended up doing 10 videos in my first year as a director, 100 in my second year and then I did 100 more and then I did 100 more and I just kept going.
DIXON:	You've worked with so many musical groups, it's ridiculous.
RESTEGHINI:	Yes. I'm actually quite proud of the fact that there has been no other director in the history of the medium to direct over 100 rock videos and over 100 hip hop videos.
DIXON:	Do you have a regular crew that your work with? Like your favorite DP [director of cinematography], your favorite AD [assistant director], people like that?
RESTEGHINI:	Absolutely. If I needed to shoot in Virginia tomorrow, I could put my hands on a crew like that. I have four or five guys I use as DPs on a regular basis and four or five ADs. Depending upon the market – whether it's Atlanta, Miami, Texas, LA, New York or the Midwest – I have people I work with all the time.
DIXON:	Your directing style is really visceral. It seems that a lot of music video directors more or less stand back and observe the

band and their videos are kind of knocked out on an assembly line basis. But you're part of the action, always right behind the camera, exhorting the artists to seemingly break through the screen and confront the viewer. So I'm wondering: do you storyboard? Do you brainstorm with the bands you work with for ideas? How do you keep each video fresh when you've done so many?

RESTEGHINI: Well, I only feel the need to storyboard when there are a lot of elements going on at the same point in time and there's a high dollar amount that has been given to the production that I'm accountable for. If a scene involves potential bodily harm or danger of any sort to the talent, then I storyboard, just to make sure everything comes out okay. But other than that, it never works for me. I didn't come up in a storyboard world. The other day, I was meeting with Bob McMinn and Gary Lucchesi over at Lake Shore Entertainment. They got to me through my agent at ICM after seeing my reel and Bob said, "Quite frankly, we don't like too many music video directors, but something about your rock stuff more than your hip hop stuff grabs us," and made them want to meet me.

Bob was asking me the same sort of questions you are right now – "how do you set it up, how do you visualize it, do you storyboard?" – stuff like that. I said, "Listen, I could go scout today and it could be an exterior shot or interior shot and then I show up two days later and we could be right at the same location, but there could be something completely different with the sun, the clouds, the lighting or the talent could show up in a different mood. And, suddenly, something would just at that moment reveal itself to me and I act on that." And Bob started smiling and he said, "You're an artist, you're a painter," which is always nice to hear. I'm happy that somebody can appreciate my work because, honestly, I do feel what I do is extremely difficult, but some people just don't get it. They say, "All you're doing is saying 'action-cut, action-cut'" – we both know it's much more than that. I have to get the essence of the artist into the video; otherwise, it doesn't work.

I always have to adapt to changing circumstances; I had to embrace what happened the other day in Omaha, for example. The song was called "Balance" by the band Emphatic and we wanted to use a few hydraulic cars and some sexy girls and it was meant to be an outdoor shoot, sort of like Aerosmith meets

Linkin Park. But it snowed outside, so the label guys are saying, "What do we do, what do we do, it's snowing, it's snowing," and the hydraulic car guys refused to show up. So I said, "Okay, we'll just make it a makeshift VIP room with the lead singer and two girls, one on each arm, with the windows all steamed up. We'll use just one light source – a ring light coming in through the window – and we'll film it inside."

And sure enough, looking at it, I felt, "This is great, this is great." So something as simple as thinking on my feet like that makes me more valuable than someone else who would be just hanging around and saying, "I'm waiting for conditions to change, I'm waiting for this, I'm waiting for that." I'm responding to the moment, asking, "What does this moment have to offer?" That's the key. I'm able to survive in chaos. I literally can thrive when the whole world is falling down. So, rather than thinking like a producer –"Let me stop this, that's not what we planned, this isn't going to work" – I say, "Take what the moment offers you, finish the day and move on." I think the experience of being locked up, of going to jail, puts all of that into perspective. Once you have gone through that, there is nothing to be afraid of; you can face anything. It's all just dealing with music video politics.

DIXON: So what are your favorite bands? What kind of music do you like?

RESTEGHINI: I get that question a lot.

DIXON: I'm sure.

RESTEGHINI: When I listen to music, it's either New Age music, or it's '80s music – my high school years, the music I grew up with. I love Phil Collins. I like music that lets me think. There are moments when I want something aggressive; when I'm working out or something. If I'm writing a script, I'm writing a scene or if I'm directing a scene, there's music I love for those moments. But when asked about the kind of music I love listening to, it's really '80s stuff that moves me; one of my favorite bands of all time is Asia.

DIXON: Which do you prefer to shoot: film or HD [high-definition video]?

RESTEGHINI: Well, I prefer film. But for the last year or two years, it's all HD. I would say of my last 100 videos, 90 were shot in HD formats. I love film because it's a simple process. Film just looks better; you can do so much more with it. There's more warmth to it, more depth, more detail. There's so much information on one frame of negative film and you can go in so many different directions with color and temperature, but with HD, it's kind of cold, it's limited and you have less to work with – it's not something immediately tangible, yet it's there. But right now, HD rules.

DIXON: How are you going to make the jump to features? Are you working on a script?

RESTEGHINI: Well, I have two scripts. One is over at Sony Studios and I'm working on that with two producers over there on the lot, as well as a new writer. I wrote it back in 1998, so that's one project. There is another project I'm attached to direct. It's a science fiction–themed film that Mark Morgan, who produced [Catherine Hardwick's] *Twilight* [2008], is working on; it's his next franchise. It's called "Unearth". I'm also attached to direct a film called "Last Gasp", based on a book by a British writer named Trevor Hoyle. It's about the last days of Earth. John Fitzgerald, who is one of the founders of the Slamdance Film Festival, is producing it.

DIXON: On a more personal note, how did you meet your wife and business partner, Kim, and what part does she have in your company, Raging Nation?

RESTEGHINI: Well, I was living in Baltimore and on my way out of one relationship. I was rollerblading from where I lived uptown, on 157th Street, all the way down to 38th Street to catch a bus and go to work as an extra on Sydney Pollack's remake of *Sabrina* (1995). On the way, I made eye contact with Kim as she was walking back from her lunch break at work. We exchanged numbers, stayed in touch over the course of a few months and eventually got together as a couple. We've been together ever since, something like 16 years. She runs the business end of Raging Nation. When I met her, she was working at David Burton Associates, which is an entertainment marketing research firm; she's 100 percent business. She's the business side and I'm the creative side.

DIXON: One of your personal mantras in the business is, "Let the sleepers sleep and the haters hate." Could you expand on that?

RESTEGHINI: I actually came up with it while working on my first film, and Redman is really the one who coined it. A "sleeper" is someone who won't give you credit for your work; someone who won't acknowledge the validity of what you do. So then that person would be "sleeping" on you, not paying attention to you.

The "haters" are obvious. They're the people who are jealous of what you're doing and try to tear you down. You have to ignore people like that and find people who support your work. "Sleepers" and "haters" don't want to see your growth, they don't want to acknowledge your success. In this business, you learn that there are some people who want to see you win and some people who don't.

I want to get back to talking about working on the set. Naturally, we use a video tap on the camera – even if I don't have to – and I always have my eye on the monitor to see how things are going. But you should really concentrate on the performers themselves and not spend all your time staring at the screen. If I'm looking at a singer or a rapper on the set and there's something going on dramatically, if I don't feel it personally, if my eyes don't believe it or if my "director gauge" doesn't believe that this is really happening, then it's not going to work in the final product. You should be on the set, working with the actors directly. It really comes down to my personal approach to directing. I didn't go to film school, I went to the school of hard knocks. I work the way I do because that's what works for me. I need to be listening to the actors, making sure that dialogue scenes are as they should be. In music videos, I lean a little bit more towards performance. In features, it's more intimate; you're working with human emotions more.

I still remember directing some of the scenes of *Colorz of Rage* like it was yesterday and they really hit home. And being able to get those performances out of all those people is the key to the whole thing. A music video is usually done in one or two days and you have all kinds of people hanging around the set, but it's still about getting that personal connection with the actor, the singer, the rapper or the rocker – to make sure I get the absolute most out of them. It gets tiring after three, four, five takes for them because they still think they are giving their all, but it's starting to slow down so you have to amp up even more. I will know literally in two or three takes if it's going to get any better or not. But I'm not going to do that many takes on any one scene; you just can't. You have a budget and a timeline and you have to stick to it.

DIXON: Do you follow through in post-production or editing, or pretty much exit the project after the shoot?

RESTEGHINI: I always follow through, be it via the Internet or if I'm able to sit down with the editor throughout the process. That's essential.

DIXON: Music videos use a lot of flashy cutting and special effects. Features have a very different editorial rhythm. How do you expect to adapt your style for theatrical films?

RESTEGHINI: I never force any style on a project. Style comes from within the material itself – the performers and the circumstances of the shoot. I take each project, no matter how different or similar than others before it, and then let the material, the artist and the day do the rest. I strongly feel that I make the best creative decisions "in the moment," rather than two or three weeks out. You can plan, but in the end, you have to respond to what's happening in front of you and so forcing your vision on the material never works; you work with the performers and you create something together. As far as cutting goes, certain projects call for visual effects and a more energetic style of editing while others work better with traditional editorial patterns and camerawork. You have to ask yourself, "What does this material need to get across to the viewer?" That's the key. It has to be real, it has to connect.

At this point, having done so many videos, I enjoy it when an artist has an idea or a concept to start with. If it needs to be scaled up or down, I make this happen. Sometimes, when I don't get awarded a particular video assignment and see what they went with, I'm often less than impressed; not because I didn't get the gig, but because I feel that what makes me a tad more valuable than a lot of others is my ability to know that, in the end, it's about selling stuff and making money for the ones who hire me. So, a lot of times, I'll forgo something more artistic for something far more commercial and visceral because you can never miss with that.

DIXON: What about 3D? Do you think it's a gimmick or do you think that it actually has possibilities and is going to stick around?

RESTEGHINI: I think it's both a gimmick and something that can be useful. It's hard for me to fathom every film being shot in 3D, just because for most of my life it's been a 2D world – making that as amazing and sonically wonderful as you possibly can for a moviegoer. 3D opens up some doors, but it also changes the game of making films and sometimes it gets in your way. But sure, I'd work with 3D in a second. It all depends on what the project is.

DIXON: There are now so many delivery systems for feature films. You have theatrical, streaming, DVDs. What do you see as the future of movies? Do you think theatrical screenings are going to continue? When you're designing a film now, you have to visualize it not only for theaters but also for TV, computers, cell phones, streaming video and other formats. What do you have to say about that?

RESTEGHINI: I believe that the movie-going experience is always going to be around. Even though the studios are beginning to toy with having some films released as "On Demand" titles for home viewers on the same day they come out in theaters, I believe that people still want to go get popcorn, a Coke and have the experience of going to a movie. Ultimately, theatrical is still going to be where the studios get the big, big dollars because every studio needs that big opening weekend to push the film over the top, which is what they build their marketing plan around. You need fan buzz buildup before the opening or otherwise you lose out on kids texting each other, "I just saw this movie and here's what I thought" right while they're watching the film! These are instant, peer-based reviews and they're more important than what any critic has to say. You open, you get one shot and that's it. You want to make sure nothing leaks out before the theatrical release – which is getting harder and harder to do – but other than teasers and trailers, the more you can control the flow of information on a film, the better off you are. Even if the buzz on a film goes viral, you can still ride that wave and make money if you know what you're doing.

I keep hammering home to the studio executives and producers I meet with that, "Guys, this is a new world." I hold up my cell phone and say, "Kids text and, for the most part, they don't want to see procedural, long-winded dialogue scenes between several actors. It's all about what's happening right now. They want to see something up on the screen they can't see in real life." They want the movie going experience, sitting in the dark, escaping the real world for a couple of hours. I believe the "real estate" of theatrical presentations, in both the physical and theoretical sense – of being able to show a film with a big buildup over a weekend, opening on Friday – is the only way to make sure you get as much money out of the film as possible. The studios need to hold on to that because, otherwise, it's going to become like music, where there are so many studios releasing films that new films are going to get lost. They're going to get lost because there's nothing to make it special. Right now, there's an avalanche of music online available for digital downloads, but if you don't know what you're looking for, you're never going to find it. So, as much as these other new technologies are good for ancillary distribution, for mainstream, big budget film, theatrical is the only way to go.

Chapter 11

MARGIN CALL: AN INTERVIEW WITH J. C. CHANDOR*

When I first saw J. C. Chandor's debut feature *Margin Call* (2010), I was deeply impressed by the film's script, direction and restraint, and also struck by the fact that the film seemed almost classical in its construction, as if it harkened back to the analogue era of *The Birds* (1963) in the precision of its shot setups and editorial construction. Along with Lars von Trier's *Melancholia* (2011), it's the finest work I've seen from anyone in quite some time – all the more impressive because, aside from a long apprenticeship as an actor, still photographer and director of short films and documentaries, *Margin Call* is Chandor's first fully-realized feature film, despite the fact that he tried to get an earlier project off the ground (see below), only to have financing evaporate at the last minute.

Margin Call documents the frenetic activity at a never-named brokerage firm on the night that the 2008 stock market collapse really took hold. The film is triggered by the firing of a longtime stock analyst, Eric Dale (Stanley Tucci, in a typically immaculate, world-weary performance), who, in his last hours at the firm, discovers that the company is deeply over-leveraged in the derivatives market. As he is being ushered out of the building, Dale passes a flash drive with his findings on to the young Peter Sullivan (Zachary Quinto) with a solemn warning. Sullivan quickly realizes the dimensions of the impending disaster and begins alerting a chain of superiors, who hatch a desperate plan to dump all the questionable assets in one day – the next morning – to save the firm, but at a terrible price.

Despite the dire nature of the crisis, Chandor's direction – from his own script, which he pounded out in a four-day (yes, *four-day*) frenzy of inspired typing and then pitched to co-producer Zachary Quinto, typos and all, to get the film off the ground – is calm, contemplative and brings the various characters in the film to the screen in three dimensions. Neither heroes nor villains for the most part, they're just working stiffs who have overextended

---

* A version of this chapter was first published in 2012 as "Margin Call: An Interview with J.C. Chandor," *Film International* 10(3): 6–15.

Figure 11. J. C. Chandor and Zachary Quinto.
Source: Author's collection.

themselves and now find that they're being called to account in the most terrible fashion possible. There are no flashing screens with meaningless numbers in the film, no rapid-fire MTV cutting, no overheated boardroom fights – just the beginning of the systematic unraveling of the United States' economy: quiet, deadly and inexorable. All in all, the film is a remarkable achievement and I decided to speak to Chandor in detail to get his take on the runaway success of the film. We spoke by phone; Chandor was in New York working on a new project on 15 November 2011.

J. C. CHANDOR: I don't know if "fan" is the right word, but I've read a lot of your work, so I'm expecting this to be a little more off the beaten track than the usual interview, which I'm looking forward to.

WHEELER WINSTON DIXON: Well, I'll try not to disappoint you. So, first off, tell me something about your childhood. When and where were you born and what were your earliest memories like?

CHANDOR: I was born in suburban New Jersey, outside of New York City. I grew up there and in London, England – I'll get to that later. My dad was a banker.

DIXON: Who worked for Merrill Lynch for 35 years, right?

CHANDOR: Yes, exactly, so it was a very stable existence; he was a successful guy – not overly so – but I had a very nice, upper middle class

	childhood and adolescence. I spent most of my early childhood in the New Jersey/New York area, but I lived in London for the 7th, 8th, 9th and 10th grades – prime years in one's upbringing. We were over there for three-and-a-half to four years, so it was pretty key in my early education. I had a great time. But I was always vaguely aware of the stress my father was under, even though he tried to make everything seem very stable. Working in the financial profession is very, very tough.
DIXON:	At this point, did you have any inkling that you were going to become involved in film at all?
CHANDOR:	Yes. I came at it from both still photography and then acting. So those two things kind of merged into moving images, but I was a fairly involved actor. For a very long time, I was extremely interested in still photography – through most of my middle school and high school years and into college as well. I started getting into film, sort of, in late high school and into college, but I had always taken still photographs and did a lot of acting. Mainly high school drama stuff, but then I did apply to acting conservatories. It was kind of my mom's idea. I was a very "mixed" student and so her theory was to get me into a better school than I could have otherwise gotten into by getting me into a first-rate acting program.
DIXON:	That's interesting. This is something that really hasn't come out in your previous interviews on the film; you're really coming to *Margin Call* from a very strong acting background. That explains part of the success of the film to me; I think you got remarkable performances from all the people that are involved. So, when was the first time you picked up a camera?
CHANDOR:	I had a VHS video camera that my sister, Heather, and I used to make some short films – which my mom has just transferred from VHS to DVD, by the way, because the originals were kind of disintegrating. So, Heather and I made a film called *George Washington Meets Abraham Lincoln*, which is the first project I really remember, when I was about 10 years old.
DIXON:	Sounds ambitious. So what happened when Washington met Lincoln?
CHANDOR:	[Laughs] I think they went for, like, a carriage ride; it isn't exactly a masterpiece. Not earthshaking or anything. We were playing with very rudimentary editing – some in-camera editing when we made that. Then I moved into a whole Christmas extravaganza for my next project, which was more of a musical revue. But

they were fairly elaborate productions, in their way; we got the neighbors involved and everything. We made three or four films altogether. Then we tried to do a horror movie, but that one didn't actually turn out very well. Then I gave up making film for awhile, but then I really dove back into it in basically my sophomore year of high school. I acted all throughout my high school years and I was lucky because the American School in London has a very, very strong drama program.

I was there for the 7th, 8th and 9th and half of 10th grades and then I was at Ridge High School, which is in Basking Ridge, New Jersey, which also had a great drama program at the time. There was a teacher there named Jaye Barre who was really sort of an inspiring woman. During that time in New Jersey, the arts were being slashed – sort of like today – and she basically kept the entire drama program going. Actually, we've kept in touch and she just came to a screening that I had of *Margin Call* in my hometown. I saw her and now they're building a theater with that drama program outside of the high school, so there's actually going to be an independent theater there, which is all her work. She's incredible and she taught me a lot.

DIXON: As you were growing up, were there any particular film directors whom you admired?

CHANDOR: Well, I'm 37 years old right now, so I was a total '80s kid who loved Steven Spielberg's films – *Raiders of the Lost Ark* [1981], all that sort of stuff. These are sort of the movies of my childhood; I think I was literally the target audience for *E. T.* [1982]. I would have been in 3rd or 4th grade when that film came out. I really rode Spielberg up through his early prime, shall we call it.

DIXON: But your films are nothing like his work.

CHANDOR: No, they're absolutely not. This was just the stuff I grew up on. But then I got interested in a little deeper stuff – all in still photography, like Ansel Adams, Diane Arbus, though I probably wasn't smart enough to actually have gotten into her until later on in college. But what turned me on the most was landscape photography, so for starters, it was definitely Ansel Adams. Then, when I got to college, in my freshman year at the College of Wooster, I created my own major in cultural film studies trying to merge all my interests into one discipline.

DIXON: Was your aim in doing this to combine film and video production with theory and aesthetics?

CHANDOR: Yes, that's absolutely right. With the straight communication major, you had to do a lot of advertising classes and stuff, but they had an independent study program which I basically figured was a really neat opportunity to expand my horizons. I had already done two production internships between my senior year of high school and freshman year of college. But, during my freshman and sophomore years of college, I *really* got into internships – one of which was an internship on the production side of MTV in the summer of 1993. I actually worked for a division of Viacom that did specials for MTV and it was a fun job actually. Then, the next summer, I started to take additional film classes at NYU because I knew I needed to add something on top of what I was doing at Wooster.

DIXON: Now, for your senior project in college, you shot a film which you have described, and I quote, as "a total overreach, too vast in scope and scale, but I got jobs right away after graduation based on it." Can you tell me about that film?

CHANDOR: It was a road trip film that was my attempt to really add something new to the genre that should have been David Lynch's *The Straight Story* [1999]. I saw that years later and that was what I was trying to do, but it was beyond me then. That's the film I should have made. But, though it didn't really work, I actually learned so much from that experience. We drove across the country, made this film, but frankly, it just didn't cut together. I tried, but it was a student film and it showed. The writing was the best part of it, but, in the end, it was just a bunch of scenes that were all very good acting exercises, for lack of a better word, but they didn't build to anything that really worked. But it was fascinating to do and there were so many lessons learned. It kind of scared me into realizing that I *thought* I knew so much more than I actually *did* – which is, of course, when you are 21 years old, how you feel: you know it all, even when you don't.

DIXON: But it must have had some level of success because, as you say, it almost immediately got you work. You graduated in 1996 and, almost immediately, you're directing music videos, documentaries, commercials, fashion videos. Can you tell me something about this time?

CHANDOR: Well, I was an intern on a sitcom for a little while – a very short while. That scared me out of the "writing room" world, where a bunch of people sit around and slam a script together. I'd rather write on my own, not bounce ideas around with a bunch of other people.

DIXON: Right.
CHANDOR: I did a bunch of fashion videos for different brands like Valentino and 23 KU, which is a Japanese brand, and some ads for Subaru cars; I did a whole series of ads for Sambazon energy drinks, Carhartt outdoor clothing – the crazy sort of fun things that you do when you're trying to make a living in the business. And, in the middle of that whole world, I did a short film that was my first success called *Despacito*, which I wrote and directed. It's 12 minutes long, starring Will Arnett in his pre-*Arrested Development* days; he was just about to shoot the pilot of *Arrested Development* when we made the film. It's about two brothers who are roofers and an immigrant worker they've hired to help them who are roofing a huge, huge barn in the winter while the rich people that own the place are away. But, they underestimate the logistics of the project and they get stuck on the scaffolding 60, 70 feet off the ground. So, the three of them are stuck on the roof on a freezing, freezing cold night and their father is showing up the next morning to check in on the job. The last thing that they want to have happen is their dad see his two idiot sons having been stuck on a roof. I leave it unresolved; you're just sort of up on a roof with these guys. It was very concise, very tight. I was quite proud of that film and so I used it as a calling card to shoot a feature, which I worked on for six or seven years to try and get made and then it fell apart at the last minute, which absolutely killed me. Everything was ready to go and then the financing collapsed. I was shattered.

DIXON: That was in 2005. What was the feature going to be about?
CHANDOR: It was about a family living in one of those huge "McMansions" in a gated community, with all the houses all right next to each other – about a guy on his second marriage, but the script really followed his daughter and what was happening to her. It wasn't a commercial story at all; somewhat *American Beauty*-esque, but basically a family drama – very quiet. People reacted very, very strongly to the script – which I wrote – but didn't feel it was very commercial, so it took us a long time to try and raise the money for it.

DIXON: And then financing collapsed a week before filming?
CHANDOR: Yes, literally. Sam Shepard was going to play the lead, Marisa Tomei was asked and Michelle Yeoh was also involved and then the whole thing fell apart. And that blew my mind, so I walked away from the business for a while. My wife and I had just had a

	baby at the time and I kept a couple of documentary projects that I was doing going; I actually still have those in the works all these years later. I didn't fully walk away, but emotionally, I needed to see if I could make a living doing something else. You're at the mercy of too many people in that situation and it's just kind of a tenuous existence. I wanted some security for my wife and child. Frankly, it was a very, very difficult time in my life. I was trying any way possible to come up with being able to make a living while also keeping the dream of a feature film alive.
DIXON:	So then you decided to get involved in real estate and renovate a building into condominiums with some partners, but right in the middle of construction the godfather of one of your partners says, "You've got to sell out right away because everything is going to go to hell in the stock market?" This is in 2007.
CHANDOR:	Essentially, but there were other reasons. We had run into lots of problems; frankly, we were in over our heads – that's the real reason. But yes, the godfather of this guy who was an investor in the project could see that the big crash was coming and he told us we had to get out now and make a small profit and be happy with that. At the time, I was annoyed, but of course, in hindsight, he was right. So, a year later when the market literally starts imploding, I started thinking back on what it must have been like for that guy to be walking around with that knowledge. Knowing all that stuff and knowing that it was about to happen.
DIXON:	Then you wrote the 81 page draft of *Margin Call* in four days flat, right? Did you feel like you were almost taking dictation when you were writing it; in a sense, that it just came out of all the experiences of your life?
CHANDOR:	Yes; it was interesting. I was desperate. When I write, I have a real problem at times focusing. The strength of my writing lies in the fact that I feel that, by wandering along as you write, eventually you get to where you are supposed to be. So, normally it doesn't happen as fast as this did and I'm not a person who can just write every day. I have periods of very intense work and then I have to kind of go away from it, thinking about it and figuring it out and then, all of a sudden, it reaches kind of a download point. I knew the voice of each of these characters individually and I could actually hear them talking and each had a distinctive voice, so I was pretty much writing it at white-hot speed.
	It was knowing each of these characters through different avenues and then locking these people into one space, which

came from the production limitations placed on myself. I wasn't writing this script to sell it. I was writing it to direct it myself and so the whole concept for the movie came from what was the best way to have a performance-driven movie – a movie about actors. So it was, "How do you write a compelling movie about a topic that essentially spans the world, but do it in one location?" My original thought was, "How do you keep this moving?" It came from my concept of: "How do you make a movie for under a million dollars about the stock market crash?" and my idea was to trap them on one floor and then you let the performances lead you through the story.

DIXON: This is the same strategy that producer Val Lewton used in his classic low-budget horror films of the 1940s: keep most of the action on one set so you don't lose time moving people around and you don't blow a lot of money on sets; you can concentrate on the story and the performances.

CHANDOR: Yes, I call them "submarine movies" – put them in a submarine and then you can shoot it really cheap. So, *Margin Call* is a ticking time bomb submarine movie. They're totally isolated from the outside. It sounds kind of ridiculous, because it *is* such a topical film, but I didn't want it to be a current events movie. This was supposed to be essentially a character-driven drama, like Sidney Lumet's *12 Angry Men* [1957]. Put them in a room, lock the door and see what happens. It's timeless.

DIXON: One thing I thought was really effective was the lack of chattering computer screens rattling off meaningless statistics. I don't think you ever really see a close-up of a monitor in the film; you just see close-ups of the actors' faces reacting to the impending disaster, starting with Zachary Quinto's look of complete disbelief and shock when he initially realizes just how bad the whole thing is.

CHANDOR: I agree with you totally, but again, this was partly economics; we couldn't really afford to do that sort of stuff. This is so much more effective. But again, it's letting the budget limitations work for you, rather than against you. What I'm constantly trying to do in *Margin Call* is to give the audience only the information that they have to have and then the rest of it becomes about the performance.

DIXON: So, who helped you get this film off the ground financially?

CHANDOR: Well, Zachary was in from the ground floor, along with his producing partner Neal Dodson – so, Neal and Zachary and I, along with producer Corey Moosa, always felt like the money would follow the cast, so to speak, and so our approach was to see who we could get to read the script. Ben Kingsley and Carla Gugino were the first two people involved, but sadly, neither of them is in the finished film. Ben was going to play John Tuld, the head of the firm, and Carla was going to play Sarah Robertson, who gets the firm involved in derivatives and then gets axed as a result, but both had to bow out due to scheduling conflicts, which is sad because they came on and supported me and really got the film moving. But they had to back out because of other commitments by the time we got the money. It took a long time.

DIXON: So, was the negative budget really $3.5 million?

CHANDOR: The negative budget minus tax incentives was actually $2.8 million.

DIXON: And the whole thing was shot in 17 days, am I right?

CHANDOR: Yes, with one "B" day to do the helicopter stuff and then, during the trading sequence at the end of the film, that second unit stuff was done on one other "B" unit day.

DIXON: Are there any particular directors whose work really impresses you, either classical or contemporary?

CHANDOR: Well, I always feel a little sort of touchy diving into that subject because you always feel like you're marginalizing some people and you don't mean to, but David Fincher is fantastic and Walter Salles, who did *Central Station* [1998], and, of course, David Lean. If I could be any director and have their career, it would be David Lean. I think he got to live in a pretty interesting era and his films really evolve and move into various different genres and do a lot of different things; some are small scale, some are epic. He could do it all. I'm a huge, huge fan of pretty much anything he touches.

DIXON: You shot *Margin Call* on a mixture of film and video, but it's mostly film, right?

CHANDOR: I've got to be honest – it's mostly shot on the RED digital camera. We were shooting so much and we were shooting with incredible speed throughout the entire shoot. A lot of the film was shot with two cameras – certainly all the boardroom scenes and everything.

DIXON: Really? I would have thought it was a single-camera film.

CHANDOR: Yes it is, in its primary structure, and the editing makes it look like a single-camera movie. It's the way I like to set things up. But we had to use two cameras because we were working so fast. We had no choice. Time was the important thing and to let nothing get in the way of the performances. In fact, one of the boardroom sequences was three cameras, actually. It was insane to orchestrate. This movie lives and dies with the performances, so that was the most important thing to capture. Frankly, between you and me, I'm a one-camera guy – that's the style I like to shoot a movie in. Still, in the end, I would say probably 65 to 70 percent of the movie was shot single-camera. But there were five or six really key scenes where it was actually wonderful to have two cameras because it allowed these performances to really live and work off of each other. But the neat thing also with having two RED cameras and shooting in that environment was that we were able to have one camera aiming out the windows when we didn't need it, doing all that wonderful time lapse stuff literally as we were shooting. If we weren't using the camera, we would set up a six hour time lapse and it was kind of neat to have that be part of the shooting environment, sitting in the corner doing its own thing while we were working.

DIXON: How closely did you work with [director of cinematography] Frank DeMarco? He got a really cold, slick look for the film, devoid of warmth or humanity, I thought.

CHANDOR: *Very* closely. To shoot a movie that quickly, he had to be the right person for the job and Frankie just *killed* it. He was the best.

DIXON: Nathan Larson's music was almost subliminal. How much input did you have on that?

CHANDOR: He and I worked very, very closely together. There was also a woman named Suzana Peric who helped with that, who is a wonderful music editor and consultant. Her specialty is, for lack of a better word, placement. We had a rough cut of the film, but the music wasn't working and none of us could figure out what was going on. Suzana came in and just moved it around and shuffled it and made the whole thing work. I never wanted the music to feel like it was taking over the movie, but it certainly was necessary to keep the movie moving forward.

DIXON: You shot the film in 17 days, but you finished Stanley Tucci in three days and Jeremy Irons in three days. How the hell did you do that? How many setups did you do a day? Really, that's incredible.

CHANDOR: Yes, the Jeremy Irons section was unbelievable because he was supposed to work on the film for five days, but because of the visa thing he could only work *three*. So we did the entire boardroom scene with Jeremy Irons in one night on the shortest night of the

	year, or close to it. So that was one day and so we were doing twelve pages a day on some days.
DIXON:	One of the things that really impressed me, though, is the restraint of all the performances. Left to their own devices, some of the actors involved might have taken it over the top, in my opinion; but, since you're coming from an actor's standpoint on the film, it seems to me that you really got everyone involved to play it very close to the vest, without any melodramatic histrionics.
CHANDOR:	Well, every one of these actors is obviously unbelievably experienced and accomplished in their own right and the amazing thing about them is, once they get confidence that the director – in this case, the writer/director – actually knows what they want, they will be willing to let you guide them towards that goal.
DIXON:	Would you say it would be fair to say you were saying, "Take it down?"
CHANDOR:	In some cases, yes, and in others it was "take it up." Different people need different things. I had to have the confidence to let these guys know what I was looking for and that's hard to do, but it's essential. If you don't have the respect of the cast, if you don't have the vision and you don't communicate it, you're not going to get what you want. The great thing I got from this film – and it's a great lesson for me moving forward with new films – is that you have to know *exactly* what you want when you go on the floor and you should never shoot something if you don't.
DIXON:	*Margin Call* is shot and edited in a very classical style, almost like John Ford, believe it or not. The camerawork is never flashy; it's just there where it needs to be, in the right place at the right time. You don't do a lot of flashy jump cuts or change speeds in mid-shot; in my book, cheap tricks all. So, it looks like a very classical film. Totally intentional, right?
CHANDOR:	Absolutely.
DIXON:	Okay. How do you feel about that MTV-ized direction?
CHANDOR:	It's a little more experimental. But with this setup, I felt that the material and the way that it was handled, I didn't need to get in the way of the story of the actors, which is what stuff like that does – it calls attention to itself. I wanted the audience to forget the camera was there. I sort of needed to get out of the way.
DIXON:	Absolutely. Strip it down and make it clean. Would you say that, in your view, there are no villains here, no heroes, just human beings who screw up?

CHANDOR: Yes and I think, even more interestingly, that everyone in the film is both a hero *and* a villain. Hopefully this is a window into an authentic vision of how people would act under these circumstances.

DIXON: Now you have a two-picture deal writing at Warner Brothers, working on the script for a film called *Portofino* for Leonardo DiCaprio. It seems to me that you are exactly where Christopher Nolan was in 1999 when he released his small, black-and-white, no-budget film, *Following*. I don't know if you've ever seen it. You're about to break through to the big time.

CHANDOR: Indeed, I have; it's a great little film. And obviously, I think that, since then, Christopher Nolan has managed to make commercial and also intelligent films. I would take Mr. Nolan's career in about 32 seconds! Right now, I'm closing the actor deal on a film that would be very different from *Margin Call* – with a bigger budget, a sort of experimental action movie. So, that is what I'll be shooting in January if that goes. And then I would like to do a bigger movie for a much wider audience. I should point out that the Warner Brothers gig, though, is strictly a writing gig; this is a completely different project. They're two different things.

DIXON: As the budgets get bigger, it seems to me that the essential thing is to maintain your artistic integrity. As André Gide famously noted, "art is born of constraint and dies of freedom." Do you agree?

CHANDOR: Absolutely. I love the business side of this business and I think wonderful things can come out of the constraints, the limitations. The driving force of *Margin Call* did not come out of thin air; it came out of how to tell this particular story well and quickly and on a tight budget. The Warner Brothers gig is a wonderful, wonderful opportunity to learn the larger studio system. I don't know if any of these scripts will ever get made into a movie, but it's a great learning experience.

DIXON: Well, thanks for your time and I guess the very last question is this – what does J. C. stand for?

CHANDOR: Jeffrey Chandor is what I have been called since birth, so J. C. doesn't make sense because my middle name is McDonald. So it should be J. M., but my parents, for some reason, called me J. C. So it's Jeffrey McDonald Chandor.

Chapter 12

"ALL MY FILMS ARE PERSONAL": AN INTERVIEW WITH PAT JACKSON*

I first became aware of Pat Jackson's work through one of his later and lesser-known films: the suspense thriller *Don't Talk to Strange Men* (1962), a sharply observed little film shot on a shoestring budget, centering on a serial killer in a small British country village who selects his victims by ringing an isolated phone booth near a bus stop and waiting to see who answers. When Jean Painter (Christina Gregg) picks up the phone late one afternoon, the anonymous caller on the other end of the line begins to chat her up in soothing, seductive tones. Lulled into a false sense of security, Jean agrees to meet him later at an isolated rendezvous. Only the timely intervention of Jean's much younger, but far more perceptive, sister, Ann (Janina Faye), saves Jean from a violent death. Interestingly, we never see the killer, who is photographed only from the back, blocking out much of the frame in each scene in which he appears; all that identifies him is his voice, which seems unnervingly calm and composed.

Originally released on the bottom half of a double bill with Tony Richardson's classic *The Loneliness of the Long Distance Runner* (1962), *Don't Talk to Strange Men* is a deft example of low-budget filmmaking at its most effective and typical of much of the work that Pat Jackson did in the 1960s – which also included a number of episodes of the visionary television series *The Prisoner* (Jackson was the person who "discovered" *Prisoner* star Patrick McGoohan and directed the actor's first screen test), as well as episodes of *The Saint*, *Danger Man* (aka *Secret Agent* in the United States), *Man in a Suitcase* and other hour-long television dramas. But Jackson's career goes back to the mid-1930s. Born on 26 March 1916, Jackson was just turning twenty when he started off as an assistant on Harry Watt and Basil Wright's classic documentary *Night Mail* (1936) and later Humphrey Jennings and Harry Watt's *London Can Take It*

---

* A version of this chapter was first published in 2011 by Taylor & Francis as "'All My Films Are Personal': An Interview with Pat Jackson," *Journal of Popular Film and Television* 39 (4): 150–61.

Figure 12. Pat Jackson (extreme right, white shirt) on set.
Source: Author's collection.

(1940), a stirring piece of agitprop shot during the Nazi blitz. Even at this early stage, Jackson was leaving a personal imprint on the films he worked on; it is his voice, for example, doing the main narration on *Night Mail* – or, as he put it, "[E]verything but [W. H.] Auden's poetry" on the soundtrack. On *London Can Take It*, Jackson was one of many cameramen on the project; as he told me, "We all shot stuff for that film."

From there, Jackson moved on to what has become his signature film: the feature-length docudrama *Western Approaches* (1945), which he also scripted, directed and acted in. A tribute to merchant seamen in the British Navy during World War II, *Western Approaches* has the distinction of being the first film shot in sync sound three-strip Technicolor in near-documentary conditions. Shot in 1943–44, when the outcome of the war was far from certain, the film unforgettably conveys the sense of sacrifice and urgency that dominated England at the height of the conflict with Hitler's Germany. This earlier part of his career has been amply documented in a number of essays and Jackson's autobiography, *A Retake Please!* (1999), but little attention has been paid to his later work.

To remedy this, I wrote to Jackson and we agreed to an interview by telephone on 25 and 26 March 2011 to discuss his later films. Even in his mid-nineties, Jackson was a formidable figure who sometimes would open up on certain subjects and then shut down on others. Irascible, blunt and very much his own man, Jackson remained an indisputably individual talent until the end of his life; sadly, this was his last interview. Pat Jackson died on 3 June 2011.

WHEELER WINSTON DIXON: Hello, Pat. How are you?

PAT JACKSON: Oh, ticking away at my ripe old age. I'm ninety-five now, you know!

DIXON: Well, a great deal of writing on your films – including your own book *A Retake Please!* – has dealt with your earlier work, such as *Western Approaches* and films you worked on as an assistant or apprentice. It's fascinating stuff, but I did want to talk to you about your other films, which haven't been discussed that much.

JACKSON: Yes, sure.

DIXON: Okay, so let's pick it up from *White Corridors* [1951], after your unhappy experience at MGM. You had been working quite successfully in England, but then you succumbed to the lure of Hollywood and found that it was a creative straitjacket, as you make clear in your memoirs. It seems that they thought you were just another director for hire – when, of course, you'd been working on personal films of one sort or another and doing most of your own scriptwriting since the mid-1930s and started out with a very experimental film unit, the GPO [General Post Office film unit], under John Grierson.

JACKSON: Well, I left Hollywood when I received the script of *White Corridors* and I never looked back. I knew I could make *White Corridors* work and I knew it was a quality project; that and *Western Approaches* are my two favorite films. I was thankful to get back to England because MGM had not picked up my option because it was too expensive. Alexander Korda had put me under contract and they would have had to pay me a lot of money at MGM to keep me. So they dropped me.

DIXON: Is it true that MGM wanted to put you on a *Lassie* picture [*Challenge to Lassie*, 1949] that Richard Thorpe wound up directing?

JACKSON: Yes, but I wouldn't do it. I never made a film I didn't believe in. When Dore Schary took over MGM from Louis B. Mayer, he called me into his office and said, "We're giving you an assignment and we want you to do it. But I hear that you don't want to do it. Am I right?" I said, "Do you expect directors to go on the floor not believing a word of what they are going to do? If that's the way you work, I'm not interested. You better sack me right away."

DIXON: You wrote one resignation letter after another.
JACKSON: Oh, yeah. I was constantly trying to leave MGM; it just wasn't working.
DIXON: In your letters, you would more or less say, "Since you are not using my services and you are giving me projects I don't believe in, maybe it's best if we just pack it all in right now," am I correct?
JACKSON: That's right.
DIXON: But every time this would result in a meeting with Schary and his assistants and they would say, "We will have something for you in three weeks," but nothing ever came of it.
JACKSON: That's about it. But then I met [the MGM contract writer and producer] Robert Sisk, who knew I was interested in a story that he was working on with Bill Ludwig, which became *Shadow on the Wall* [1950]. Originally, it was called *Death in a Doll's House*, which they had to change because somebody finally realized [here, a distinct note of sarcasm creeps into his voice] that someone named Ibsen had written a play with roughly the same title! Robert helped a lot with the script; it was a fairly good suspense thriller and I agreed to do it. So they gave it to me to do and then we went over schedule by nearly two days after three weeks of shooting. Nancy Davis promptly came down with the mumps or some damn thing. So that made it very difficult. But we finally finished under schedule and on time. That had a pretty good cast: Zachary Scott and Ann Sothern were the leads and they were quite competent. It was a five week schedule, which is fairly luxurious. But, after that, nothing worked out at MGM and I was glad to get back to Britain.
DIXON: Your first film after that was the hospital drama *White Corridors*, which is one of your favorite films. You cover that in your book. But let's talk about your segment of *Encore* [1951], a multipart film based on three stories by Somerset Maugham; your segment was "The Ant and the Grasshopper."
JACKSON: That was lovely. That starred Nigel Patrick and Roland Culver; it was a very pleasant assignment, very literate – a great script. But the schedule was short; I had only a week to shoot it. The title sums the whole thing up; one brother is a worthless layabout while the other is constantly striving to get ahead in business. But the layabout, Tom [Nigel Patrick], gets the girl! A nice twist ending, typical for Maugham. It was an easy piece to shoot.
DIXON: Your next feature was *Something Money Can't Buy* [1952], which you co-wrote with James L. Hodson; it's about a returning World War II veteran who can't adjust to civilian life and is threatened

by his wife's job as head of an employment agency. Unwilling to sit at home, he goes into the catering business with some of his former comrades. What can you tell me about that?

JACKSON: Well, that was the famous novelist James L. Hodson. He was a survivor of the first World War, who wrote a wonderful book called *Return to the Wood*. We had a long history together. I first met him in 1943. We had gone to Rome together because, when Rome fell, Prime Minister Churchill thought it would be a very good idea to make a film on the theme of the "Return of the Four Freedoms" in the first captured enemy capital. Churchill had his own 35mm copy of *Western Approaches* and he loved the film, so he thought I was the man for the job. So, I was summoned to the Ministry of Information and they said, "The Prime Minister wants this film made on the Four Freedoms."

I said, "Freedom in any form is pretty abstract for a film, but I suppose if you let me use a sync sound setup, we should be able to understand what Rome is thinking about being liberated by the Allies and it will be interesting." But they didn't want to give me a sound unit; they wanted me to shoot the whole thing silent and dub it in later. I said, "Without sound, it will be a travelogue with British soldiers looking at the Coliseum and the Vatican and that's going to be a fat lot of good, isn't it?" So they said, "Well, that's up to you to provide the right visuals." I said, "I'm not your man. I think it's a crazy idea without sync sound and it's going to be a waste of time." So we argued about the assignment and so on.

Finally they said, "Well, if James Hodson is prepared to go, I don't see why you shouldn't." That piqued my interest. So we met over lunch and I told Jim that, "Without sync sound, this is an absolute waste of time." He said, "I agree with you. But we're in a difficult position because the Prime Minister wants this film made. I agree with you that without sync sound it's going to be a waste of time, but the least we can do is to go there, have a look at Rome and report." Then, with a twinkle in his eye, he said, "Anyway, it would be an interesting experience, wouldn't it?" And so we got a trip to Rome out of it, at least, and the film never did get made. But, it led to a long friendship between Jim and myself. So, when we got to *Something Money Can't Buy*, we were old friends and could draw on a lot of shared experiences.

DIXON: There's a credit for you in most sources as a co-director on an early Hammer film, *Scotland Yard Inspector* [1952], which was directed to Sam Newfield.

JACKSON: No, I never worked for Hammer, never would.
DIXON: What about *The Gentle Touch* [1956]?
JACKSON: Oh yes, that was a nursing film. I wrote the script to that and directed it; a lot of other people were originally involved, but I pretty much swept them out of the way and took over the whole thing. It was about student nurses in a National Health Service system in the 1950s. After that I made *The Birthday Present* [1957] about a salesman who brings home an expensive watch to his wife and gets caught with it at customs and winds up in jail! Tony Britton and Sylvia Syms were the stars; it was Jack Whittingham's script. We made it on a five week schedule. Sylvia Syms was delightful to work with and so was Tony Britton. Actually, there were a lot of good people in that film: Geoffrey Keen, Thorley Walters, Howard Marion-Crawford and even Ian Bannen, in a small bit as a junior customs officer. Then I did an interesting little film, *Our Virgin Island* [aka *Virgin Island*, 1959], which I co-scripted with Ring Lardner, Jr. [from a novel by Robb White, who later went on to write a series of horror films for director William Castle]. That one had a really good cast: John Cassavetes, Ruby Dee, Sidney Poitier and it was shot by Freddie Francis, who went on to win two Academy Awards and also directed a number of films. It's about two people who go to live on a tropical island and become entangled in a smuggling ring.
DIXON: Yes, I knew Freddie very well; a fabulous cinematographer.
JACKSON: After that I directed *Snowball* [1960], a very interesting little crime thriller, very short – just over an hour – with Gordon Jackson, Kenneth Griffith, Zena Walker and a little boy who became a famous actor and is still going strong: Dennis Waterman. Then came *Seven Keys* [1961], another crime thriller, and then a horror comedy, *No Place Like Homicide* [aka, *What a Carve Up!*, 1961], which was sort of an unofficial *Carry On* [comedy series] film, with Sidney James and Kenneth Connor and a great supporting cast: Shirley Eaton, Dennis Price, Michael Gough. I loved doing it because I thought, "I'll take the Mickey out [i.e., mock the seriousness] of horror films," but it was so well done that everybody thought I was playing it straight.
DIXON: Now I want to get into your TV work. How did you get into television?
JACKSON: Well, I brought Patrick McGoohan to the screen. I'll tell you how that happened. When Orson Welles came to London, he produced a theatrical version of Herman Melville's novel *Moby*

Dick, entitled *Moby Dick Rehearsed*, in 1955. A wonderful thing to have done. The whole thing was done in modern dress with practically no props. Welles even shot a film of the production in one weekend, but it's now apparently lost. Can you believe it; to shoot the whole thing and then lose it? Anyway, I went to see it in the theater and it was fantastic! What a cast: Gordon Jackson, Christopher Lee, Patrick McGoohan, Joan Plowright, Kenneth Williams – Kenneth Williams, mind you, from the *Carry On* films, in a serious production, playing multiple roles – just amazing! Welles had a real eye for talent because, at that point, *none* of these people were really known. Anyway, Patrick played the first officer, Starbuck, and as soon as he came on the stage, he had the audience in the palm of his hand. He had a wonderful voice. I had never heard of him, never seen him. It was one of his very first parts; he was a completely unknown actor.

So, I got in touch with him and said, "I want you to come down, if you would, and do a screen test." So he said, "Yes, all right, fine. But I've never done any film work, you know." I said, "Well, it doesn't matter because you're a wonderful actor. That's all that matters." So I met him a few days later at Pinewood [Studios] about 8:00 in the morning, outside the canteen. He drove up in his little car and got out, as white as a sheet. He came up to me and said, "Pat, I'm sorry. I don't think I can go through with this." I told him, "Relax. One thousand feet of film is no more important than a roll of toilet paper. You've got nothing to lose. Don't be a fool, of course you're ready to do it." So I shot 1,000 feet of his face, close-ups, long shots, different lighting – a real run through of what he looked like on screen. Well, he did a *wonderful* test and immediately was put under contract by J. Arthur Rank – and then, of course, he became a TV star with *Danger Man*. So, I directed his first test and pretty much discovered him, which is why we worked together so well on *The Prisoner*, much, much later.

DIXON: Now what can you tell me about the TV series *Rendezvous* [1957–61]? You directed twelve episodes of that.

JACKSON: More than that. I did half of them. You must see it because Peter O'Toole is in it and Patrick is in one of the episodes, "The Executioner," which I directed in 1961. It was one of Peter O'Toole's first appearances on film or television; we shot it all on film.

DIXON: Was this a big hit in Britain?

JACKSON: No. It died the death. It was ahead of its time. *Rendezvous* was a whole series of short stories – half-hour short stories. There was no continuity; it was an entirely new cast and plot line every week. But the British audience, by that time, insisted on soap operas or serials. They couldn't take a new short story every week. Getting used to characters they had never seen before was simply too much work for British TV viewers, even then, and so the series lingered for a while and then died. It was too bad because it was very good. Peter O'Toole was delightful to work with.

DIXON: Now we come to *Don't Talk to Strange Men*.

JACKSON: Well, that was a great little suspense thriller produced by Derick Williams. It was shot very quickly, on a very modest budget. But it holds up very well. It had a great script by Gwen Cherrell and a solid cast: Christina Gregg, Janina Faye and Cyril Raymond were all very good. The voice of the killer, incidentally, is done by Tony Britton, who gets no credit anywhere in the film; he did it as a favor to me. But, as you know, you never see his face; he's always got his back to the camera. We never find out who the killer is, even at the end. It doesn't really matter *who* he is. He could be anyone. That's the point of the whole film. You think you know people, but you don't. The fact that you don't know who it is makes the whole film that much more sinister.

DIXON: What I thought was interesting – among many other things in the film – was how much you did with atmosphere. Simple things. When Jean is in the phone booth and you're listening to the killer talk to her, you cut outside to the woods around the phone booth, but there's really nothing obvious there. You get the sense that there's *something* back there, but you can't see what it is. It gives a sense of unease to the whole thing. I thought it was just a brilliant piece of work – memorably sinister. And now, of course, it's on DVD, so a whole new generation of viewers can see it.

JACKSON: Yes, I was quite surprised by that. I like the film, but I'd prefer it if *White Corridors* came out on DVD; it's really a better film, I think. And after *Don't Talk to Strange Men*, I directed a sort of kid's film, *Seventy Deadly Pills* [1964], about a group of young kids – a gang called "The Rockets" – who find a bunch of pills that could kill them; the film becomes a race against time to recover the pills before one of the kids takes them. That was also for Derick Williams, who produced *Don't Talk to Strange Men*.

	"ALL MY FILMS ARE PERSONAL" 155
DIXON:	Right after that, you directed one episode of *The Saint*, entitled "The Revolution Racket" [1964]. Roger Moore has gone on record as saying, "I'm not an actor and I've got 50 films to prove it." Would you more or less agree?
JACKSON:	He was all right, in a limited way. That was just more or less an assignment. It was shot in five days; assembly line work. And, around the same time, I also did some episodes of *Man in a Suitcase*, an hour long drama about an American spy [McGill, nicknamed Mac, played by American actor Richard Bradford] who has been kicked out of the service unjustly and winds up in London. From there, he takes whatever work he can while at the same time trying to restore his reputation. It's a good premise, but the show was just routine. I did three episodes: "The Bridge," "Man from the Dead," and "Variation on a Million Bucks: Part 1," all in 1967. It paid the rent.
	But, around the same time, I got the chance to do an episode of *Danger Man* – "The Hunting Party" in 1966. That was a whole different story. Patrick was such a good actor and, even though it was a TV show, with a tight schedule, he just had so much more range that the whole thing just clicked right from the start. I just did one episode of *Danger Man*, but then, of course, that led to *The Prisoner*, which was very much a personal project for Patrick. I directed four episodes of *The Prisoner*, which was *way* ahead of its time: "Hammer into Anvil," "The Schizoid Man," and "A. B. and C.," all in 1967, and "Do Not Forsake Me, Oh My Darling" in 1968.
	As you know, there were only seventeen episodes shot in the entire series and then it was done. Today, of course, it's a classic. Patrick had almost complete total control over it. We had five days to shoot each episode and because the whole thing was so well planned out, it went off just like clockwork. Television moves very quickly and you have to get things done bang on schedule; when you have a good crew and a good cast, the whole thing moves right along. But *The Prisoner* was a one-of-a-kind series; they tried to remake it a year or so ago for television and it simply didn't work. Without Patrick's vision, *The Prisoner* would never have existed.
DIXON:	Do you storyboard your films and television shows?
JACKSON:	It's much more than that. I plan everything – and I mean *everything* – out in advance. Every camera movement is worked out, every movement of the artist is worked out, because otherwise you

don't know what your camera is going to do. I don't arrive on the floor and see what the actors have blocked out; I work all that out beforehand. It has to be precise. I plan the whole thing out in advance. It's the only way to do it, particularly when you have to get it done on time and on schedule. And, of course, I moved into directing a lot of television; my last work was on the TV series *Arthur of the Britons* in 1973 – I did six episodes of that – and, after that, a kid's show, which was very popular – *The Famous Five*, in 1978 and 1979. I shot eleven episodes of that; both were half-hour series. Again, without preplanning everything, you're never going to get it done on time, so I always plan every last detail before I go on the set.

DIXON: You worked with people like Harry Watt and John Grierson in the glory days of the GPO with *Night Mail* and *London Can Take It*. But who were the people in the 1960s you worked with? How did you feel about how the cinema had changed over the years?

JACKSON: Well, I didn't have any real connection to other directors in the 1960s. I was freelance. Every time I made a film, it would be a different lot of people. I was a floating object, floating on the sea. Anybody who was interested got in touch. Because I hadn't got an agent. So, on my later films, we shot them and we didn't think they would have any great future, but we did films like *Don't Talk to Strange Men* because it was an interesting story.

When you make a film and it goes down well in the press, you feel you've done something, that it's all been worthwhile. Some films I've made, like *Western Approaches*, are obviously personal films I have control over from start to finish. And then working on *The Prisoner*, that was Patrick's personal vision – he even directed some of the episodes himself – and so that was very satisfying. Some work I've done simply to pay the bills. But, in everything I've done, I've tried to give it an edge, something that's mine alone. Of course, I've written a lot of the scripts for my films and I wish I had a chance to do more of that – and I have several scripts that I would like to have done, but never got the chance to do, for various reasons. But, when I look back on my work, I'm pleased with it; I got a chance to do a lot of interesting projects and my best work, like *White Corridors*, still holds up today. I was never an organization man; as you know from my abortive sojourn at MGM, Hollywood holds no allure for me. All of my films are personal, to one degree or another. That's the only way to do it.

Chapter 13

WORKING WITHIN THE SYSTEM: AN INTERVIEW WITH GERRY O'HARA*

Gerry O'Hara is a true original and, if he never really got the chance to definitively climb out of the ranks of assistant directors into the realm of full-fledged feature directors, he nevertheless managed to carve out a solid career in the cinema working with such luminaries as Sir Laurence Olivier, Ronald Neame, Michael Powell, Sir Carol Reed, Anatole Litvak, Ken Annakin, Terence Fisher, Sidney Box, Otto Preminger and many more in his early years, before striking out on his own with several low-budget sixties British films – the most memorable of which is *The Pleasure Girls* (UK, 1963), recently rereleased as part of the BFI's "Flipside" series of lesser-known films that nevertheless deserve attention. Despite its unfortunate title, *The Pleasure Girls* is, in reality, a deeply moving feminist document of '60s London, shot in a real apartment building as four young women come to London to make their way in the world.

Throughout his career, O'Hara has had to do a number of projects he didn't really want to do, but he also got a chance to work with some of the greatest talents in the history of the cinema and is frank about his past, including the biggest mistake of his career: walking off *Lawrence of Arabia* (dir. David Lean, UK, 1962) as first assistant director during early preproduction, after which he alleges that Columbia Pictures effectively blacklisted O'Hara within the industry as "unreliable." I couldn't possibly cover all of his credits even in this lengthy interview, but suffice it to say that Gerry O'Hara was extremely active from the early 1940s on, working with all the major talents in the field; he certainly left his mark on the cinema industry. But let him tell it in this interview conducted on 3 December 2010.

---

* A version of this chapter was first published in 2011 by *Screening the Past* (online) as "Working Within the System: An Interview with Gerry O' Hara" (number 30): http://www.screeningthepast.com/2011/04/working-within-the-system-an-interview-with-gerry-o%E2%80%99hara/.

Figure 13. Gerry O'Hara on set of *The Pleasure Girls*.
Source: Author's collection.

WHEELER WINSTON DIXON: You were born in 1924.
GERRY O'HARA: Correct.
DIXON: And your father was a bookmaker?
O'HARA: That's right. He was just small time. He was the equivalent of what was called a street bookie. In those days, it was illegal to take cash for wagering. He was just a very small-time bookie in a little country town – Boston Lincolnshire – where I was born.
DIXON: What about your early schooling?
O'HARA: Very primitive. St. Mary's Catholic School – it was what was called then an elementary school. They just taught you the three R's for three hours a day and, being a Catholic school, a lot of religion. Plus a little geography, a little history. But I never finished; I left school at 14. I was really more interested in getting out into the world and finding my own way. So, I became a cub reporter on a failing Labour newspaper in a conservative town, the *Boston Guardian*. It was on its last legs and it lasted for about 18 months at the outside, but when it folded, we were all picked

DIXON: And what was your beat?
O'HARA: Deaths and weddings, christenings, charity dinners – that sort of stuff. I was 14 when I got the job on the *Guardian*. It's odd, really, because of course at 14 now you wouldn't have a chance at something like that. They might allow you to sell newspapers on the street, but they wouldn't make you write them. But anyway, I kept at this for some time, until one day in 1941, the *Lincolnshire Standard* sent me out to interview [director] Michael Powell, who was shooting *One of Our Aircraft is Missing* [co-directed with Emeric Pressburger, UK, 1942] on location. We were told in the newspaper office that there was a film unit down at the swing bridge – which was a railway bridge across the river – and I went down there on my bicycle and saw what was happening. Ronnie Neame was the cameraman – who, of course, later became a very famous director – and I watched the crew working all day. I got an interview in the evening with Michael Powell, who was very open and forthcoming. I went home thinking about what I'd seen and it looked very intriguing. After a few weeks, the penny dropped and I thought, "Hey, that looks like a pretty good job."

It was during the war, of course, but I was young and full of ambition, so I wrote to Michael asking for a job, which took some nerve, I guess. Surprisingly, Michael wrote back and said, "Yes, come and see me if you come down to London." So I went off to meet him, but I went to the wrong place. I went to his office in the city, which was an accountant's office, when of course I should have gone to Pinewood Studios or Denham, where he was shooting. But they took pity on me. I was 17 and pretty green – with straw in my hair, as it were. So the accountants said, "Look, we represent Michael Powell, but since you have come all this way, there is a film company around the corner, a documentary company run by Sidney Box and we also look after them. Why don't you try your luck there?"

DIXON: That was Verity Films, wasn't it?
O'HARA: That's right. I got a job there at 3 pounds 7/6 a week. I started as a trainee in the script department because, theoretically, I was a journalist. But I was just running errands for the script department, carrying film cans and stuff like that. Then Ken Annakin, who became quite famous later on, was a young assistant director there; he sort of took me under his wing and

	I switched to being a runner and errand boy in the assistant director's department.
DIXON:	So, basically, you were working on documentaries as an assistant director?
O'HARA:	Yes. How to put out a firebomb and stuff like that. It was a lot of wartime work, of course, and most of it was civil defense stuff, films for hire.
DIXON:	Did you work on any films for the GPO – for the General Post Office?
O'HARA:	Yes, the Ministry of Information. We did a sort of copy of Carol Reed's *The Next of Kin* [UK, 1942] called *Jigsaw* [UK, 1942], which was a naval version of how to keep secrets and so forth. I did a film called *Old Mother Riley at Home* [dir. Oswald Mitchell, UK, 1945] with Arthur Lucan, which was drag comedy, very simple stuff; oddly, Lucan came from my hometown and his whole drag act as Old Mother Riley was very, very popular with working class audiences. I was a second assistant on that and so I kept working and gradually moved up to first assistant. I think the first one was a film called *The Loyal Heart* [dir. Oswald Mitchell, UK, 1946]; it was about a faithful sheepdog, shot very quickly at British National. The cinematographer on that was Arthur Grant, who later went on to do a lot of work for Hammer in the '60s; he was very, very fast on the set. We shared a bedroom in Cumberland for about three or four months during that period. Percy Marmont and his daughter, Patricia, were in it, but it wasn't very good. I think it ran for about three days in two cinemas and they took it off. I think, at that time, I seemed to waver between first and second assistant, which happened a lot. I was still very young then – only about 18 or 19. But it was a great apprenticeship; it was incredible. So I kept working on small-budget films and then I got a shot at working on *Boys in Brown* [dir. Montgomery Tully, UK, 1949], a very famous British film about a prison for boys – what we call a Borstal. That had a really top-flight cast, all of them at the beginning of their careers: Sir Richard Attenborough (who wasn't a "Sir" then), Dirk Bogarde and Jack Warner, who was a fixture in British crime dramas and also in the Huggett films, which were family comedies. Later, he had a big success playing one character over and over again: Sgt. George Dixon, Dixon of Dick Green.
DIXON:	Did you have any particular feelings that these people were going to go on to be major names?

O'HARA: Well, I think people had their eye on Dirk because he had begun to get quite a good reputation in the theater. He was known to be a talent, but he was a little reserved – a very nice guy but very private. One never got to know him. Dickie Attenborough knew him very well. Dickie used to give me a ride up and down to the studios every day and Dickie came from Leicestershire, which is quite near where I came from. And so we had a very, very slight affinity.

Boys in Brown was shot using what they called "the independent frame system," which nobody remembers, but which was just crazy. It was the third and last film made with the independent frame process, which was devised by a production designer. The idea was that you could prefabricate the set off the stage and wheel them in on rostrums so you didn't occupy the stage for too long. And you'd shoot most of it with front screen projection or rear projection. You'd go out and do all the exteriors when the weather was good and then you'd come in and shoot the rest of the film against a bunch of projection plates. They shot one more film with the process after that – *The Astonished Heart* [dirs. Antony Darnborough and Terence Fisher, UK, 1950], a Noel Coward vehicle, which he wrote and starred in – but then they only used elements of it. The process was just too constricting.

DIXON: You can clear something up for me here: Terence Fisher and Antony Darnborough are credited as co-directors on *The Astonished Heart*, a somewhat unusual arrangement. But did they really co-direct it?

O'HARA: Yes. Terry Fisher was really an editor; he was graduating from the cutting room and moving into the director's chair. And, of course, like Arthur Grant, Terry also wound up at Hammer, making lots of horror films, which made his reputation. Terry had made some smaller films before that, but this was a Noel Coward film, so it was a big deal.

DIXON: So how did they collaborate on that film?

O'HARA: Well, Antony Darnborough was a very nice guy, but he was a sort of high-flyer – kind of a toff [aristocrat]. Antony did most of the direction of the actors and Terry worked on the camera setups because he knew what would cut together, being an editor. Antony was a very decent guy, but he was actually better off as a producer. He did one more with Terry, *So Long at the Fair* [UK, 1950], which I was also first AD on. That had a pretty stellar cast, too: Jean Simmons, Dirk Bogarde, David Tomlinson, Felix

	Aylmer, André Morrell and a young Honor Blackman. Again, Antony directed the actors while Terry tended to the camera setups, but after that, Antony vanishes from cinema history while Terry's career took off. Terry was a very quiet, very determined director; chain smoked all the time; always kept on time and on schedule.
DIXON:	Yes. So, do you have any memories of *So Long at the Fair*? That was an "A" picture, of course.
O'HARA:	Yes, it was a big movie. We went to Paris for about four weeks to do the location stuff.
DIXON:	Really? I thought the whole thing was shot in the studio.
O'HARA:	No, we did a lot of location work at the Tuileries Gardens in Paris. Of course, we then went back and shot a lot of the film in the UK; we had a mock up of the base of the Eiffel Tower in the studio and used that for a lot of the dialogue work. I don't remember exactly how much we shot in Paris, but you know, in those days, things were more relaxed.
DIXON:	How many setups would you do in a day on something like *So Long at the Fair*?
O'HARA:	Well, on an "A" movie, probably about 8 to 10 setups. If it was a quickie, more like 15 to 18 setups.
DIXON:	Next comes *Trio* [dirs. Ken Annakin and Harold French, UK, 1950], which is a portmanteau film, with three stories all written originally by Somerset Maugham, who also appeared in the film. You were really going from one film to the next very rapidly.
O'HARA:	Yes, I certainly was. I worked on only one episode of that, "The Verger," which was directed by my old friend Ken Annakin, who by now was moving up very rapidly. James Hayter and Michael Hordern starred in that; it was a nice short piece of work. Geoffrey Unsworth shot that; he was a fine cameraman. It was produced, oddly enough, by Antony Darnborough, who by this time had decided to step back from direction and work strictly as a producer.
DIXON:	There was really quite a vogue for these Somerset Maugham "anthology" movies at the time; there was *Trio*, *Quartet* [dirs. Ken Annakin, Arthur Crabtree, Harold French and Ralph Smart, UK, 1948] and *Encore* [dirs. Harold French and Pat Jackson, UK, 1951].
O'HARA:	I worked on *Trio* and *Quartet*; both times with Ken. We did one episode of *Quartet*, "The Colonel's Lady." Cecil Parker, Wilfrid Hyde-White and Nora Swinburne were in that; Reginald Wyer

shot it – a very fast and efficient cameraman. It was a beautiful segment about a very tough-nosed colonel who couldn't live with the fact that his wife had written a book of erotic poetry. That was shot at Gainsborough Studios in Islington. It was a very small studio, one stage built on top of the other. In fact, it was a converted factory.

DIXON: Next up is the crime thriller *The Clouded Yellow* [UK, 1950]. That was directed by Ralph Thomas. What was he like as a director? Jean Simmons and Trevor Howard were in that.

O'HARA: Ralph Thomas was okay. He was an awful snob. His brother, Gerry Thomas, was much more amusing, much more fun – he was much more approachable. Ralph took himself quite seriously. You had to call him "Rafe," not "Ralph." I remember that he was very proud of the fact that he was a member of the Cavalry Club, which was a very exclusive London men's club. Supposedly, he had a long affair with Betty Box.

DIXON: Gerry directed all the *Carry On* films, right?

O'HARA: Absolutely. I didn't work on any of those, but I knew him slightly. Both Ralph and Gerry were editors who became directors. They were what we call "working directors"; they got the film in on time and on schedule, but they certainly weren't mainstream talents.

DIXON: Next, I have a film called *Meet Mr. Callahan* [UK, 1954], directed by Charles Saunders, based on Peter Cheney's character of the slightly down-at-the-heels private detective Slim Callaghan. The Slim Callaghan novels were wildly popular in the '50s, but now nobody seems to read him except for Jean-Luc Godard, surprisingly. What was that like?

O'HARA: That was fine; a small picture, but easy to make. Charlie Saunders again was an ex-editor. Those kinds of guys like Charlie, Ralph Smart and Ralph and Gerry Thomas were what I used to call "meat and potatoes" directors. They knew how to cut up the script and how to choose the right setups to get it in the can as rapidly as possible. Charlie's brother produced the long running Agatha Christie play *The Mouse Trap*, which opened in 1952, is still running to this day; some 24,000 performances!

DIXON: The next picture that I have for you, though, is a distinct step up: Sir Laurence Olivier's *Richard III* [UK, 1955]. You've been essentially working in "B" films and on smaller "A" films, but this is quite a promotion. How did you get the job on that?

O'HARA: Well, I was working on *The Divided Heart* [dir. Charles Crichton, UK, 1954] at Ealing Studios, which was based on a true story published in *Life* magazine. It was a really good picture, very solidly told. It was about a little boy whose entire family, including his mother, was presumed killed by the Nazis during World War II. After the war, the boy is adopted by a German couple in the Bavarian Alps, where he grows up and considers the adoptive couple his real parents. But then, out of nowhere, his birth mother suddenly reappears and fights tooth and nail through the courts to get the child back. Really well done; Theodore Bikel, Yvonne Mitchell, Geoffrey Keen, Alexander Knox and Liam Redmond were all in it and they were first rate.

But here's the thing: Ealing Studios was grooming me to be a staff member there, which I didn't really want to be. I didn't realize that at the time, but I didn't care for Ealing Studios. They were a bit snobbish, you know? They were quite nice, but there were all university guys and they were a bit kinky. So I didn't really fit in. But I made one good friend; the cameraman on that was a lovely guy named Otto Heller. He was a Czech refugee and his English was appalling. He was a very funny, very sweet guy but he couldn't read the scripts, so that was a real problem! The Ealing people didn't really care for him, but they hired him for the very good reason that he was fast. Really, really fast on the set. But Otto couldn't read the script, so I used to tell him what the scene was every day. Each scene. Charlie Crichton was a bit standoffish; he "couldn't be bothered" to tell Otto what was going on, you know. So that's why we became quite good pals, Otto and I.

And then Otto came to me one day and said, "Gerry, what is this *Richard III*?" And I said, "Well, it's Shakespeare; it's a play about a very cruel British monarch." That's as best as I knew, you know, since we hadn't studied Shakespeare at school. "Why do you ask?" I wondered. "Well," Otto said, "I'm going to speak to Mr. Olivier tonight" – he called him "Mr. Olivier" – "because he wants me to shoot a film for him." Larry was playing at the Phoenix Theatre in Terence Rattigan's *The Sleeping Prince* with Vivien Leigh and he wanted Otto to drop by after the performance for a job interview. Otto was beside himself; he really wanted the job, but he had no idea what *Richard III* was about! So he asked me, "Could you find out for me what it's about, what the plot is, so I don't look like an idiot?" "Sure," I said, so I sent for one of Michael Balcon's trainees, Michael Birkett, who later became Lord Birkett – a very nice guy.

Anyway, I called Michael on the set – he was only about 18 or 19 years old at the time – and said, "Look, I want a 'once upon a time' version of *Richard III*, only a couple of pages long, and I want it by 5:00 tonight." And Michael did it. Otto and I went to a coffee bar after day's shooting. I told him the story and he went to see Larry. Larry wanted Otto because he was fast; he had a much-deserved reputation for doing great work really, really quickly. Larry had worked with some of the great cameramen of the British cinema in his earlier films, but they'd taken up the lion's share of production time getting the set lit, with the actors waiting around and he didn't want to do that again.

So, somebody had told him that Otto was quality and quick and, after a very brief interview with Larry, he got the job. But, as Otto was leaving the dressing room, he said, "There's just one thing: I need an assistant on the film. I have difficulty reading and this boy, Gerry O'Hara, really helps me with the script." So Larry said, "Send him in tomorrow night." So I went backstage the next night, spoke to Larry and got the job. Otto really did me a favor there; he made my participation in the film essential. I was first assistant on that film and it was a hell of a break for me.

DIXON: *Richard III* was shot in a very kind of "book of hours" manner – very stylized. The sets look like they came from a medieval illuminated manuscript – very theatrical – and I also noticed that Olivier and Heller used banks of colored lights on the set – lots of colored gels during shooting. Am I right?

O'HARA: Yes. Ninety percent of the film was shot inside, on the studio floor, and for the scenes of the castle ramparts, we would have a hell of a lot of light pouring down on the set. We shot the battle sequences in Spain, which was a nightmare, but most of the film was shot very quickly in the studio in long takes, which Larry loved because they got so much done so quickly. He had quite a good editor on the film – Helga Cranston. We had a very good camera operator – Denys Coop, who, of course, went on to being a very good DP. He had all these guys from the theater – very good production designers and a wonderful art director called Carmen Dillon. Sir William Walton did the music, which is one of my favorite scores for any film. So, it was top notch all the way around.

DIXON: How long a schedule did this film have?

O'HARA: Well, as I said, it all went well until we went to Spain to do the climactic battle sequence. It took forever and didn't really

	come off. It seemed to me that he was trying to redo the battle scenes from his own film, *Henry V* [UK, 1944], but it didn't work. The battle scenes for *Richard III* were shot in the same kind of stylized way as the rest of the film. We went over the battleground some days ahead and tried to plan everything out, but the weather was terrible and, in the end, we didn't really get what we wanted.
DIXON:	A very young Stanley Baker played Henry, the Earl of Richmond in the film, who finally brings about Richard's downfall. What was Baker like on the set? Would you tab him as somebody who was an up-and-comer?
O'HARA:	Yes, you would. Unfortunately, he was very arrogant because he knew he was an up-and-comer, too! And there was a terrible moment on location when Larry got shot by an arrow during the battle sequence. It accidentally hit him in the chin. So it was a tough shoot during the Spanish location work.
DIXON:	What was Olivier like as a person?
O'HARA:	Oh, he was great. Everybody called him Sir Larry. We got on tremendously well. He was a very solid, professional person; working on that film was a real eye-opener. You could make topflight stuff and still be a rather down-to-earth personality.
DIXON:	How long was the whole schedule on the picture?
O'HARA:	Quite a long one – about 18 weeks.
DIXON:	So, all in all, this was a huge jump forward for you.
O'HARA:	Yes, it was, and after that, offers of work came in droves. Anatole Litvak wanted me for *Anastasia* [UK, 1956], Ronnie Neame wanted me for *The Man Who Never Was* [UK, 1956], Robert Rossen for *Island in the Sun* [UK, 1957], Muriel Box's *The Truth About Women* [UK, 1957], Carol Reed's *The Key* [UK, 1958], which nobody seems to remember now, and I did them all. It was a really great time to be working in the industry. *Anastasia* I remember because I loved working with Anatole, but the star of the film was Yul Brynner and he was a bastard – he was a pain in the ass. Ingrid Bergman was another matter altogether; lovely to work with, but very, very private. But she used to tease Anatole because he would shoot take after take; that was just his style. He would say, "Cut, go again," and one day she finally said, "Why, why should we go again?" and he just said, "Again, Ingrid." But she was a real professional. *Island in the Sun* was a rather daring film for the time because of its interracial love aspect, with Dorothy Dandridge, James Mason, Joan Collins and

	Harry Belafonte. I remember we were specifically told not to try and get fresh with Dorothy Dandridge because her boyfriend was in the mafia. And it all came from working on *Richard III*.
DIXON:	And then, in something of a switch, you worked on *Third Man on the Mountain* [USA, 1959], a Disney adventure film about mountain climbing. This one is also somewhat forgotten, but it's a rather rousing adventure film and much of it was shot on location in Switzerland, scaling the Matterhorn. Ken Annakin directed it, with a cast that included Michael Rennie, James MacArthur, Janet Munro and Herbert Lom. That must have been a difficult film to shoot because a lot of the footage was shot on the mountain itself and not in the studio, if I remember correctly. Was there a lot of location work on that project?
O'HARA:	Yes, there was, but we also shot a lot of it on a small mountain halfway up among other mountains. There was also a great big clump of rocks that stood just outside the railway station where we were shooting and we had it scaffolded so we could do all the close-ups. Ken did send me off one day with the French Mountain Unit to do some second-unit shots with doubles and I did actually get hauled up on a rope a fair way up the Matterhorn, so yes, it was a bit challenging.
DIXON:	What about *Our Man in Havana* [dir. Carol Reed, UK, 1959]?
O'HARA:	Oh, that was a lot of fun to work on, but it didn't really turn out all that well in the end. We shot a lot of it in Cuba right around the time of Castro's revolution. Of course, that was based on Graham Greene's novel and it had a lot of star power going into the project.
DIXON:	The main character, James Wormold, a vacuum cleaner salesman who's recruited as a spy for the British government, was played by Alec Guinness. What was he like to work with?
O'HARA:	Well, unfortunately that didn't work too well between Carol and Alec; not that I was aware of anything being said, but Alec was a cold fish. Again, he was a very private man. He took us all out to dinner one at a time. I had dinner with him one night in Havana. But he didn't open up at all; it was like, "So, tell me about you." So he was more or less inspecting you in a way.
DIXON:	What about Ernie Kovacs?
O'HARA:	Oh, he was wonderful – we all loved him, he was great. It was really, really sad when he died so young in that car accident [on 13 January 1962]. Who knows what he could have done.

DIXON: And what about Noel Coward, who plays Hawthorne, the British secret service agent who taps Alec Guinness's character for spy duty?

O'HARA: Noel Coward was talent personified. When he turned up, you knew he was there; he sort of dominated the whole thing effortlessly. He didn't work on the picture that long, but he was a delight on the set – a very dry sense of humor. He was very fond of Carol, but, as I say, it didn't quite work as a film.

DIXON: Next, I have you as AD on *The L-Shaped Room* [dir. Bryan Forbes, UK, 1962], which is something of a change of pace for you, with Leslie Caron, Tom Bell and Brock Peters. It's a kitchen sink drama about some lonely misfits in a London boarding house. That's a different kind of film compared to the other work that you were doing – all interiors, a small cast.

O'HARA: Well, yes. I got into a muddle there. Before that, I was in Rome on *Cleopatra* [dir. Joseph L. Mankiewicz, USA, 1963]. But, before I went up to do *Cleopatra*, the producer Jimmy Woolf had picked me to do *L-Shaped Room*. I didn't want to do it; it was the wrong kind of film for someone like me because it was really just a small affair and I think anybody could have done it, you know. But I signed up for it.

DIXON: And you liked working on big pictures?

O'HARA: That was it, because I was having a wonderful time in Rome on *Cleopatra*, where I was first AD on the second unit. But then my time was running out. I was going to have to go back to London and shoot *L-Shaped Room*, which, as I say, anyone could have done. Walter Wanger, who was producing *Cleopatra*, wanted very much to keep me. *Cleopatra* was a huge picture and he wanted me to keep a firm hand on things. He pleaded with Jimmy Woolf to release me, but Jimmy wouldn't, which was annoying. And so I had to come back for it. But you know, on *Cleopatra*, I was originally supposed to be Joe Mankiewicz's assistant, but it turned out that, in fact, I was actually first assistant on the second unit, which was directed by Ray Kellogg ...

DIXON: I didn't know that!

O'HARA: Yes, he was an ex-Marine – a bull of a man.

DIXON: Yes, he was really a special effects guy, but later he directed stuff like *The Giant Gila Monster* [USA, 1959], *The Killer Shrews* [USA, 1959] and *The Green Berets* [USA, 1968], which he co-directed with John Wayne, who starred in the film, and also Mervyn LeRoy, who came in and directed some scenes.

O'HARA: I never met John Wayne, but Ray was of that ilk. A really tough customer.
DIXON: So, how long did you work on *Cleopatra*?
O'HARA: I was on it for about three months. But then I got a break and got out of the second unit and sort of promoted, in a rather odd way. One of the extras in the cast was embarrassed because they wanted her to appear nude in a scene and she was an Italian actress who didn't want to do that kind of stuff. I sort of interceded with Joe, who I only knew really because we used to have dinners from time to time. I got it resolved to everyone's satisfaction, so they pulled me off the second unit and made me kind of a special assistant, sorting out problems, what they call a "trouble shooter" for Joe. And that's why Walter Wanger asked Jimmy Woolf to let me stay with them.
DIXON: But he wouldn't let you, so then you wound up going back to do first AD chores on *The L-Shaped Room*.
O'HARA: That's it. It wasn't fun. I wish I could have stayed. But I was under contract and I had to do it.
DIXON: Now what about *Tom Jones* [dir. Tony Richardson, UK, 1963]? You were first AD on that and it was both a huge film and a period piece and, of course, it won many, many awards – both in the States and the UK.
O'HARA: Oh, that was wonderful. It was a big picture, but it was the happiest film I was ever on. I couldn't wait to go to work in the morning. Tony was a delight. It had a great script by John Osborne and Albert Finney was superb in it, as was Susannah York. And you're right; it did amazingly well. It won all kinds of awards. Oddly enough, Albert Finney was a friend of mine, you know; his father was a street bookie, just like my father. So was Peter O'Toole's, but I never worked with him.
DIXON: Jumping back a bit – during your career, you also drew an assignment with the notoriously, how should I put this, volcanic …
O'HARA: Otto Preminger.
DIXON: Yes, Otto Preminger first on *Exodus* [USA, 1960] and then on *The Cardinal* [USA, 1963]. Now, *The Cardinal* was a big picture, but not a particularly good one. I don't know if you would agree with that.
O'HARA: Well, give me *Exodus* any day. That was a really huge production. Probably the biggest picture I did, physically. I was the first AD on it; I worked on that with a bunch of people, one of whom was the Israeli AD, Yoel Silberg. He and I are still friends. He is now

the senior director at the Habima Theater in Tel Aviv. Another guy who worked on that, in an uncredited capacity, was George Cosmatos, who wound up directing *Rambo: First Blood Part II* [USA] in 1985 and *Tombstone* [USA] in 1993. The production of *Exodus* went on forever and forever; it was an enormously complex project in every respect – locations, cast, crew, everything. Just look at the cast: Paul Newman, Eva Marie Saint, Peter Lawford, Ralph Richardson, Lee J. Cobb, Sal Mineo, John Derek, Hugh Griffith ... the list goes on and on and on. We were in Israel and then we went to Cyprus.

DIXON: What was Paul Newman like to work with?

O'HARA: He was, again, very private. All he would ever say was, "Hi, Gerry," and that was the end of the conversation. Lee J. Cobb, though, I thought was wonderful. I loved him.

DIXON: But, after *Exodus*, I have a gap. And, during this time, it seems that you turned down the job of first AD on *Lawrence of Arabia*, amazingly enough. What happened?

O'HARA: Well, I'll tell you, but it's complex. Two or three years or so after *Exodus*, I was in Paris working on *The Four Horsemen of the Apocalypse* [USA, 1962] with Vincente Minnelli. But, after about six weeks, the picture was in trouble and we were miles behind schedule. Vincente was a lovely guy, but he was very difficult at times; he took forever to set things up and then he would change his mind. He was adorable, but nevertheless he was taking forever. Anyway, he came to me one day and said, "Look, they're pulling the picture, we have got to go back to Hollywood. But they won't let me take you with me because the Hollywood union won't allow it, so you're off the picture." But then he said, "Look, I saw Sam Spiegel [the producer of *Lawrence of Arabia*] last night in the hotel and he wants to see you." Now, I had already turned down *Lawrence of Arabia* because I had a feeling it wasn't going to work out for me, but I was suddenly out of work as it were and it would have been silly not to go, so I went to the hotel and saw Sam. And Sam said, "Look, you know, whatever your problems, if it's about money, call our guy in London and tell him what you want. I'll see you in Jordan." And foolishly I went along with it.

I left before *Lawrence* started, during preproduction, because I had been told that it was going to be just a few weeks in Jordan and the rest shot in the UK, but then they said, "No, it'll be three months in Jordan and *then* the rest of it in England." Well, I had a Jewish girlfriend and she couldn't come to Jordan. So, when I met up with David Lean in Jordan, I mentioned the schedule to him – shooting some of it in Jordan and the rest back in the UK – and he said, "Oh no, we're going to do it all here, the whole thing right here in the desert." And I thought, "Oh, fuck. That lets me out." And I'm afraid I left the picture. I just didn't like the way things were going on the project, but it was still my biggest mistake. I should have taken the job. It put me in big trouble. Columbia put the word out that I was unreliable. When I went back to London, I couldn't get work. I did get a short job as first AD on a really small British comedy, *Maid for Murder* [dir. Robert Asher, UK, 1962; originally titled *She'll Have to Go*], starring, believe it or not, Bob Monkhouse, Alfred Marks, Hattie Jacques from the *Carry Ons* and, of all people, Anna Karina, Jean-Luc Godard's wife! Then somebody offered me a little picture, a three week shoot as a director.

DIXON: *That Kind of Girl* [UK, 1963].

O'HARA: *That Kind of Girl*. And I think the guy who offered it to me, Robert Hartford-Davis, thought he was going to direct *me*! It was an exploitation picture, pure and simple, about venereal disease. I shot *That Kind of Girl* and it was a three week shoot, 17 days. The night that we finished, I went back to my flat and I was absolutely exhausted. We had no money, so we just had a few beers in a pub and that was the end of the picture party. They didn't even want me to edit it or do any of the finishing stages. I think I got 750 pounds for a three week shoot. That was probably about two years after *Exodus*. So, the night I finished it, I was at home having a drink when Otto Preminger phoned me from New York – typical Otto, right to the point. He said, "Gerry, what are you doing?" And I said, "Well, I just finished directing a film." Otto said, "Okay, I'll drink to the film's success. But let me ask you, are you going to go on directing?" I said, "No, no, they don't even want me to edit it. I'm through." Immediately, he jumped on this. "Good," he said, "I want you here in New York. Go to Columbia tomorrow, get your ticket." And that's how I got on *The Cardinal*; he put me on as a second unit director. No one else would give me a job, but Otto came through, in his own unusual way.

DIXON: And then you wrote and directed *The Pleasure Girls* [UK, 1965], which has now come out on DVD and Blu-Ray, as you know, as part of the BFI's Flipside series.

O'HARA: Yes. It was shot for something like 30,000 pounds; it's about a group of young women making their way in 1960s London.

I wrote the script and we shot it on location. Probably our biggest star was Klaus Kinski, who got 900 pounds for 10 days' work in the film, just before he went off to appear in *Dr. Zhivago* [dir. David Lean, UK, 1965]; the entire shoot was only 20 days. But then we also had Tony Tanner, Ian McShane and, of course, Francesca Annis, so it was an excellent cast. It was shot in a house in Kensington; we didn't have the money for a studio. Plus, it made the whole thing that much more realistic. Michael Reed shot it; he was very fast, very good and also wound up working as a DP for Hammer! The original title of the film was *A Time and a Place*, but that didn't last long; the producer, Michael Klinger, saw to that. Michael had a great deal of movie sense; he's the one who gave Roman Polanski a shot at directing his first English language feature with *Repulsion* [UK, 1965], which certainly launched his career in the UK. I hated the title and I hated the title music. It had nothing to do with the film! But they didn't consult me about it, so that's what happened. Still, I think the movie is rather good.

DIXON: The title music is ghastly – yes, it's true. But you can't be held responsible. But the thing that strikes me about the film is that it's a very feminist movie. It's really about a group of young women, told from their point of view, and it really gives you a sense of what the '60s were really like in London. You also have a very sympathetic gay couple in it.

O'HARA: Yes, which was quite intentional. That was the first gay kiss in the movies. They did a program on the BBC – a whole bit on it – when it came out. It was the first time anyone had seen two boys kissing in a film.

DIXON: This was your script; how long did it take you to write?

O'HARA: Well, I'll tell you how that happened. I started writing scripts on "spec," or speculation, hoping to get one of them financed. Looking for work, in other words. I had written four or five scripts and gotten absolutely nowhere. I would send them out to everyone I knew and they all wound up in the slush pile and no one was paying any attention to them. But luckily for me, Raymond Stross, the producer, was in the hospital having an operation and, to take his mind off his problems, he had his secretary send over a stack of scripts to read. I had no knowledge of any of this, but one morning around 7:30 the phone rang and it was Raymond. He said, "Listen, I read your script" – which wasn't *The Pleasure Girls*, it was another spec script

I'd written – "and I don't want to buy it, but I like the dialogue. Do you have anything else?" I said, "Yes, sure." So he said, "Well, bring it around to the hospital, which is just around the corner, and I'll read it."

So, two or three days later I got another phone call from him, with the same verdict: "I like the dialogue, but I don't want to buy it. You had better come and have tea with me when I get out of the hospital and see if we can't fix something up." So I went to have tea with him and he said, "Look, why aren't you writing about Chelsea? You live in Chelsea, you obviously hang around all the Chelsea clubs and things, the discos and all that sort of stuff. Why don't you write about that? That sounds more interesting to me than the rest of this stuff you've sent me." I went back to my flat. Now, at that time, I shared my flat with a young guy who wasn't in the film business at all, but he had a lot of common sense. He said, "Are you stupid or what? A producer takes the time to talk to you and tells you what he wants to see and you don't want to do it? Write the damned thing!" And I was so annoyed, I sat right down there with the typewriter and banged the script out. And then they bankrolled it and it turned out very well. Apart from the title and that damned theme song, I pretty much had a free hand. And the notices were very good – then and now, with the DVD release, which was a pleasant surprise.

DIXON: Now let me touch on some other work you did. You directed a couple of episodes of *The Avengers*: "The Hour That Never Was" [UK, 1965] and "Small Game for Big Hunters" [UK, 1966], with Patrick Macnee and Diana Rigg. These were two of the black-and-white filmed episodes, which I think were the best of the series.

O'HARA: I agree.

DIXON: What was Diana Rigg like to work with?

O'HARA: She was a very shrewd, very amusing girl. She had Patrick in her pocket. Patrick was just an amiable sort of David Niven kind of character. They knew exactly what they were doing; they used to rehearse in their dressing rooms and they would come down with a scene already worked out. And, if you had any sense, you went along with it. We took about 10 or 11 days to do an episode; it was quality television. But then Diana found out that the cameraman was making more money than she was and she quit. And I was hired to shoot a day's test with six women for a possible new partner for Patrick's character, John Steed.

DIXON: You were the one who was stuck with that?

O'HARA: Yes. I directed Linda Thorson's test and she got the part.

DIXON: Now, your next film as director was *Maroc 7* [UK, 1967]. What can you tell me about that?

O'HARA: Not a happy experience. Sidney Box had put me under contract after *The Pleasure Girls*. He saw *The Pleasure Girls* and he also saw *The Avengers* episodes I did and liked my work. He rang me that night that *The Avengers* went out, "The Hour That Never Was," and said, "Gerry, you know a few years ago, we would have made a movie out of that and made money with it. Come and see me." So he put me under contract. I was under contract to him for a couple of years. But nothing ever happened! Whatever we tried to set up didn't come off. And then Leslie Phillips, who was quite a good comedy actor, had seen *Pleasure Girls* and was about to produce his first feature, *Maroc 7*. So he went to Sidney and Sidney loaned me out to direct *Maroc 7*. I had nothing to say about it; I was under contract and I had to do it. Gene Barry was the star after another German actor, whose name I forget, pulled out, along with Elsa Martinelli, Cyd Charisse and Leslie Phillips, of course, acting in his own film. Not only that, but I went over budget. There were lots of problems.

DIXON: What about *Amsterdam Affair* [UK/Netherlands, 1968]?

O'HARA: That was part of my Sidney Box contract with a company called London Independent Producers. While I was with them, somebody brought along the book by Nicholas Freeling called *Love in Amsterdam*. Freeling was a British crime novelist and it was a solid piece of work. So they asked me if I would do the script. But, although I was under contract to them to direct, I wasn't under contract to them *to write*. I played this very close to the chest. I went to Amsterdam and met with Nicholas Freeling; he agreed to work with me for ten days. He wouldn't put a word on paper. He would only talk. And so we talked for ten days.

I went to Amsterdam twice. I laid out the locations, got ready to direct the film and then they called me in one day. Sidney by now had gone from the company and the guy who took over said, "Gerry, I've got some bad news for you. The completion guarantors won't accept you as the director because you went over budget on *Maroc 7*." I had been waiting for it to happen. I've always had a kind of slightly book-makerish cynicism. I knew somebody was going to pull the rug out from under me because of that, so I said, "Look, what are you going to do for a script?"

And the guy said, "What are you talking about?" I said, "Well, you don't own the script." He said, "We own it, we own the book." I said, "Sure you own the book, but you don't own the script. I own the script. I did it on spec. I'm not under contract to write, *just to direct*. So if you want my script, you'll have to let me direct." I had them over a barrel and they knew it.

So, I went to a meeting with the completion guarantors. They were very heavy characters, accountants with attitude. So, this was my one chance and I took it. Essentially I said, "Look, I'm the best possible person to shoot this movie because I have got to get off the hook with you. I guarantee to shoot this film bang on time, possibly under time. Give me a shot at it." So they sent me to Amsterdam with their own man, a very heavy production manager and he revised the schedule. He broke the script down into A, B and C scenes; scenes that were absolutely essential to the film, subplots that could be excised and then insert shots for added production value. The plan was that I would be allowed to shoot A scenes and I could shoot B scenes if I had time at the end of the day. C scenes would be shot by the second unit. Well, I shot the whole thing – A, B and C – and came in on time and under budget. By the end of the last week, I could have finished it a few days early, but I used up the time just to make this movie as pretty as I could. I'm very fond of it. It's a film I like enormously, but I can't find a copy of it.

DIXON: What about *All the Right Noises* [UK, 1971]?

O'HARA: Well, I love that film. That was Tom Bell, who was in *The L-Shaped Room*. Olivia Hussey was in that, as well. Tom had become a friend of mine and I wrote the script with him in mind. I gave it to [director and cinematographer] Nicolas Roeg – whom I've known forever – and said, "Do me a favor, Nic, and tell me what you think of this. It's been going the rounds and everybody's turned it down." Nic read it and said, "It's great, I like it very much, let me see what I can do." A few months later, Nic rang me up at half past 7 in the morning; he said, "Now, listen Gerry and listen carefully. A guy is going to call you, a guy named Si Litvinoff. I had dinner with him last night; he's the guy who produced my film *Walkabout* [UK, 1971]. Si told me that he's looking for something to do in England. I told him you had a great script, *All the Right Noises*, ready to go. He wants to buy it." And so it got made. Now, that's only because Nic told him the story. How lucky can you get?

DIXON: What about Jackie Collins' film *The Bitch* [UK, 1979]?

O'HARA: Well, that was a kind of cynical affair. I was hired to do *The Bitch* – to write it and direct it – on the condition that I did it for the same budget as *The Stud* [dir. Quentin Masters, UK, 1978], which was made a year earlier.

DIXON: And these were Joan Collins' "comeback" pictures, weren't they?

O'HARA: Yes, they were. As a result of *The Bitch*, she got the role on *Dynasty* and it ramped up her career all over again.

DIXON: Now, how did you become involved with the notoriously cost-conscious producer, Harry Alan Towers?

O'HARA: Well, when things were bad, my agent would scour around and try to get me work. And, one day, she got me to meet Harry in the late '60s and he and I established a kind of working friendship, which lasted until he died last year. But he was a real pirate, make no mistake.

DIXON: Was your version of *Fanny Hill* [UK, 1983] one of his productions?

O'HARA: That's right. He produced it; he wrote a kind of half-hour script for it. I didn't even use the script. I had a pretty good cast, though: Oliver Reed, Wilfrid Hyde-White (who died about a year later) and Shelley Winters, who was wonderful. She talked the whole time and then when you said "action" she went right into character.

DIXON: And what about *The Mummy Lives* [UK/Israel, 1993]?

O'HARA: The less said the better. That was produced by Yoram Globus, with Tony Curtis in the lead. It was supposed to be Chris Lee, but he wisely bowed out of the project before it went forward. We shot it in Tel Aviv.

DIXON: Looking back at your long and involved career, you worked with so many people. You made such a great beginning with *Pleasure Girls*, but then, after that, luck seemed to run against you. Why didn't you make the jump to a full-fledged directorial career, in your opinion? What prevented you?

O'HARA: Well, in the '60s, people like Richard Lester and those guys were all the rage. I didn't fit in with that set. My real problem was that, when Sidney Box retired, I didn't have a producer. I didn't have an advocate. I had Harry Alan Towers, who used me, but that wasn't the same. You know, he was a very tough guy and he used to phone me up and say, "Gerry, come and see me; I'm going to cross your palm with silver." But that's all it was – silver.

DIXON: He was a real operator. That was basically it. But I'm so glad for you that *Pleasure Girls* has come out and has found a new twenty-first century audience.

O'HARA: That and *All the Right Noises*. It's certainly a better picture, at least in my opinion. More money was spent. It was a nine week shoot. And, of course, it's my own script and I had pretty much total creative control, which is very rare. As I told you, Nicolas Roeg helped set that up for me and I think it's probably my best film. Some things I did simply for the pension fund. But I've done a lot of things I'm proud of, that really still hold up for me and, for that, I'm grateful.

Chapter 14

ANDREW V. MCLAGLEN: LAST OF THE HOLLYWOOD PROFESSIONALS*

Andrew V. McLaglen (he is quite insistent on retaining the "V" in his name, as part of his authorial signature) is without a doubt one of the last of the classical Hollywood filmmakers who worked during the Golden Age of the studio system. Coming of age when his father – the gifted actor Victor McLaglen – won an Oscar for Best Actor for his performance in John Ford's *The Informer* (1935; Ford himself also won as Best Director that year, as did Max Steiner for his music score and Dudley Nichols for the screenplay), young Andrew worked and lived with the cream of Hollywood's most original and idiosyncratic artists. In addition to John Ford, he knew and/or worked with John "Duke" Wayne, William Wellman, Budd Boetticher and Cary Grant and later carved out a career for himself as a director in the Western genre that few can equal. Even now, he is still going strong, directing stage productions of such classics as Arthur Miller's *Death of a Salesman* and keeping an interested eye on the business.

In all his work, Andrew V. McLaglen was a genuine artist, but one who also kept an eye on the bottom line and kept his projects moving. And, as you will see, although he is best known for his work as a director of Westerns, he feels that he did some of his best work in other genres. At 89, McLaglen is still as sharp as a tack – his memory is clear and strong and his personal history is pretty much a history of the medium itself. Most telling, he is generous to others in telling his story and eager to acknowledge the talents of the many actors and directors whom he worked with. But let him tell his story to you directly, as he did to me in February 2009.

WHEELER WINSTON DIXON: You were born on 28 July 1920 in London and your father was the actor Victor McLaglen, which makes you

---

* A version of this chapter was first published in 2009 by *Senses of Cinema* (online) as "Andrew V. McLaglen: Last of the Hollywood Professionals" (issue 50): http://sensesofcinema.com/2009/50/andrew-v-mclaglen-interview/.

roughly 15 years old when he won the Academy Award for *The Informer*. What can you tell me about your early childhood, your early growing-up years and your education?

ANDREW V. MCLAGLEN: As a young child, I was schooled conventionally, then I went to Black Fox Military in the fifth grade. From the fifth grade through the eighth grade, I went to a school on Beverly Boulevard called The Carl Curtis School [now called simply The Curtis School]. It was an academic school, along with a strong emphasis on physical education. All the kids at the school were doing gym exercises every single day – special exercises to, you know, to keep you in good shape, everything you could think of. It was a very thorough education. And, through my life, I've known what the names of all the bones in the human body are and everything just through my basic grade school education there.

DIXON: When was the first time that you realized that your father was doing something other than ordinary work, so to speak?

MCLAGLEN: Well, I think it was when he starred in Josef von Sternberg's *Dishonored* [1931] with Marlene Dietrich, which made quite a splash. But he had been in the business a long time before, of course, going back to his first film, A. E. Coleby's *The Call of the Road* [1920], which was made the year I was born. Then, of course, he moved over to the States. He and Edmund Lowe were giant stars in the late '20s, starting with Raoul Walsh's *What Price Glory* [1926], which was their first movie together. They worked together doing six or seven movies – way up into the '30s somewhere – and became a very well known team. His pictures did a *lot* of business. I remember receiving a watch my dad gave me years ago – a platinum watch that they gave him at the Roxy Theater in New York as the biggest box-office star of that time. It was when he made a personal appearance and it was about that time I realized he was working in a different sort of profession, something the public noticed.

DIXON: Did you hang around on the set when he worked? What was your relationship like with your father?

MCLAGLEN: I can remember going as a sub-teenager to the set, but not that often. I went to boarding school, so I didn't do much of it then, except when I graduated from high school in 1938 and I spent two weeks on the set of George Stevens' *Gunga Din* [1939]. Then I got to see George Stevens, Cary Grant, my father and Douglas Fairbanks, Jr. in action, which was quite an experience! I just kept out of the way because they were working hard; they had a picture to make! I had another school buddy with me at the time – we were 18 and 19 years old – and we had a terrific time. We got to know Cary and Doug, Jr. and Joan Fontaine – what a great group of people they were! And George Stevens; in years to come, whenever I bumped into him, we would always talk about those *Gunga Din* days because I think that was one of his favorite projects.

DIXON: It's a fantastic film. Now, at this point, did you get the idea that maybe you were interested in making movies?

MCLAGLEN: Yeah, I got the idea when I was in high school at Cates School in Santa Barbara [now the Cate School]. I got a 16mm camera and I got together with my friends and I made little movies there. This was in the late 1930s. That's when I first really got really interested in it – from the ninth grade onwards.

DIXON: Did you ever try to convince your father to be in any of your films at that point?

MCLAGLEN: I never did, no. These were school things that we did as a bunch of friends and we didn't get any adults involved. Well, this is very early on, you know, for people to be making movies. Then, right after I graduated, I went to the University of Virginia. I was on the freshman boxing team. I only stayed there one year because, if you really wanna know the truth, I fell in love with a gal from Stanford. One interesting thing: when I was a freshman there, [future director] Robert Aldrich was a senior.

DIXON: Did you meet him?

MCLAGLEN: Oh, yeah – he knew me and he even tried to get me into his fraternity. He was on the Virginia football team. Then I went home and World War II was just about getting started. My parents were very close friends of Robert E. Gross, who was the Chairman of the Board of Lockheed Aircraft. And he said, "Do you think Andrew would like to come and work here?" Which was funny because I was drafted right away, so it looked like that wouldn't happen, but everything turned out fine. I was as good as in the Army, you know, except when it came to my height. I stood on a scale during the induction physical and the little guy who was taking my height had a stool he had to stand on because the ruler came out of his hands. I was six feet seven. That's where I got my nickname, Big A, which stuck from that point on. Anyway, the little guy didn't know what to do. I'll always remember that he didn't say a word. He just got down and took a little yellow pad and he wrote "4F" [unfit for military service because of a physical handicap] on it and gave it to me.

Figure 14. *McClintock!*
Source: Author's collection.

DIXON: 4F! Just because of your height!

MCLAGLEN: Yeah, 4F. So, I wasn't in the Army. But, instead of being in the Army, I spent four years chasing ring corrugations for the P38 all over the factory at Lockheed. I didn't wanna do *that* for my whole life! So, by the time the war was over, the question was "What am I gonna do?" When I got out of Lockheed, my father said, "The one thing I'm gonna advise you is don't go in the picture business. It's disappointing, it's hard work, it's full of ups and downs and I just suggest that you skip that." Well, I didn't take his suggestion. Instead, I wrote a letter to Herbert J. Yates, the head of Republic Pictures. I told him who I was and I said, "I really wanna get into the motion picture business" and so on. He wrote me a letter back and said, "Come to work."

DIXON: Why did you pick Republic and not one of the major studios?

MCLAGLEN: Well, the only reason I picked Republic is 'cause, at that particular moment, my father was about to make a movie there.

DIXON: The first credit I have on you – and maybe this is wrong – is as an assistant director on Albert Rogell's 1945 film, *Love, Honor and Goodbye*.

MCLAGLEN: You're exactly right.

DIXON: So, what was your baptism of fire like as an assistant director?

MCLAGLEN: Well, I didn't start as an AD on *Love, Honor and Goodbye*. I was what we call a company clerk.

DIXON: A go-fer.

MCLAGLEN: I had to make the call sheet and check up on the weather to see if it was okay to go on location. So, yeah, you're right: a go-fer.

DIXON: Then I have a gap from you between '45 and '51 when you worked with Budd Boetticher on *Bullfighter and the Lady* [1951]. What happened?

MCLAGLEN: After two years at Republic or so, I decided I wanted to be a second assistant director. I remember I said, "Now, how in the hell am I gonna do it?" Every morning, Herbert Yates would drive in in his big limousine, get out and walk along this long path to go into his office. I hid in the bushes one morning and met him halfway. I kind of jumped out of the bushes at him. I said, "Mr. Yates, I really feel like I'm ready to become a second assistant." And he said, "Oh, I remember you, son. I'll look into it." And that was it, believe it or not. I became a second assistant, but it was when the war was just over and all the guys are coming back. So, I didn't have much job security. Then the studio said, "Sorry, Andrew, we're gonna have to lay you off now because the fellas are coming back from the war." That's when they took away my permit from the Directors Guild because, until I'd done a sixth picture, I was riding on a permit and not a full Guild membership. So, they took my permit away, but I happened to read the bylaws of The Guild and it said, "After six pictures, you're automatically a member." So, I wrote to Yates again. I said, "If you read your bylaws, I'm automatically a member of the Guild because [I had done six pictures and] I'll have to sue you." He didn't want that, so in '46 or '47, I became a member of the Directors Guild.

DIXON: I don't have any credits for you between '45 and '51.

MCLAGLEN: Oh, I did a whole bunch of movies. But, in those days, it wasn't a Guild rule that second assistant be given credit. I know I worked on some films with Budd Boetticher at Monogram with Roddy McDowall, who was just a kid then.

DIXON: Yes, that was called *Killer Shark* [1950].

McLaglen: That's it! You got it. My God Almighty, yeah.

Dixon: When I interviewed Boetticher shortly before his death, he called Monogram "really second rate."

McLaglen: Absolutely. But it was a good thing being on that picture with Budd. I was only a second assistant, but we became friends. And Budd said, "You know, I've written this script" and I said, "Listen, let me see it. Maybe I can do something with it." So I took the script and, because I'd worked with Duke [John Wayne], you know, in my very first picture as a second assistant, *Dakota* [1945] …

Dixon: Joseph Kane, who directed literally hundreds of Westerns, directed that. You were the second assistant on that?

McLaglen: Uh-huh. With John Wayne and Vera Hruba Ralston. And Wayne took a liking to me. He'd already known my father for a long time – all the way up through my years at Republic. So, when I took Budd's script to him in 1950, I was still a second. I said, "Take a look at this, Duke, and see what you think." I told Budd, "If by some miracle Duke can get Mr. Yates to make this movie, I want you to make me the associate producer." He says, "You got it." So, Yates liked it and we went down to Mexico and did *Bullfighter and the Lady*. That was when I became a first assistant.

Dixon: And you actually got credit on it as "Andy McLaglen."

McLaglen: Yeah. Whether Budd tried or didn't try, I didn't get my associate producer credit, but at least I became a first assistant. I was a first from then on. But then Mr. Yates had decided to make [John Ford's] *The Quiet Man* [1952]. They knew that I knew Duke well and that I had known John Ford since I was about 13 years old.

Dixon: But you were the second assistant on that film.

McLaglen: You're right and here's why. Yates said, "Look, we can't make you the first on that because Wingate Smith is John Ford's brother-in-law and he's his first."

Dixon: Makes sense.

McLaglen: "Would you go over as the second?" "On *that* picture?" I said. "You bet I will."

Dixon: A wise decision… and a free trip to Ireland, to boot.

McLaglen: Absolutely. Except, when I got over there, Wingate was my roommate and we got along fine. But he was an old guy by that time, so I actually was the first assistant on *The Quiet Man* for the entire movie and old Wingate stood aside and let me do it. I

	really stepped up to the plate and I'll never forget it. I worked my ass off for John Ford.
DIXON:	What was your impression of Ford? I've heard so many different stories about him – and about John Wayne – with lots of different opinions. Give me your take.
MCLAGLEN:	My take on Ford was that he was kind of a mysterious character – a very unusual personality. You'd have to almost meet him to understand something about him. Unpredictable.
DIXON:	Practically blind, right?
MCLAGLEN:	Blind in one eye and he sometimes wore an eye patch.
DIXON:	And used to chew on a handkerchief while he was shooting.
MCLAGLEN:	You're absolutely right. It was a nervous habit. He used to chew on his handkerchief all the time.
DIXON:	And he shot to the cut, didn't he?
MCLAGLEN:	He would shoot to the cut. In other words, he would pretty much shoot only what he needed. Totally economical. I mean pictures like *She Wore a Yellow Ribbon* [1949] and *Fort Apache* [1948] – he made those in like six weeks!
DIXON:	I know. It's just amazing.
MCLAGLEN:	And when he made *The Informer* with my dad, he shot that in 27 days.
DIXON:	I know. That was supposed to be a "B" picture and it broke through to an "A" status, won a bunch of Oscars and everybody was very surprised.
MCLAGLEN:	Oh, yeah, yeah. It was a real victory for my father, 'cause to win the Best Actor Oscar he had to knock off Clark Gable, Charles Laughton and Franchot Tone for [Frank Lloyd's] *Mutiny on the Bounty* [1935].
DIXON:	Tough competition.
MCLAGLEN:	Tough competition. And, as we're talking, I'm looking at my father's Academy Award that he won that night.
DIXON:	What happened after you did *The Quiet Man*?
MCLAGLEN:	I became almost a contract first assistant for Batjac with John Wayne.
DIXON:	John Wayne's company.
MCLAGLEN:	And that was another great experience because, though I didn't get to work with Ford anymore, I did four or five movies with William A. Wellman.
DIXON:	"Wild Bill" Wellman.
MCLAGLEN:	That's right. We went through *The High and the Mighty* [1954], *Island in the Sky* [1953], *Track of the Cat* [1954] and *Blood Alley* [1955].

That was one of my best experiences I've ever had because Bill Wellman was fantastic. And, boy, when you're *his* assistant, you're not just a production assistant. You were *his* assistant. He would call me up at 5:30 in the morning and say, "Hey, Andrew, good morning, what are you doing?" I'd say, "Sleeping." And he'd say, "Well, how about breakfast?" I'd say, "Okay, what time?" "How's 6:30?" So, I'd run over to his house. It was his seven kids and his wife and we'd all sit around the table and have breakfast with him. I *really* loved working with Bill Wellman. He just loved making movies and knew *exactly* what he was doing. But *Blood Alley* was my last movie as a first assistant because Bob Morrison and I found a little script and Duke knew that I wanted to be a director. So, one day, he said, "I'll tell you what. If you guys can put it together, I'll guarantee the budget at the bank."

DIXON: Wow, that's a real vote of confidence.

McLAGLEN: Not many people knew that.

DIXON: That's a hell of a kind gesture.

McLAGLEN: That's how I became a director, with a little film called *Man in the Vault* [1956]. The funny thing was, it wasn't a Western. It was a crime picture – almost a noir film – with William Campbell, Anita Ekberg and Mike Mazurki. But the thing is, when you move up to being a director and you just do a little picture, how are you gonna keep on being a director? So, Bob Morrison and I found another script, which became my next picture, *Gun the Man Down* [1956]. When I was working as first on this, the picture we made in Hawaii in the early '50s...

DIXON: Edward Ludwig's *Big Jim McLain* [1952].

McLAGLEN: ...yeah, *Big Jim McLain*... I'd gotten to know Jim Arness very well. And Jim Arness happened to be under contract to Duke. And, all of a sudden, Jim became a big star with the TV series *Gunsmoke*.

DIXON: Which made him totally bankable.

McLAGLEN: Yeah. So, I went and saw the vice president of United Artists and said, "What if I give you Jim Arness and Angie Dickinson in this script and shoot it in ten days?"

DIXON: Ten days? That's a very tight schedule.

McLAGLEN: I put Harry Carey, Jr. into that also and Bill Clothier was the cameraman. That was my second one.

DIXON: What was the budget on that, if I may ask?

McLAGLEN: Oh, my gosh. You know, the budgets were so small then...

DIXON: A hundred grand, something like that?

McLAGLEN: Yeah, a little more than that. I know I was making $2,500 a week back then, which today is like nothing. But, in 1956 dollars, it was quite a lot. So, after I finished *Gun the Man Down*, my next thought was, "What am I gonna do next?" You can't stop; you've gotta keep looking for that next project. We found another script and what do you think that was? Budd Boetticher's *Seven Men from Now* [1956].

DIXON: But you didn't wind up directing that film.

McLAGLEN: No, I didn't. I just took it for granted that, if we made the picture, I would direct it. But Bob Fellows, who was Duke's partner, for some reason told Warners that he'd much rather have Budd Boetticher direct it. So, Budd directed it and that was that. I did get a producer credit out of it, but that wasn't what I wanted. I wanted to keep on directing.

In the meantime, Arness had done a year of *Gunsmoke*. And he said to CBS, "Why don't you try McLaglen on a couple of *Gunsmoke* episodes? I just did a movie, *Gun the Man Down*, with him and that worked out well." So, I signed up for a couple of *Gunsmoke*s. And, to cut it real short, I hold the record for the number of episodes of *Gunsmoke* directed: 96 between 1956 and 1965. Each of those episodes was done in six days; that's it. You couldn't go over. Anyway, during that period, they made a pilot for *Have Gun – Will Travel*. They took me off *Gunsmoke* for a little bit and put me on *Have Gun – Will Travel* and, the next thing you know, I had directed 116 episodes on *that*!

DIXON: Tell me about Richard Boone [star of *Have Gun – Will Travel*].

McLAGLEN: He became a very close friend of mine. We worked together for six solid years. But, during that time, I also did five movies. I went to CBS and said, "Look, will you let me off for three or four weeks, I wanna do a little movie." And they said, "Okay." That's when I did *The Abductors* [1957] and *The Little Shepherd of Kingdom Come* [1961].

DIXON: What was it like directing your father in *The Abductors*? This was an odd little period crime drama about two men trying to hold Abraham Lincoln's body for ransom. Your father was joined by George Macready, Fay Spain and some other talented actors in this little film.

McLAGLEN: Yeah, I loved it. I made the picture in ten days. He just did it as a favor for me.

DIXON: Then, back on television, you directed a bunch of *Perry Masons* and seven episodes of *Rawhide* with Clint Eastwood. What was Eastwood like at that point in his career, which is very early on?

MCLAGLEN: He was great; he was just starting out. You know, it's funny – on that show, Eric Fleming [an actor who appeared in the series] was sort of the boss. He was kind of a grumpy guy. I remember Clint as being a good guy, easy to work with, always on time, always knew his lines. It's a kick when I think back. If then you were gonna tell me that Clint was gonna become one of the biggest icons that's ever hit the screen, I wouldn't have believed you. But he's done some incredible work in his career.

DIXON: Well, the next picture I have you directing is a big budget Western, *McLintock!* [1963].

MCLAGLEN: Oh, *McLintock!* was my big break – with Duke and Maureen O'Hara. Big box-office hit, big picture. And that put me in the big time.

DIXON: That film was tied up in some rights problems for years and years and you couldn't see it anywhere. Now it's come out on DVD in the past couple of years. You know anything about that or not?

MCLAGLEN: Well, it might have been because Duke's family owned it. When Michael Wayne – Duke's oldest son – died, his widow took over all the pictures. And she went over to Paramount and struck a DVD deal. That was on all the pictures that I did with Duke. I think he owned *Chisum* [1970], too.

DIXON: But after *McLintock!*, you actually went over and did an episode of *The Virginian*, which was the first 90-minute television series.

MCLAGLEN: One episode. That's it. No more. It was okay, but I didn't wanna slip back to TV when I was doing so well as a feature director. I got another feature off the ground fast, *Shenandoah* [1965] and then *The Rare Breed* [1966]. That came right after *Shenandoah*.

DIXON: What was it like working with Jimmy Stewart?

MCLAGLEN: I loved it. He was a great actor, always professional, knew what he wanted – a real solid actor. I did four pictures with him.

DIXON: You worked a lot with Maureen O'Hara too.

MCLAGLEN: I did two with Maureen and with Jimmy, including *Bandolero!* [1968] and my favorite of all, *Fools' Parade* [1971].

DIXON: How would you describe the way that you approached directing actors? When you have somebody like Jimmy Stewart, who knows what he's doing, or John Wayne, would you just run through it and then just shoot it? What's your approach to working with actors?

McLAGLEN: Well, by the time I was directing Duke and Jimmy, I had done 200-plus TV pictures. And, you know, there's one thing about doing television: you're taught to, without sacrificing anything in the way of production values, keep things on time and move forward. You find yourself doing things on budget, on schedule, no problems. And Duke and I got along fine. That's the only reason, after *McLintock!*, I did five more movies with Duke. He knew what he was doing and so did I. He had a lot of faith in me.

DIXON: I understand what you're saying because directing television is great practice for getting things done on time and under budget.

McLAGLEN: You can't beat it. You either get it done or they find someone else.

DIXON: How many setups did you have to do a day on *Gunsmoke*?

McLAGLEN: Oh, my – I don't remember it. But I remember my first day on the *Man in the Vault* vividly. I did 51 setups. Don't ask me how. It was crazy, but that's what you had to do. That's what you gotta do. I was well prepared. That's one important thing: you have to know the next setup and exactly what you're doing.

DIXON: Do you storyboard?

McLAGLEN: I never used a storyboard very much. I didn't like those too much. If I did my homework, I knew what I wanted to do and I didn't have to hunt around until noon to get my first shot.

DIXON: Would you more or less set up the master and then go in for the close-ups and do it that way?

McLAGLEN: Well, yeah. It depends on what the scene is, but that's usually how I'd do it.

DIXON: How did you then get involved with *The Ballad of Josie* [1967] with Doris Day?

McLAGLEN: Oh, that was because I had a multiple picture contract at Universal. My time came up to do a movie and they said, "Would you do a picture with Doris Day?" I said, "You bet." She was another complete professional. That was a lot of fun to shoot.

DIXON: And then, after that, you went over to Disney to make *Monkeys, Go Home* [1967].

McLAGLEN: That's Maurice Chevalier's last movie.

DIXON: I know, with Dean Jones and Yvette Mimieux.

McLAGLEN: I gotta tell you, I *loved* working with Maurice Chevalier. That's the main reason I took on the picture – just to get a chance to work with him. He was a terrific guy, just a terrific guy. Total pro, knew his lines. Everything was good about him, you know. As a matter of fact, that picture was kind of fun because I had those damn chimpanzees to work with. [Laughs]

DIXON: Your next film was *The Way West* [1967].

MCLAGLEN: *The Way West* was, to me, one of the things I dream about today because I thought it was a terrific picture. I had Richard Widmark, Kirk Douglas, Bob Mitchum and Sally Field, in her first movie. She was incredible; you could tell, even then, that she'd be a big name in the business. It was fun to shoot and UA thought it was great. I was really happy with it. But then, after the whole thing was shot, they called me up and said, "We're releasing the picture, but we want to cut 22 minutes off the beginning." I thought it was just perfect as it was. But they thought it was too long and we had to bring it back in, which cost a fortune because we had to cut it *after* we released it. I mean, how dumb can you get? It's stupid. So I had to go over to the Goldwyn Studio and sit with my producer, Harold Hecht, and try and nip and tuck here and there to cut some footage out. And I think I hurt the picture because, in that movie, I showed you the beginning of each character and their whole story and how the whole thing developed. It was a great novel [by A. B. Guthrie, Jr.] and it was a great screenplay. Ben Maddow wrote the screenplay and Bob Mitchum was very tickled doing the movie 'cause he loved the novel.

DIXON: You shot that on location in Bend, Oregon, didn't you?

MCLAGLEN: Bend, Oregon and Eugene.

DIXON: After this, we go to *The Devil's Brigade* [1968], a war picture with William Holden and Cliff Robertson.

MCLAGLEN: *The Devil's Brigade* took me all over the map and finally to Italy. Originally, they sent me up to Salt Lake City to do the picture. And the art director was hunting all over the side of a mountain, trying to find the right place to build a village here. The producer was David L. Wolper, who did a lot of stuff for TV, and I said, "Jesus, you're gonna spend all that money to build a set? It's gonna be a lot cheaper for us to go to Italy and find a little town." He said, "Well, maybe you're right." So they went to the studio and guess what? They agreed with me; it *was* cheaper. That's when we went to Italy. Now, I showed the finished cut to United Artists and they just loved *The Devil's Brigade*. They said, "Well, we never try to tell you what to do artistically, but I wouldn't touch anything and especially the stuff with Bill Holden." But the producer had a big projection room in his house and he showed the movie for a solid week to a hundred

	people and I think a hundred people had ideas of what we should do with the movie.
Dixon:	Oh, God.
McLaglen:	And without me having any input – I didn't have the last say – they cut the movie and, in the end, it was not nearly as good as it could have been. I had a great ending and a lot of good stuff in there and he didn't know what he was doing. I still worry about that.
Dixon:	Your first directorial credit was a crime film, *Man in the Vault*, but you rapidly became the "go-to" guy for Westerns.
McLaglen:	I know it.
Dixon:	Do you have a real love for the Western genre?
McLaglen:	No, that was really by mistake.
Dixon:	You're kidding.
McLaglen:	It was totally by mistake because first I did *Man in the Vault*. Then I got a Western, *Gun the Man Down* [1956], because I knew Jim Arness. Then, as I told you, I wound up doing a whole bunch of *Gunsmoke* episodes. I then became the "Western Director" – the star over at CBS. Then everybody thinks, "Jesus, that's his big specialty."
Dixon:	How did you feel about being typed as a Western director?
McLaglen:	Not good, not good.
Dixon:	That's interesting 'cause I always thought that you had a real affection for it.
McLaglen:	No, I didn't. It was what happened. It's the way my course was laid for me.
Dixon:	So, what other kind of films would you have liked to have done?
McLaglen:	Well, that's a big question. There are probably a lot of would-haves. But, as it is, I consider myself very fortunate having had a career and having worked with so many great people. I know that that time has gone by now. I've had more calls [for interviews] lately than I've ever had. Maybe 'cause I'm the only one around.
Dixon:	Did you enjoy making *Hellfighters* [1968], which was a "non-Western" project?
McLaglen:	*Hellfighters* was fun because it was a story about "Red" Adair, the guy who made a living putting out oil well fires all around the world. Duke was in it, of course, and Red was my technical advisor on the film. We shot that down in Houston, Texas and Casper, Wyoming and, of course, it had one of my favorite people to work with, Katharine Ross. I put her in her first movie. That was *Shenandoah*. Before that, I had her in television.

DIXON: And now we come to *Chisum* [1970], one of the last classic Westerns, with John Wayne and Forrest Tucker.

MCLAGLEN: Duke owned the negative on that baby. Warner Brothers released it; it was originally made for Fox and then Fox sold it over to Warner Brothers. That's got a really amazing cast. In addition to Duke and Forrest Tucker, it had Christopher George, who was a damned good actor, and his wife, Lynda Day George, to say nothing of old timers like Bruce Cabot and Patrick Knowles, who both go way, way back. Patrick Knowles had a big, big part because *Chisum* was a true story about "Billy the Kid." The Englishman [J. Henry Tunstall in the film] was a real character who befriended "Billy the Kid," who was played in the film by a guy named Geoffrey Deuel. Knowles' character eventually got killed by the bad guys for his trouble.

DIXON: Then you did *One More Train to Rob* [1971].

MCLAGLEN: *One More Train to Rob* was one of my Universal pictures that I did with George Peppard, which was just an okay movie. It's played an awful lot on TV, but it isn't my favorite by a long shot. After that, I did *Cahill U.S. Marshal* in 1973, which was a good picture and another chance to work with the Duke. Then I had a little bit of a lapse. I did a couple of family pictures for Disney on television and then I got called back to Twentieth Century Fox to do a picture with Charlton Heston and James Coburn, *The Last Hard Men*, which was shot in 1975 and released in 1976.

DIXON: But then you did a big picture, *The Wild Geese* [1978], which is emphatically *not* a Western.

MCLAGLEN: Oh, man, that was fabulous! That was a whole new start for my career, man, are you kidding? That was great. A really solid action war picture with a superb cast: Richard Burton, Roger Moore, Richard Harris, Stewart Granger – just incredible. This producer called me up. I'd only met him once before – Euan Lloyd, an English producer. And he said, "You know, I was talking to John Ford one day just before he died [in 1973]," and Ford asked him who was gonna direct *The Wild Geese* and he said they hadn't thought of a director yet. So Ford said, "Well, you ought to try that young McLaglen 'cause he really knows how to make pictures." Well, I never knew that, except when he told me that Ford had really helped me there. But he was like that – he would sort of help you behind your back. And so, I did the film. Hell, I loved that movie. It had a great script by Reginald Rose, who's a damn, damn good writer. I thought, "I'm back in the big time, thank God," because I had a little slump there. After that, I did *The Sea Wolves* [1980], which was another big war picture and, again, I was working with a top shelf cast: Gregory Peck, Roger Moore, Trevor Howard and David Niven. I was back on top. I then did another film in Berlin with Richard Burton and Rod Steiger, which came out here as *Breakthrough* [1979], which was a good film. But then, in '81, I got what I really enjoyed doing – seven hours of *The Blue and the Gray* [released in 1982]. It was for television, but it had a first-class budget and a great script. It was nominated for four Emmys. Again, an incredible cast: Stacy Keach, Lloyd Bridges, Rory Calhoun, Coleen Dewhurst, Geraldine Page, Rip Torn, Robert Vaughn, Sterling Hayden, Paul Winfield and Gregory Peck. How can you go wrong?

DIXON: You did all seven hours of that?

MCLAGLEN: All seven.

DIXON: That's a hell of an accomplishment.

MCLAGLEN: That was a big, big thing on TV. And it's out on DVD now too, you know.

DIXON: And then the last picture I have for you is *Return from the River Kwai* [1989].

MCLAGLEN: *Return from the River Kwai*, yes. A good picture – a sort of sequel to the David Lean film. That was shot in '88; it came out in '89. And then I did another picture in Europe. Took me all over Europe: *Eye of the Widow* [1989]. That is one we don't even wanna go into. It had a Corsican producer. I came home at Christmas, then was going back to finish cutting it. But he just stole the whole movie and took it to Paris. That was the last I heard or saw of it. I know it was released all over Europe. I'm still getting slight, little returns on it, but it drives you nuts to have something like that happen. I figured that was enough. So I just retired from making movies in '90. Then, in '97, I moved up here on this island and I've got a beautiful spot here. You wouldn't even believe it.

DIXON: This is on San Juan Island in Washington State. I understand that you're still directing plays for the San Juan Island Community Theater.

MCLAGLEN: Absolutely right. We have a 300 seat, state-of-the-art legitimate theater here.

DIXON: So, you're still directing.

MCLAGLEN: Well, I've just finished my seventeenth play in 17 years.

DIXON: What kind of stuff do you do?

McLaglen: *Death of a Salesman.* All of the first-rate stuff, everything you can think of. Chekhov's *Uncle Vanya*, *The Cherry Orchard*, things like that. We do a lot of Neil Simon's plays.

Dixon: I understand that your son, Josh, is an assistant director and works in a lot of big pictures.

McLaglen: Well, Josh is to, to me… Okay, I'm bragging now.

Dixon: That's okay.

McLaglen: I think he's probably one of the three top first assistant directors in the whole business. And, of course, what really got him off is that he was first assistant on [James Cameron's] *Titanic* [1997]. That was a big production and he's been doing nothing but big pictures ever since.

Dixon: And your daughter, Mary, is an executive producer and a unit production manager.

McLaglen: Yes, she's doing a lot of good stuff. I also have another daughter, Sharon, who for 20 years was a script analyst at Warner Brothers and, after that, was a script analyst for ten years at MGM. And she's my oldest daughter and she lives up here now, where I live. Mary has a house right next door to me here.

Dixon: What do you think about some of the recent Westerns, like George P. Cosmatos' *Tombstone* [1993]?

McLaglen: Oh, I love *Tombstone*.

Dixon: What do you think of Clint Eastwood's movies as a director?

McLaglen: I have nothing but admiration for Clint. I just think he's great. I love his Westerns and also his newer stuff, like *Gran Torino* [2009], which is a damn good film. The thing I like about *Gran Torino* is that he shot the film in about 30 days on location, no nonsense – "Get in and get out," you know? Do you remember when Clint got the Oscar for directing *Million Dollar Baby* [2004]? He thanked everybody and started to walk away from the microphone. Suddenly, he jumped back in and said, "And I shot it in 37 days, too." I always got a kick out of Clint for that. I love it when someone can do something very economically. At this point, he can do anything he wants to do and I also love *Changeling* [2008].

Dixon: I agree. I'm really happy to hear that you're keeping up on all this stuff.

McLaglen: I do. You have to. That's what life's about.

Chapter 15

POP STAR, DIRECTOR, ACTOR: AN INTERVIEW WITH MICHAEL SARNE*

Michael Sarne has had a multifaceted career as a director, actor and even a pop singer and managed along the way to direct one of the most notorious films of all time: *Myra Breckinridge* (1970). Needless to say, he's had a fascinating career and I jumped at the chance to interview him. Born in 1940 in London, Sarne spent most of the early 1960s singing and had a British pop hit with the novelty tune "Come Outside," with assistance from Wendy Richard; during this period, Sarne also worked intermittently as a TV quiz show host. Sarne pretty much knew everyone who was part of the scene that became known as "Swinging London" and soon he was moving in the inner circles of the entertainment business. Sarne has also directed a number of television commercials, done film criticism for various cinema journals – such as *Sight and Sound* – and continues to moonlight as a pop singer in his spare time, in addition to numerous acting gigs. Through a series of chance encounters, blind luck, coupled with shrewd calculation, Sarne was soon directing the lavish Technicolor musical *Joanna* (1968) and then parlayed that into a contract with Twentieth Century Fox in Hollywood. Since then, he's been involved in a variety of other projects, but let him tell it in this interview from 30 April 2011, arranged by Jill Reading of the BFI.

WHEELER WINSTON DIXON: Well, I've been looking over all of your credits and it seems as if you did just about everything at one point or another in your career, so I'm just going to basically touch on a lot of that. First off, you were born Michael Scheuer on 6 August 1940 in London?

MICHAEL SARNE: Yes.

---

* A version of this chapter was first published in 2011 as "Pop Star, Director, Actor: An Interview with Michael Sarne," *Film International* 9(5): 30–6.

Figure 15. Raquel Welch and Michael Sarne on the set of *Myra Breckinridge*.
Source: Author's collection.

DIXON: I was intrigued by the 1962 pop record you made, "Come Outside," as one of your early ventures into show business; you were about 21 or 22 at the time.

SARNE: That was produced by Robert Stigwood. A lot of my bios say that it was produced by Joe Meek, the guy who did the instrumental hit "Telstar" with The Tornadoes, but it isn't so. I did meet Joe a couple of times and I made a record called "Just Like Eddie" with him, which didn't chart. Joe and Stigwood were going through a little breakup at that time. During that time, Joe made a couple of records with a guy called John Leyton [a pop personality of the era], whom I actually saw yesterday.

DIXON: Yes, he was in [the pop musical with Freddie and the Dreamers] *Seaside Swingers* [aka *Every Day's a Holiday*, dir. James Hill, 1965], wasn't he?

SARNE: Yes and so was I. As it happens, we just did a gig last night – John Leyton and I – the first time we'd done a gig together in 50 years or something. We went back on the road and sang our old songs.

DIXON: What are some of those song titles?

SARNE:	Well, he did "Johnny, Remember Me" and I did "Come Outside" and "Will I Want" and I did some Chuck Berry numbers like "Roll Over Beethoven," "Johnny B. Goode" and things like that. Can you imagine, after 50 years?
DIXON:	But you're already working in film at the time; I have a credit for you as an extra in *Sink the Bismarck* [dir. Lewis Gilbert, 1960].
SARNE:	Yes, well, I had one line I think.
DIXON:	How did you get into the film business?
SARNE:	Well, I was in college at London University. My mother was in Paris at the time. My parents split up, so I lived with my father in London – he was an archeologist and a traveling salesman in dental goods. They were both refugees from Europe, my parents. They managed to get across the border from Czechoslovakia. So, I was living at the time in Soho with my father and going to college. I lived on Compton Street and worked in a coffee bar. So, I was a waiter there and I was studying Russian at the university and, at the same time, I was looking for work as an actor or singer because I had already done a bit of singing and guitar playing before. I was in a skiffle group and met this guy, Robert Stigwood, who later managed the Bee Gees and became quite a force in the music industry.

Through him, I met his partner, Stephen Komlosy, and he asked me if I wanted to do any modeling. I didn't meet Stigwood – I met his partner, Stephen Komlosy. They were partners and Komlosy ran the modeling end of the agency while Stigwood ran the musical end of it. So, I went off for a weekend to do a Kodak modeling commercial; it was all advertising. That went very well and I actually got paid! Then Stigwood asked me, "Can you sing?" and I said, "Yes, I'm trying to do a bit of singing" because I was trying to get into theater doing musical comedy numbers, Howard Keel numbers, Frank Sinatra numbers, the whole bit. So, Stigwood was working with Joe Meek and John Leyton had done a few records with Joe, so they decided to do one with me. Well, Joe Meek came up with a song called "Fountain of Love," which was really stupid – "Jack and Jill let's climb up the hill to the fountain of love" – and it finished with the strangest line, which I never understood, even to this day – "It's where you go to share your load, it's the finest pub in the old Kent Road." |
| DIXON: | That's ridiculous. |
| SARNE: | Totally, absolutely didn't make any sense. And then he said, "Well, what are we going to do for a B side?" So the arranger – |

a chap called Charles Blackwell, a very nice man – had a song called "Little Doll," kind of an Americanized dance track. Well, I changed the title to "Come Outside" and, as I was singing it at the piano with Charles Blackwell, Stigwood had the brilliant idea of saying, "I can hear a girl talking back to you, saying, 'Why do you want to take me out, what do you want to do?'" And then we got Wendy Richard in the studio and the thing just clicked. Stigwood is brilliant; there's no getting around it.

DIXON: So, what about your film work? How did you jump from pop music to *Sink the Bismarck*, where you get one line?

SARNE: Well, there was a club near where I lived called the Old Theater Club and I would hang around there with Michael Caine, Terence Stamp, people like that, looking for work. We would go up for small parts, extra parts, and because I could speak German and Russian and French, I would go up for parts with different agents, banking on this. *Sink the Bismarck* needed somebody who could say a couple of lines in German and then the same thing for *The Guns of Navarone* [dir. J. Lee Thompson, 1961] and then *Beware of Children* [dir. Gerald Thomas, 1961], for which I did a French accent and also a slightly bigger part. I also worked on *The Avengers* – the TV series – in 1961, but that was all done live then, with live switching and multiple cameras, so I don't know if any of that survives. By then, John Leyton and I had had our hits and "Come Outside" had already become a hit. So, I started working pretty regularly and I wrote a couple of extra songs for *Seaside Swingers*. That was a year or so later. Believe it or not, Nicolas Roeg shot that; you know, of course, that he went on to much bigger things. I also did the TV series *Man in a Suitcase*, another hour-long action show from that period. I got a lot of small acting jobs and it kept me alive.

But then I got a chance to direct a film of my own: *Road to St. Tropez* [1966]. I had been kicking around the basic outline of the film in my mind for quite some time; it was about a guy who's a gigolo, with an older woman, and the whole thing was going to look like a travelogue. A short film; I figured about 20, 30 minutes long. By then I had a girlfriend, Gabriella Licudi, whom I loved very much. She was in the south of France acting in the James Bond spoof, *Casino Royale* [dirs. Val Guest, Ken Hughes, John Huston, et al., 1966]. I got hold of Udo Kier, who's a great actor, and Melissa Stribling, who had been in all these Hammer horror movies and was married to Basil Dearden, the director.

DIXON: Really? I didn't know that.

SARNE: Well, I met Basil when I was one of the leads, for a change, in his crime thriller *A Place to Go* [1963] – one of the best roles and best directors I had worked with up to that point. I admired him a lot and, in fact, he was the one who said, "You should direct pictures because you've got the eye for it." Well, we shot the film, Twentieth Century Fox picked it up and the amazing thing is that this little picture I made for 10,000 pounds made 100,000 pounds for Fox.

DIXON: As a short?

SARNE: As a short. Because there was a plan called the Eady Levy in those days, where British films would return 50 percent or 40 percent to the producer of successful films. Now, this little picture of mine went out with a film called *In Like Flint* [dir. Gordon Douglas, 1966]. And the films were cross-collateralized because my film went along with *In Like Flint* as a package, so if you played that film, you had to play mine, and so *Road to St. Tropez* got a chunk of *Flint*'s box office. And this got the attention of Dick Zanuck, who was running Fox.

By then, I had written a script called *Joanna*, which I had and was pitching around town as the female *Alfie* [dir. Lewis Gilbert, 1966]. Zanuck liked that angle and gave me a million dollars to shoot the film and, at the same time, gave Bob Freeman a million to shoot what became *The Touchables* [1968]; Bob had shot a lot of album covers for The Beatles and things like that and this was his big chance. The thing is, all of this happened on a street corner, outside Zanuck's hotel, in a matter of seconds. Zanuck just looked at me, looked at Bob, and said, "I'm going to give each of you a million to do your pictures" and that was that. Imagine that happening today? I don't think so.

But the thing was, *Joanna* didn't get all that good a reception from the public when it came out, especially in Britain. Actually, the English hated it because they were into this very bitter, cynical left-wing black-and-white movie phase – something like *Darling* [dir. John Schlesinger, 1965] – so to do something in color, in Panavision, and be a cross between a musical, a comedy and a drama was something they didn't expect or understand. There was also a Felliniesque quality to *Joanna* that didn't go over well – especially the ending, where you see the whole cast and crew in the train station all dancing and singing. It did open well in America, though; *Time* magazine gave it a great review, titled

"Hail, *Joanna.*" The posters were better, too; poppier and sunnier, with the slogan "Your smile is like CinemaScope," something that John Springer, the veteran publicist, came up with. But the rest of the press thought it was pretty kitsch, which it is – but I concealed any serious message well below the surface. You have to dig for it.

When we were getting ready to release *Joanna*, Fox thought it would be a good idea if the film played at Cannes and got some advance publicity there. My friend, Roman Polanski, was head of the jury at the time. I thought I would get a prize. But then the Festival got shut down by the events of May 1968 and the whole thing collapsed. Henri Langlois had been fired as the head of the Cinematheque Française by Charles de Gaulle and the whole country went nuts. Truffaut was the ringleader of the shutdown and that was it. And the whole country was collapsing, so Polanski and I escaped to Rome. So, *Joanna* didn't exactly have the smoothest of launches, if you know what I mean.

DIXON: Okay, but how did you go from here and make the jump to *Myra Breckinridge*, which to me is sort of an experimental movie that you got Twentieth Century Fox to pick up the tab for?

SARNE: Well, it's nice of you to put it like that. They couldn't do anything with that movie. They had the novel, but they didn't know how to put it on the screen. I wrote the final script for the film, which turned the whole thing into a dream, working with David Giler, who was also one of the producers, but it was clear to me from the outset that the entire project was going to be almost impossible to do. I had to spend a lot of time thinking about what to do and also I had ideas that the producers didn't want in the final cut and so there was endless conflict on the set. I was given total control of the film, supposedly, but at the same time I was constantly having to fight over every little detail. As it was, the film got an "X" rating, which was the kiss of death [a 1978 recut was given an "R" rating].

DIXON: I have always heard that the set was totally contentious. True? Not true?

SARNE: Totally. Mae West didn't like Raquel Welch and it went on and on –

DIXON: It is true that when John Huston finished his work on the picture, he turned to you and the rest of the cast and said, "Goodbye, people. You're never going to pull this thing together?"

SARNE: No, that's apocryphal. John was actually very happy to do it and working with him on the set was one of the best parts of making the movie. At the end of the shoot, I gave everybody on the film a present from Gucci and, for John, I bought the most beautiful humidor for cigars because he quite famously liked cigars. But shooting was tense every day and I had a feeling as we were shooting it that it was going to be a tough sell.

DIXON: So then *Myra Breckinridge* comes out and everybody just piles on.

SARNE: Everybody.

DIXON: And what happened?

SARNE: Nothing. I get assassinated, I keep looking for a rope that is strong enough to hold me up so I can hang myself some place. No, I hang around in LA with Lou Adler and John Phillips and we work on something called "The Byron and Shelley Project," which doesn't come off. Then I went to Brazil, where I was invited to shoot a film and wound up making a film called *Intimidade* [co-dir. Perry Salles, 1975] which is a slightly surrealistic film in Portuguese. *Intimidade* won a few prizes and then I get back to England and the first thing I hear – we go down to this nightclub in London and there is this punk band and I'd never heard anything like it. I'd been listening to bossa nova music for two years and this was a real wakeup call. I couldn't stand disco. That's why I acquired this book called *The Punk*, which I made that into a movie in 1993 [also known as *The Punk and the Princess*]. Then what happened was the kids who were working with me on *The Punk* said, "Hey, we're going to take the weekend off and go drop acid at the music festival in Glastonbury." Well, I told them that wasn't the best plan; instead, I told them to shoot film of the whole event – Super 8, 16mm, 35mm, anything at all and then they could edit the whole thing together and make what became *Glastonbury the Movie* [1995]. I'm the producer/director on the film, but I didn't cut the picture together.

DIXON: It's basically all their footage. You facilitated it and produced it, but it's their footage and they did the editing and everything?

SARNE: That's right. The only thing I told them was, "Here's the first shot and the last shot and the rest you can fill in what you want." So, that was entirely their project and they did a really good job of it, too. And, in the meantime, I did a lot of acting to keep busy, mostly in British television – in *The Minder*, *Howard's Way*, the remake of the '60s series *Randall and Hopkirk (Deceased)* and, of course, in David Cronenberg's film *Eastern Promises* [2007], which was a great experience, playing a character named Valery. It was really great working with Cronenberg because he's a fantastically professional guy. I got that part through my friend, Jerzy Skolimowski, a director whose work I really admire. They know each other and I think Jerzy must have said to David, "You know, Mike speaks Russian." Jerzy has finished directing a wonderful picture called *Essential Killing* [2010]. There is not one word of dialogue in it. It's a new picture, just came out – absolutely brilliant.

DIXON: One thing I notice here is that, in an odd twist of fate, you played a minor role in Nick Moran's biopic *Telstar: The Joe Meek Story* [2008].

SARNE: Oh, yes – well, why not? It was a nice, small part. The producers put all the people who were from those days – like John Leyton and all these other guys – and they gave them little parts in this picture. That's why I was one of them.

DIXON: So, how do you feel now that *Joanna* is coming out on DVD and everybody is like raving about it now?

SARNE: Well, the thing is that when I shot the film, I never imagined that such a thing would happen. When I made the picture, I sent a picture – I sent one print to the BFI in a taxi and said, "Oh, it's for you, just put it in your vault" and that was it. And many, many years later I said, "Well, how about showing it at the BFI Southbank theater?" which is a really excellent facility. So, a lot of people showed up from the industry, raved about it and then the BFI said, "Well, can we release it as a DVD?" and, naturally, I agreed. So, the other day they took me to lunch and said, "What do you think? After all, it's been 40 years – what do you think now about what's happening?" I said, "You boys have made all my dreams come true." It's really nice to see the film finally get an audience and not just sit in the vault.

DIXON: So, what's next for you?

SARNE: I'm working a couple of other projects. I'm working on a screenplay of something called "The Battle of Cable Street." It's set before World War II, when the East End of London erupted in fury because of the activities of Sir Oswald Mosley, who was a British Nazi sympathizer who founded the British Union of Fascists. Mosley and his black shirts came marching into the East End [on 4 October 1936] and the lower classes staged a big riot and stopped the march from happening. Something like 400,000 people fought Mosley and the police – who were trying to let the march proceed – but they stopped it cold. And, in a way, because of that, you could say that it was on that date that the English began their resistance against Hitler. If you like, it's a mini-revolution. That's what I'm working on now. There are so many real stories – good stories like that – around and they deserve to be told.

WORKS CITED AND CONSULTED

Abraham, Jugu. 2013. "The Late Argentine Director Fabián Bielinsky's *El Aura (The Aura,* 2005): A Mind-Bending Thriller that Takes You Beyond Guns, Women and Lucre." Moviessansfrontiers.blogspot.com, 23 April. Online: http://moviessansfrontiers.blogspot.com/2010/08/104-late-argentine-director-fabian.html (accessed 28 April 2013).

Anderson, Christopher. 1994. *Hollywood TV: The Studio System in the Fifties.* Austin: University of Texas Press.

Arledge, Sara Kathryn. 1947. "The Experimental Film: A New Art in Transition." *Arizona Quarterly* (summer): 101–12.

———. 1981. "Brief Statements." *Canyon CinemaNews* 1980.6–1981.1:5.

Backstreet, Jack. 2007. "Biography for Ben Judell." Internet Movie Database, 31 May. Online: http://www.imdb.com/name/nm0431879/bio (accessed 28 January 2013).

Balun, Chas. 1996. *Lucio Fulci: Beyond the Gates.* San Leandro, CA: Blackest Heart Books.

Banes, Sally. 1993. *Greenwich Village, 1963: Avant-Garde Performance and the Effervescent Body.* Durham, NC: Duke University Press.

Barbour, Alan G. 1970. *Days of Thrills and Adventure.* New York: Macmillan.

Barshay, Robert. 1974. "Ethnic Stereotypes in *Flash Gordon.*" *Journal of the Popular Film* (Winter): 15–30.

Battcock, Gregory. 1967. *The New American Cinema.* New York: Dutton.

Behlmer, Rudy. 1965. "The Saga of *Flash Gordon.*" *Screen Facts* 2(4): 53–62.

Belasco, Daniel. 2007. "Barbara Rubin: The Vanished Prodigy." *Art Signal,* May. Online: http://art-signal.org/pdfs/asm-numero0.pdf (accessed 11 February 2013).

Berg, Gretchen. 1967. "Nothing to Lose: An Interview with Andy Warhol." *Cahiers du Cinema in English* 10: 38–42.

Bogdanovich, Peter. 1975. "Edgard G. Ulmer Interview." *Kings of the Bs: Working Within the Hollywood System.* Edited by Todd McCarthy and Charles Flynn, 376–409. New York: Dutton.

———. 2012. "Legendary Director Peter Bogdanovich: What If Movies Are Part of the Problem?" *Hollywood Reporter,* 25 July. Online: http://www.hollywoodreporter.com/news/dark-knight-rises-shooting-peter-bogdanovich-353774 (accessed 11 February 2013).

Bottin, Josephine. 2010. "Gerry O'Hara." Booklet, DVD release of *The Pleasure Girls,* 14–15. London: BFI Flipside.

Bourdon, David. 1989. *Warhol.* New York: Abrams.

Bresson, Robert. 1986. *Notes on the Cinematographer.* Translated by Jonathan Griffin. London: Quartet.

Burckhardt, Rudy. 1983. "Warren Sonbert." *Film Culture* 70/71: 176.

Butler, Judith. "Burning Acts – Injurious Speech." In *Performativity and Performance*, edited by Andrew Parker and Eve Kosofsky Sedgwick, 197–227. New York: Routledge.

Cameron, Ian, ed. 1970. *The Films of Robert Bresson*. New York: Praeger.

Canyon Cinema. 1992. *Canyon Cinema Catalogue No. 7*. San Francisco: Canyon Cinema Collective.

Carvajal, Doreen. 2007. "The New Video Arcade in Spain Might Be the Movie Theater." *New York Times*, 26 February.

Chanan, Michael. 2006. "Fabián Bielinsky: Fresh New Spirit of the Mainstream Cinema in Argentina." *Guardian*, 19 July. Online: http://www.theguardian.com/news/2006/jul/20/guardianobituaries.argentina (accessed 28 April 2013).

Cocteau, Jean. 2001. *The Art of the Cinema*. Translated by Robin Buss. London: Marion Boyars.

Colalongo, Mariano and Alvaro Fuentes. 2006. "Entrevista con Fabián Bielinsky" [Interview with Fabián Bielinsky]. *La Ventana Indiscreta*, 21 April. Online: http://laventanaindiscretacineyfilosofia.blogspot.com/2006/05/entrevista-con-fabinbielinsky.html (accessed 28 April 2013).

Cummings, Doug. 2004. "*Les Dames du Bois de Boulogne*." *Movie Mail*, 27 July. Online: http://www.moviemail.com/scripts/article.pl?articleID=144 (accessed 12 February 2013).

Cunheen, Joseph E. 2003. *Robert Bresson: A Spiritual Style in Film*. New York: Continuum.

Curtis, David. 1971. *Experimental Cinema*. New York: Universe.

Daily Variety. 1943. "PRC Has Growing Pains: Record Year Marked by Five Forward Steps." *Daily Variety*, 29 October: 489. Collection of the Margaret Herrick Library, Academy of Motion Picture Arts and Sciences, Los Angeles.

_____. 1944a. "Film Baby Walks By Self: PRC Makes Big Strides with More Coin and More Stars." *Daily Variety*, 16 October: n.p. Collection of the Margaret Herrick Library, Academy of Motion Picture Arts and Sciences, Los Angeles.

_____. 1944b. "PRC Announces Takeover of Major Indie Producer: Reveals Theater Ownership." *Daily Variety*, 3 August: n.p. Collection of the Margaret Herrick Library, Academy of Motion Picture Arts and Sciences, Los Angeles.

_____. 1944c. "Vote Today on 15 Million Combo of Neufeld and PRC." *Daily Variety*, 24 June: n.p. Collection of the Margaret Herrick Library, Academy of Motion Picture Arts and Sciences, Los Angeles.

_____. 1951. "*Dragnet* Review." *Daily Variety*, 17 December: 7.

_____. 1952a. "TV-Film Production Chart." *Daily Variety*, 7 January: 9.

_____. 1952b. "TV-Film Production Chart." *Daily Variety*, 11 February: 9.

Dawson, Tom. 2002. "Fabián Bielinsky: *Nine Queens*." BBC, 2 July. Online: http://www.bbc.co.uk/films/2002/07/02/fabian_bielinsky_nine_queens_interview.shtml (accessed 28 April 2013).

Denby, David. 2007. "Big Pictures: Where Are the Movies Heading?" *New Yorker*, 8 January. Online: http://www.newyorker.com/arts/critics/atlarge/2007/01/08/070108crat_atlarge_denby (accessed 13 February 2013).

Dixon, Wheeler Winston. 1993. "The Early Films of Andy Warhol." *Classic Images* 214 (April): 38–40.

_____. 1997. *The Exploding Eye: A Re-visionary History of 1960s American Experimental Cinema*. Albany: State University of New York Press.

_____. 1999. "Review: *Les Dames du Bois de Boulogne*." All Movie Guide, 20 September. Online: http://www.allmovie.com/movie/les-dames-du-bois-de-boulogne-v98436/review (accessed 13 February 2013).

———. 2001. "Twenty-Five Reasons Why It's All Over." In *The End of Cinema As We Know It*, edited by John Lewis, 356–66. New York: New York University Press.

———. 2004. "'How Will I Get My Opium?': Jean Cocteau and the Treachery of Friendship." In *Bad: Infamy, Darkness, Evil and Slime on the Screen*, edited by Murray Pomerance, 127–41. Albany: State University of New York Press.

———. 2005. *Lost in the Fifties: Rediscovering Phantom Hollywood.* Carbondale: Southern Illinois University Press

———. 2008. "Tomorrowland TV: The Space Opera and Early Science Fiction Television." *The Essential Science Fiction Television Reader*, edited by J. P. Telotte, 93–110. Lexington: University Press of Kentucky.

Dixon, Wheeler Winston and Gwendolyn Audrey Foster. 2011. *21st-Century Hollywood Movies in the Era of Transformation.* New Brunswick: Rutgers University Press.

Doherty, Thomas. 2005. *Cold War, Cool Medium: Television, McCarthyism, and American Culture.* New York: Columbia University Press.

Edwards, David. 2002. "Fabián Bielinsky: *Nine Queens.*" TheBlurb.com, 26 September. Online: http://www.theblurb.com.au/Issue21/FabianBielinskyInt.htm (accessed 28 April 2013).

Ellis, John. 1982. *Visible Fictions: Cinema, Television, Video.* London: Routledge.

Euker, Jake. 2007. "*Les Dames du Bois de Boulogne.*" Filmcritic.com, 15 October. Online: http://movies.amctv.com/movie/1945/Les+Dames+du+Bois+de+Boulogne (accessed 11 February 2013).

Fahsbender, Federico. 2005. "Le dije que no a Hollywood. Allá no tenés libertad para crear" [I said no to Hollywood. There you have no freedom to create]. *Gente.* Online: http://www.gente.com.ar/nota.php?ID=10471 (accessed 28 April 2013).

Falicov, Tamara L. 2012. "Argentine Cinema and the Crisis of Audience." In *The Argentine Film*, edited by Daniela Ingruber and Ursula Prutsch, 207–18. Münster/Berlin/Vienna/Zurich: LIT Verlag.

Filmmakers' Cooperative. 1967. *Filmmakers' Cooperative Catalogue No. 4.* New York: New American Cinema Group.

Flaubert, Gustave. 1875. Gustave Flaubert in a letter to George Sand, December. From Wikiquote. Online: http://enwikiquote.org/wiki/Gustave_Flaubert (accessed 4 October 2013).

Flynn, Charles and Todd McCarthy. 1975a. "The Economic Imperative: Why Was the B Movie Necessary?" In *Kings of the Bs: Working Within the Hollywood System*, edited by Todd McCarthy and Charles Flynn, 13–47. New York: Dutton.

———. 1975b. "Interview with Joseph Kane, 2 September 1973." In *Kings of the Bs: Working Within the Hollywood System*, edited by Todd McCarthy and Charles Flynn, 313–24. New York: Dutton.

Foster, Frederick. 1954. "Filming the *Dragnet* TV Show." *American Cinematographer* (April): 188–9, 198–200.

Fraser, Harry L. 1990. *I Went That-A-Way: The Memoirs of a Western Film Director.* Edited by Wheeler Winston Dixon and Audrey Brown Fraser. Metuchen, NJ: Scarecrow Press.

Galloway, Chris. 2010. "That Kind of Girl." Criterion Forum.org, 3 January. Online: http://www.criterionforum.org/DVD-review/the-pleasure-girls/bfi-flipside/744 (accessed 19 February 2013).

Gronlund, Melissa. 2007. "Artfilm's New Haven." *Sight and Sound* 17(1): 28–9.

Grossman, Gary H. 1981. *Saturday Morning TV.* New York: Delacorte.

Hammer, Barbara. 1981. "Sara Kathryn Arledge." *Canyon CinemaNews* 1980.6–1981.1: 3–4.

Harley, Kevin. 2006. "Fabián Bielinsky." *Independent*, 20 July. Online: http://www.independent.co.uk/arts-entertainment/theatre-dance/features/fabianbielinsky--director-of-nine-queens-408566.html (accessed 28 April 2013).
Harper, Sue. 2010. "Getting on with Their Own Happiness: *The Pleasure Girls*." Booklet, DVD release of *The Pleasure Girls*, 1–5. London: BFI Flipside.
Harvey, Stephen. 1984. "The Mask in the Mirror: The Movies of Jean Cocteau." In *Jean Cocteau and the French Scene*, edited by Arthur King Peters, 185–208. New York: Abbeville Press.
Hayde, Michael J. 2001. *My Name's Friday: The Unauthorized but True Story of Dragnet and the Films of Jack Webb*. Nashville, TN: Cumberland House.
Hayes, R. M. 2000. *The Republic Chapterplays: A Complete Filmography of the Serials Released by Republic Pictures Corporation, 1934–1955*. Jefferson, NC: McFarland.
Henderson, Jan Alan and Burr Middleton. 2001. "Behind the Ming Dynasty: Revelations from the Emperor's Grandson, Burr Middleton." *Filmfax* 85: 50–8, 87.
Hollywood Citizen News. 1944. "Film Merger Plan Revealed: PRC to Combine with Another Company." *Hollywood Citizen News*, 3 August: n.p. Collection of the Margaret Herrick Library, Academy of Motion Picture Arts and Sciences, Los Angeles.
Hollywood Reporter. 1944. "PRC President Outlines Company's Expansion Plans." *Hollywood Reporter*, 3 August: n.p. Collection of the Margaret Herrick Library, Academy of Motion Picture Arts and Sciences, Los Angeles.
Horak, Jan-Christopher. 2012. "Janna Jones: *The Past is a Moving Picture*." UCLA Film and Television Archive Blog, 27 July. Online: htpp://www.cinemaucla.edu/blogs/archivalspaces/2012/07/27/janna-jones-past-moving-picture (accessed 30 January 2013).
Indiana, Gary. 1942. "I'll Be Your Mirror." *Village Voice*, 5 May: centerfold section, 2–3.
Jin-seo, Cho. 2006. "Phone to Carry Video Projector." KoreaTimes.co.kr, 13 April. Online; page no longer available.
Jonas, Susan and Marilyn Nissenson. 1994. *Going Going Gone: Vanishing Americana*. San Francisco: Chronicle Books.
"Jose," pseudonym. 1951. "*Dragnet* (review)." *Weekly Variety*, 19 December: 27.
Kaufman, Anthony. 2002. "World Cinema Report: Argentina's Next Wave Struggle Sustains Momentum Amid Economic Collapse." Indiewire, 20 March. Online: http://www.indiewire.com/article/world_cinema_report_argentinas_next_wave_struggles_to_sustains_momentum_ami (accessed 28 April 2013).
Keenan, Vince. 2009. "Too Soon Gone: the Noir Legacy of Fabián Bielinsky." Vincekeenan.com, 3 July. Online: http://blog.vincekeenan.com/2009/07/too-soon-gone-noir-legacy-of-fabian (accessed 28 April 2013).
Kehr, David. 2010. "Film Riches, Cleaned Up for Posterity." *New York Times*, 14 October. Online: http://www.nytimes.com/2010/10/15/movies/15restore/html (accessed 30 January 2013).
Khasnis, Giridhar. 2012. "*Aura* of a Master." Deccanherald.com. Online: http://www.deccanherald.com/content/116235/ipl-2012.html (accessed 28 April 2013).
Kinnard, Roy. 1998. *Science Fiction Serials*. Jefferson, NC: McFarland.
Kinnard, Roy, Tony Crnkovich and R. J. Vitone. 2008. *The Flash Gordon Serials: A Heavily Illustrated Guide*. Jefferson, NC: McFarland.
Klawans, Stuart. 2006. "Imitation of Life: A Valediction for Fabián Bielinsky." *Parnassus: Poetry in Review* 30.1/2: 347–54.
Knipp, Chris. 2006. "Fabián Bielinsky: *The Aura*." Filmleaf.net, 19 December. Online: http://www.chrisknipp.com/writing/viewtopic.php?f=1&t=712 (accessed 28 April 2013).

Kusmin, Nicolás. 2006. "Fabián Bielinsky." Leedor.com, 3 July. Online: http://www.leedor.com/contenidos/cine/fabian-bielinsky (accessed 28 April 2013).

Lahue, Kalton C. 1968. *Bound and Gagged: The Story of the Silent Serials*. New York: A. S. Barnes.

Library of Congress. 1953. *Motion Pictures 1940–1949: Catalog of Copyright Entries: Cumulative Series*. Washington, DC: Library of Congress.

Lee, Nathan, Kent Jones and Paul Arthur. 2007. "Movies That Mattered." *Film Comment*, January–February. Online: http://www.filmcomment.com/issue/january-february-2007 (accessed 12 February 2013).

Lerer, Diego. 2006. "Fabián Bielinsky, 1959–2006." Fipresci.org, July. Online: http://www.fipresci.org/news/archive/archive_2006/bielinsky_dlerer.htm (accessed 28 April 2013).

Letelier, Jorge. 2006. "El apoyo de la crítica para las películas pequeñas es decisivo" [The critical support for small movies is turning]. *Mabuse*, 29 January. Online: http://www.mabuse.cl/entrevista.php?id=72022 (accessed 28 April 2013).

Look Magazine. 1938. "*Flash Gordon's Trip to Mars*." *Look Magazine*, 15 March: n.p.; 29 March: n.p.; 12 April: n.p.

Los Angeles Times. 1973. "Jean Beutier Wed to Joel C. Newfield." *Los Angeles Times*, 29 November: C10. Collection of the Margaret Herrick Library, Academy of Motion Picture Arts and Sciences, Los Angeles.

Lucanio, Patrick and Gary Coville. 1993a. "Behind Badge 714: The Story of Jack Webb and *Dragnet* (Part One)." *Filmfax*, August–September: 51–61, 98.

_____. 1993b. "Behind Badge 714: The Story of Jack Webb and *Dragnet* (Part Two)." *Filmfax*, October–November: 37–42, 78–80.

Lukas, Amadeo. 2009. "An Interview with Fabián Bielinsky." Odeon.hu, 9 April. Online: http://www.odeon.hu/megkerdeztuk/phtml?id=31 (accessed 28 April 2013). Originally appeared in *Raíces del Cine*, 2005.

MacCormack, Patricia. 2004. "Great Directors: Lucio Fulci." *Senses of Cinema* 31 (22 April). Online: http://sensesofcinema.com/2004/great-directors/fulci (accessed 12 February 2013).

MacDonald, Scott. 1998. *A Critical Cinema: Interviews with Independent Filmmakers*. Berkeley: University of California Press.

Maddow, Ben. 2000. "Acts of Friendship." In *Gerard Malanga: Screen Tests, Portraits, Nudes 1964–1996*, edited by Patrick Remy and Marc Parent, 120–25. Göttingen: Steidl Publishers.

Malanga, Gerard. 1967. "A Letter to Warren Sonbert." *Film Culture* 46: 20–21.

_____. 1976. "The Secret Diaries (excerpt)." *Cold Spring* 9: 4–10.

_____. 1988. "Working with Warhol." *Art New England* (September): 6–8.

Martorell, Carlos Rodríguez. 2010. "Columbia U. Holds Tribute to Mario Montez, a Boricua Drag Performer from Warhol's Era." *New York Daily News*, 31 March. Online: http://www.nydailynews.com/entertainment/tv-movies/columbia-u-holds-tribute-mario-montez-boricua-drag-performer-warhol-era-article-1.173194 (accessed 12 February 2013).

McCreadie, Marsha. 1983. *Women on Film: The Critical Eye*. New York: Praeger.

Mead, Taylor. 1998. "Notes on *The Flower Thief*." Anthology Film Archives Program Notes, January–February: 2–5.

Mekas, Jonas. 1972. *Movie Journal: The Rise of the New American Cinema*. New York: Collier.

Michel, Jean-Claude. 1990. "Directed by Lucio Fulci, Italy's Gore Master." *Fantasy Film Memory*, 2 October: 1–36.

Millar, Daniel. 1970. "*Les Dames du Bois de Boulogne.*" In *The Films of Robert Bresson*, edited by Ian Cameron, 33–41. New York: Praeger.
Misek, Richard. 2004. "Jean Cocteau." *Senses of Cinema* 30 (12 February). Online: http://sensesofcinema.com/2004/great-directors/cocteau (accessed 12 February 2013).
Mitchell, Robert. 1981. "*Flash Gordon.*" In *Magill's Survey of Cinema: English Language Films*, Second Series, Volume II, edited by Frank N. Magill, 796–9. Englewood Cliffs, NJ: Salem Press.
Moore-Gilbert, Bart and John Seed, eds. 1992. *Cultural Revolutions: The Challenge of the Arts in the 1960s*. London: Routledge.
Motion Picture Herald. 1942. "Increased Film Budget Planned for PRC Product." *Motion Picture Herald*, 31 June: n.p. Collection of the Margaret Herrick Library, Academy of Motion Picture Arts and Sciences, Los Angeles.
———. 1944a. "Fromkess Elected PRC President." *Motion Picture Herald*, 22 July: n.p. Collection of the Margaret Herrick Library, Academy of Motion Picture Arts and Sciences, Los Angeles.
———. 1944b. "PRC Pictures Plans National Distribution." *Motion Picture Herald*, 5 February: n.p. Collection of the Margaret Herrick Library, Academy of Motion Picture Arts and Sciences, Los Angeles.
Moviefone. 2013. "Fabián Bielinsky Biography." Moviefone.com, 23 April. Online: http://www.moviefone.com/celebrity/fabian-bielinsky/2004240/biography (accessed 28 April 2013).
Moyer, Daniel and Eugene Alvarez. 2001. *Just the Facts, Ma'am: The Authorized Biography of Jack Webb*. Santa Ana, CA: Seven Locks Press.
Myers, Louis Budd. 1967. "Marie Menken Herself." *Film Culture* 45: 37–9.
Neufeld, Sigmund, Jr. 2007. Telephone interview with the author, 2 June.
Neufeld, Stanley. 2007. Telephone interview with the author, 3 June.
Nietzsche, Friedrich. 1992. *Ecce Homo*. Translated by R. J. Hollingdale. London: Penguin.
Nord, Cristina. 2005. "Dead Skin." Fipresci.org, December. Online: http://www.fipresci.org/festivals/archive/2005/havana/havana_nord.htm (accessed 28 April 2013).
O'Brien, Geoffrey. 1995. *The Phantom Empire: Movies in the Mind of the 20th Century*. New York: W. W. Norton.
O'Hara, Gerry. 2002. "You're Fired!" *Veteran* 97: 3–4.
———. 2003. "Critic's Choice." *Veteran* 99: 7–9.
———. 2010a. "Gerry O'Hara Recalls Writing and Directing *The Pleasure Girls*." Booklet, DVD release of *The Pleasure Girls*. London: BFI Flipside, 7–10.
———. 2010b. Unpublished letter to the author, 16 November 2010.
Parish, James Robert and Michael R. Pitts. 1977. "*Flash Gordon.*" In *The Great Science Fiction Pictures*, edited by James Robert Parish and Michael R. Pitts, 125–7. Metuchen, NJ: Scarecrow Press.
Quandt, James. 1998. *Robert Bresson*. Toronto: Toronto International Film Festival Group.
Rabinovitz, Lauren. 1991. *Points of Resistance: Women, Power, and Politics in the New York Avant-Garde Cinema, 1943–1971*. Urbana: University of Illinois Press.
Rainey, Buck. 1999. *Serials and Series: A World Filmography 1912–1956*. Jefferson, NC: McFarland.
Ratner, Megan. 2007. "A Legacy Slight But Substantial." *Bright Lights Film Journal* 55 (February). Online: http://brightlightsfilm.com/55/bielinsky/php#.UgLekJWxpG4 (accessed 28 April 2013).
Reader, Keith. 2000. *Robert Bresson*. Manchester: Manchester University Press.

Ressner, Jeffrey. 2012. "The Traditionalist." *DGA Quarterly* (Spring). Online: http://www.dga.org/Craft/DGAQ/All-Articles/1202-Spring-2012/DGA-Interview-Christopher-Nolan.aspx (accessed 30 January 2013).
Rice, Ron. 1983."Note from Ron Rice to Jonas Mekas." *Film Culture* 70/71: 100–111.
Roud, Richard. 1959. "The Early Work of Robert Bresson." *Film Culture* 20: 44–52. Reprinted in *The Film*, edited by Andrew Sarris, 34–8. Indianapolis: Bobbs-Merrill, 1968.
Rovin, Jeff. 1977. *"Flash Gordon": From Jules Verne to Star Trek*. New York: Drake Publishers, 44–5.
Samuels, Charles Thomas. 1970. "Encountering Directors: Robert Bresson." Robert-Bresson.com, 3 October. Online: http://people.ucalgary.ca/~tstronds/robert-bresson.com/Words/CTSamuels.html (accessed 11 February 2013).
Sargeant, Jack. 1997. *The Naked Lens*. London: Creation.
Schimmel, Paul. 1998. *Out of Actions: Between Performance and the Object, 1949–1979*. Los Angeles: Museum of Contemporary Art.
Schlockoff, Robert. 1982. "Interview with Lucio Fulci." Translated by Frederic Levy. *Starburst* 4.12 (August): 51–5. Originally printed in *L'Ecran Fantastique*.
Schutz, Wayne. 1992. *The Motion Picture Serial: An Annotated Bibliography*. Metuchen, NJ: Scarecrow.
Scorsese, Martin. 1991. Unpublished interview with Dennis Coleman, 21 March. Hollywood, CA.
Scott, A. O. 2007. "And You'll Be a Moviegoer, My Son." *New York Times*, 5 January. Online: http://www.nytimes.com/2007/01/05/movies/05note/html?ex=1325653200&err=37847e400fd50d2a&ei=5088&partner=rssnyt&emc=rss (accessed 11 February 2013).
Shaviro, Steven. 1993. *The Cinematic Body*. Minneapolis: University of Minnesota Press.
Sloan, Jane. 2007. "Chapter II: Critical Survey." Robert-Bresson.com, 5 October. Online: http://people.ucalgary.ca/~tstronds/robert-bresson.com/Words/Sloan_Bresson_Survey.html (accessed 11 February 2013).
Sperber, A. M. and Eric Lax. 1997. *Bogart*. New York: Morrow.
Stark, Scott. 2009. "The Flicker Pages", 13 December. Online: http://www.hi-beam.net/cgi-bin/flicker.pl (accessed 11 February 2013).
Steegmuller, Francis. 1970. *Cocteau*. Boston: Little, Brown.
Steinbrunner, Chris and Burt Goldblatt. 1972. *"Flash Gordon": Cinema of the Fantastic*. New York: Galahad Books, 125–50.
Sterritt, David. 2010. *"Targets."* Fipresci.org 6.4. Online: http://www.fipresci.org/undercurrent/issue_0609/sterritt_targets.htm (accessed 11 February 2013).
Strock, Herbert L. 2000. *Picture Perfect*. Lanham, MD: Scarecrow Press.
———, 2004. Interview by the author, 20 January, telephone.
Taubin, Amy. 1995. "Warren Sonbert, 1947–1995." *Village Voice*, 20 June: 48.
Terrace, Vincent. 1986. *Encyclopedia of Television Series, Pilots and Specials 1937–1973*. New York: Zoetrope.
Thrower, Stephen. 1999. *Beyond Terror: The Films of Lucio Fulci*. Guildford: FAB Press.
Truffaut, François. 1981. "André Bazin, the Occupation, and I." *French Cinema of the Occupation and Resistance: The Birth of a Critical Esthetic*. Edited by André Bazin. Translated by Stanley Hochman. New York: Ungar.
Turner, George. 1983. "Making the *Flash Gordon* Serials." *American Cinematographer* (June): 56–62.
Tuska, Jon. 1982. *The Vanishing Legion: A History of Mascot Pictures 1927–1935*. Jefferson, NC: McFarland.

Tyler, Parker. 1969. *Underground Film: A Critical History*. New York: Grove.
Ulman, Erik. 2001. "*Les Anges du péché*." *Senses of Cinema* 17, (20 November). Online: http://sensesofcinema.com/2001/cteq-anges/ (accessed 12 February 2013).
Urban, Andrew. 2002. "Four Aces for *Nine Queens*." Urbancinefile.com, 26 September. Online: http://www.urbancinefile.com.au/home/view.asp?a=6562&s=interviews (accessed 28 April 2013).
Usai, Paolo Cherchi. 2001. *The Death of Cinema: History, Cultural Memory and the Digital Dark Age*. London: BFI Publishing.
Vermilye, Jerry. 2008. *Buster Crabbe: A Biofilmography*. Jefferson, NC: McFarland.
Whitezel, Karl. 2000. "Buster Crabbe: An All-American in Outer Space." *Filmfax* 79: 52–9.
Whitman, Charles. 1966 "Suicide note." 31 July. From the Collections of the Austin History Center. Online: http://alt.cimedia.com/statesman/specialreports (accessed 4 October 2013).
Wikipedia. 2013. "*Flash Gordon* (serial)." Wikipedia.org, 28 July. Wikimedia Foundation, Inc. Online: http://en.wikipedia.org/wiki/Flash_Gordon_(serial) (accessed 4 October 2013).
Willis, Donald, ed. 1985. *Variety's Complete Science Fiction Reviews*. New York: Garland.
Witney, William. 1996. *In a Door, into a Fight, Out a Door, into a Chase: Moviemaking Remembered by the Guy at the Door*. Jefferson, NC: McFarland.
Young, Neil. 2007. "A Fitting Epitaph?: Fabián Bielinsky's *The Aura*." Neil Young's Film Lounge, 24 June. Online: http://www.jigsawlounge.co.uk/film/reviews/a-fitting-epitaph-fabian-bielinsky-s-the-aura-7-10/ (accessed 28 April 2013).
Youngblood, Gene. 1970. *Expanded Cinema*. New York: Dutton.
"Zagria," pseudonym. 2008. "'Whatever Happened to Mario Montez?' A Gender Variance Who's Who," 25 July. Online: http://zagria.blogspot.com/2008/07/whatever-happened-to-maria-montez.html#.UgLhArwwzys (accessed 13 December 2009).

ABOUT THE AUTHOR

Wheeler Winston Dixon is the Ryan Professor of Film Studies, coordinator of the Film Studies Program, professor of English at the University of Nebraska, Lincoln, and editor-in-chief, with Gwendolyn Audrey Foster, of the *Quarterly Review of Film and Video*. His newest books are *Streaming: Movies, Media and Instant Access* (University Press of Kentucky, 2013), *Death of the Moguls: The End of Classical Hollywood* (Rutgers University Press, 2012), *21st Century Hollywood: Movies in the Era of Transformation* (co-authored with Gwendolyn Audrey Foster; Rutgers University Press, 2011), *A History of Horror* (Rutgers University Press, 2010), *Film Noir and the Cinema of Paranoia* (Edinburgh University Press/ Rutgers University Press, 2009) and *A Short History of Film* (co-authored with Gwendolyn Audrey Foster; Rutgers University Press, 2008; second revised edition, 2013). Dixon's textual blog of media commentary, *Frame by Frame*, and a series of brief videos by Dixon on film history, theory and criticism, also entitled *Frame by Frame*, are available online.

INDEX

3D features 131

The Abductors 187
Acid Mantra: Re-Birth of a Nation 100
acting 91–3, 103–4, 137, 142, 144–5, 198–9, 201
actors 144, 145
Adair, Red 191
Adams, Ansel 138
advertising: *see* television commercials
Ahlgren, Martin 125
Aldrich, Robert 181
Alexander, Ben *32*
All the Right Noises 175
Ambassador Pictures 64
Amphetamine 101
Amsterdam Affair 174–5
Anastasia 166
Les Anges du péché 82
Ann Arbor Film Festival 101
Annakin, Ken 159, 162
Apology for Murder 67
Argentina, filmmakers 47–8
Arledge, Sara Kathryn 102–3
Arness, Jim 186
Arthur, Paul 113
Arthur of the Britons [TV series] 156
The Astonished Heart 161
Atwill, Lionel 28
The Aura 48–57
The Avengers [TV series] 173–4, 198
awards 44, 55, 185

BFI Southbank 202
Babluani, Géla 46
The Ballad of Josie 189
Balun, Chas 16

Barre, Jaye 138
Batman (1943) 28
Becker, Jacques 86
Becky Sharp 109
Belasco, Daniel 99
Bell, Tom 175
Bergman, Ingrid 166
The Beyond 11, 15–17
Bielinsky, Fabián 43–57, *44*
Birkett, Michael 164–5
The Birthday Present 152
The Bitch 175–6
The Blue and the Gray [TV miniseries] 193
body as performative site 95–103
Boetticher, Budd 183–4, 187
Bogdanovich, Peter 3–7; *Who the Devil Made It* 3
Boone, Richard 187
Box, Sidney 174
Boys in Brown 160
Brakhage, Stan 98
Bresson, Robert 77, 78, 79–81, 83, 86–7
Britton, Tony 154
budget limitations 142, 146, 186
Bullfighter and the Lady 184
Butler, Judith 102
buzz, commercial value 132

The Call of the Road 180
camerawork 145
Cannes film festival 200
Captain Gallant of the Foreign Legion [TV series] 73
The Cardinal 171
Carr, Thomas 29
Casarès, Maria 79–80
Chanan, Michael 50

Chandor, J. C. 135–46, *136*
Chevalier, Maurice 189
Chisum 192
Christmas on Earth 99–100
Chumlum 93–4
Cinegames, Madrid 113
cinema, history xvii, 108, 112
City of the Living Dead 11
Cleopatra 168–9
The Clouded Yellow 163
Coburn, Kip 98
Cocteau, Jean xvii, 77, 79, 82, 86–7, 108
Collins, Joan 176
Colorz of Rage 124–5
Columbia Pictures 28–9
Commando Cody [TV series] 27–8
Corman, Roger 3
Cosmatos, George 170
Coville, Gary 39
Coward, Noel 168
Crabbe, Buster 23–6
Criminal 45
The Crimson Ghost 27
Cronenberg, David 201–2
cross-platforming 111
Cummings, Doug 80
Curtis, David 114

DCPs xii
DVD technology xiii
Les Dames du Bois de Boulogne 77–9, *78*, 83–6, 87–9
Danger Man [TV series] 155
Darnborough, Antony 161–2
Day, Doris 189
de Hirsch, Storm 98
DeMarco, Frank 144
Dearden, Basil 198–9
Delpeut, Peter 108
Denby, David 111
Despacito 140
The Devil's Brigade 190
digital: cinematography 143; image, vulnerability 108; technology, uses of xii, 114–15; video, quality 110–11
Digital Cinema Packages (DCPs) xii
digitization xii–xiv, 105–15

directing 124, 130–31, 135, 186, 188–91; style 126–8; television 156; theater 193–4; videos 125
directors xvi, 21–2, 91–2, 97–103, 122, 124, 143, 163
Dishonored 180
The Divided Heart 163–4
Don't Talk to Strange Men 147, 154
Douy, Max 87
Dragnet [radio series] 33
Dragnet [TV series] 31, *32*, 34–42; cinematography 34–5

Eady Levy rules 199
Eagle Lion Pictures 71
Ealing Studios 163–4
Eastern Promises 201–2
Eastwood, Clint 188, 194
editing 131, 163
editors 163
Emshwiller, Ed 98
Encore [multipart film] 150
Escuela Nacional de Experimentación y Realización Cinematográfica (ENERC) 43
Essential Killing 202
Evans, Robert, *The Kid Stays in the Picture* 123
Exodus 169–70
experimental cinema 91–104
Eye of the Widow 193

The Famous Five [TV series] 156
Fanny Hill 176
fetish films 108
film: 16mm 106; critics 109, 113; history xvii, 108, 112; stock 106–7; with video 143
filmic medium xi, 110, 128–9; fate of 105–15
filmmakers xvi, 47, 91–9, 97–103; *see also* directors
films: on DVD 202; digitized xiii; as entertainment 69; music 144, 165, 172; screening 132; *see also* fetish films; genre films; horror films; motion picture serials; portmanteau films; short films; thrillers; war pictures

Fisher, Terence 161–2
Fithian, John 112
Flaming Creatures 92, 96
Flash Gordon [serial] *20*, 23–7
Flash Gordon Conquers the Universe 26
Flash Gordon trilogy 29–30
Flores, Dolores [pseud.] 96
The Flower Thief 93
Fools' Parade 188
Ford, John 185, 192
The Four Horsemen of the Apocalypse 170
France, Vichy regime 88–9
Francis, Freddie 152
Fraser, Harry 22
Freeling, Nicholas 174
Freeman, Bob 199
Fromkess, Leon 69
Fulci, Lucio 11–18
Fuses 100

GPO 160
Gainsborough Studios 163
Gassan, Arnold 98
General Post Office films (GPO) 160
genre films 13, 49, 69
The Gentle Touch 152
Geography of the Body 103
gialli 13
Gide, André 146
Glastonbury the Movie 201
Goldwyn, Samuel 110
Gran Torino 194
Greenhalgh, Jack *62*, 72
Gronlund, Melissa 112
Guinness, Alec 167
Gun the Man Down 186
Gunga Din 180–81
Gunsmoke [TV series] 187

Hammer Films 71
Have Gun – Will Travel [TV series] 187
Heller, Otto 164–5
Hellfighters 191
high-definition video 113, 128–9
hip hop 126
Da Hip Hop Witch 125
Hitler: Beast of Berlin 65
Hodson, James L. 151

Hoffman, Sabine 125
Horak, Jan-Christopher xiv
horror films 152
human body on film 95–103
Huston, John 200–201

Iljin Display Company 111
image overload 114
In Like Flint 199
The Informer 179, 185
internships 139
Intimidade 201
Irons, Jeremy 144
Island in the Sun 166

Jackson, Pat 147–56, *148*; *A Retake Please!* 148
Jaremelu 100–101
Jerovi 100–101
Jigsaw 160
Joanna 199–200, 202
Jones, Kent 113

Kaufman, Anthony 48
Keenan, Vince 55
Kehr, Dave xiii
Kellogg, Ray 168
Klawans, Stuart 46–7
Klinger, Michael 172
Knowles, Patrick 192
Komlosy, Stephen 197
Kovacs, Ernie 167
Kusama, Yayoi 102
Kusama's Self Obliteration 102

The L-Shaped Room 168
Larson, Nathan 144
Lawrence of Arabia 170
Lean, David 143
Lee, Nathan 113
Lerer, Diego 53
Levine, Naomi 100
Levine, Nat 22
Leyton, John 196, 197
Lippert, Robert 71
Lloyd, Euan 192
London Can Take It 147–8
The Longest Most Meaningless Movie in the Whole Wide World 114

Lost City of the Jungle 28
Lost Continent 71–2
Lowe, Edmund 180
The Loyal Heart 160
Lucan, Arthur 160
Lucanio, Patrick 39

MGM 149–50
Maas, Willard 103
MacCormack, Patricia 13
MacRae, Henry 24
Maid for Murder 171
Malanga, Gerard 97, 99, 109
Mamet, David 49
Man in a Suitcase [TV series] 155, 198
Man in the Vault 186, 189
Manhunt of Mystery Island 27
Margin Call 135–6, 141–5
Mario Banana No. 1 96
Markopoulos, Gregory 101
Maroc 7 174
Marsyas 98
Martinez, Enrique 113
McGoohan, Patrick 152–3, 155
McLaglen, Andrew V. 179–94
McLaglen, Josh 194
McLaglen, Mary 194
McLaglen, Sharon 194
McLaglen, Victor 179–80, 185
McLintock! *182*, 188
McMinn, Bob 127
Mead, Taylor 93, 94–5
Meek, Joe 197
Menken, Marie 103
Meshekoff, Mike 39
Meyer, Barry 112
Micha, René 93
Middleton, Charles 27
Millar, Daniel 78
Minnelli, Vincente 170
Monkeys, Go Home 189
Montez, Maria 96
Montez, Mario 96–7
Moore, Roger 155
Moser, Jim 39–40
motion picture serials 19–30; directors 21–2; silent 19–21; *see also* science fiction serials

movies, economics xiv; theatrical experience 132; *see also* films
moving image, defining 107; recording/display technology 105, 111; *see also* films; video
music: *see* films, music; music videos; pop songs
music videos 119, 125–6, 130
Myra Breckinridge 200–201

Nelson, Gunvor 98
Neufeld, Sigmund *62*, 62–3, 65, 69, 71, 73, 74
Neufeld, Sigmund Jr. 61, 65, 67, 69, 70, 71, 72, 74
Neufeld, Stanley 61, 72, 73, 74
New American Cinema 91–104
New Argentine Cinema 47
The New York Ripper 14
Newfield, Sam 61, *62*, 63–75; pseudonyms 65–6; silent films 64; two-reel shorts 64
Night Mail 148
Nine Queens 44–50; awards 55
Nolan, Christopher xi, 146
non-narrative structure 11
Nueve Reinas 44–50

O'Brien, Geoffrey xvi, 108–9
O'Hara, Gerry 157–77, *158*, 160
O'Kelly, Tim 4, *4*
Old Mother Riley at Home 160
Olivier, Laurence 164, 165, 166
One More Train to Rob 192
O'Toole, Peter 153
Our Man in Havana 167
Our Virgin Island 152

PDC 65
PRC 65–6, 69–71, 74
performance, definitions 91–3, 102–4
performativity, in art 102; as content 92–93
Peric, Suzana, 144
The Perils of Pauline [serial] 19
Pete Kelly's Blues [radio series] 40
The Phantom Empire [serial] 22
Phillips, Leslie 174

photography 138
A Place to Go 199
The Pleasure Girls 157, 171–3
pop culture, destructive 7–9
pop songs 196, 198
portmanteau films 162
Powell, Michael 159
Preminger, Otto 169, 171
The Prisoner [TV series] 147, 155
Producers Distribution Corporation (PDC) 65
Producers Releasing Corporation: *see* PRC
production systems 22
program pictures 64
psychological thrillers 49
The Punk/The Punk and the Princess 201
The Purple Monster Strikes 27

Quartet [multipart film] 162
The Quiet Man 184
Quinto, Zachary *136*

Rage 119–33
Raging Nation Films 119
Ramar of the Jungle [TV series] 73
rappers 126
Ratner, Megan 56
Rebatet, Lucien (François Vinneuil) 88
Reed, Michael 172
Rendezvous [TV series] 153–4
Republic Pictures xiii, 27–8, 182–3
Resistance cinema 89
Resteghini, Dale "Rage" 119–33, *120*
Rice, Ron 93–94
Richard III 163, 165–6
Rigg, Diana 173
Road to St Tropez 198–9
rock videos 126
Rodriguez-Soltero, José 100
Roeg, Nicolas 175, 198
Rose, Reginald 192
Rosenberg, Robert 38–9
Ross, Katharine 191
Roud, Richard 79
Rubin, Barbara 99–100

The Saint [TV series] 155
Sarne, Michael 195–202, *196*

Schary, Dore 149
Schmeerguntz 98
Schneemann, Carolee 100
science fiction serials 27–30
Scorpio Rising 91
Scorsese, Martin 61
Scott, A. O. 111
screenwriting 139–40, 141–2, 156, 172, 174, 200, 202
The Sea Wolves 193
Seaside Swingers 198
serials: *see* motion picture serials; television series
Seventy Deadly Pills 154
Shadow on the Wall 150
short films 64, 124
Silberg, Yoel 169
Sink the Bismarck 198
Sisk, Robert 150
Skolimowski, Jerzy 202
slasher films, 7
Sluizer, George 46
Smith, Jack 96
Smith, Wingate 184
So Long at the Fair 161–2
Something Money Can't Buy 150–51
Sonbert, Warren 101–2
Spielberg, Steven xi, 138
Stephani, Frederick 23
Stern Brothers Company 63–4
Sternbach, Bert *62*
Stewart, Jimmy 188
Stewart, Peter [pseud.] 65
Stigwood, Robert 196, 198
Stoller, James 101, 102
The Straight Story 139
Strock, Herbert L. 33–5, 37; *Picture Perfect* 34
Stross, Raymond 172
studios, control by xii
Superman [serial] 29
Superman [TV series] 29
synchronized sound technology 151

Targets 3–9, *4*
"Tattoo the Earth" rock tour 126
Technicolor 109–10, 148
teleseries: *see* television series

television 7–8, 73, 74, 152–6; acting 201; commercials 48, 140, 197; directing 173, 187–9; series 29, 30; *see also by name*
That Kind of Girl 171
theaters 113, 132, 202
theatricality and improvisation 91–2
Third Man on the Mountain 167
Thomas, Gerry (Gerald) 163
Thomas, Ralph 163
thrillers 49
Tom Jones 169
Touch of Evil 123
Towers, Harry Alan 176
Trio [multipart film] 162
Truffaut, François 81, 88
Twentieth Century Fox 199–200
two-reel shorts 64

Ulmer, Edgar G. 66
United Artists 186, 190
United Kingdom, Ministry of Information 160
Universal 28
Urban, Andrew L. 45
Usai, Paolo Cherchi 107, 109

Van Meter, Ben 100
Verity Films 159
video: with film 143; gaming, communal 113; projectors, in mobile phones 111; stores xiv, 110
Vinneuil, François [pseud.] 88
violence, in US culture 6

Virgin Island 152
The Virginian [TV series] 188

Wanger, Walter 109, 168
war pictures 190, 192, 193
Warhol, Andy, experimental films 96–7
Warner Bros. 192
The Way West 190
Wayne, John 184, 186, 188–9
"Wear" [pseud.] 24
Webb, Jack 31–5, *32*, 37–42
websites, archival 74
Welch, Raquel *196*
Welles, Orson 152–3
Wellman, William A. 185–6
Western Approaches 148
Westerns 191
What Price Glory 180
White Corridors 149
Whitman, Charles 5
The Wild Geese 192
Wiley, Dorothy 98
Williams, Derick 154
Winters, Shelley 176
Witney, William xiii
Wolper, David L. 190
World War II, Occupation of France 81–3, 88–9
Wyer, Reginald 162

Yalkut, Jud 102
Yates, Herbert J. 182–3

Zanuck, Dick (Richard) 199

www.ingramcontent.com/pod-product-compliance
Lightning Source LLC
Chambersburg PA
CBHW021825300426
44114CB00009BA/326